INTEGRATED BRANDING

Lynn M. Parker

Integrated Brand Model

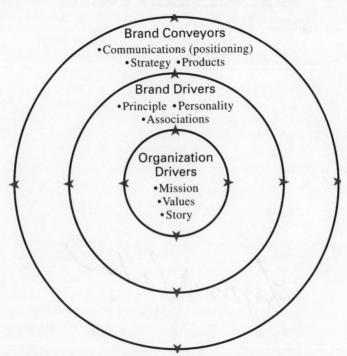

The Integrated Brand Model provides an overview of how to become a brand-driven organization. It outlines the three levels of activity—brand conveyors, brand drivers, and organization drivers—that define brands.

INTEGRATED BRANDING

becoming
brand-driven
through
company-wide
action

F JOSEPH LEPLA & LYNN M PARKER

KOGAN
PAGE

First published in the United States by Quorum Books in 1999
Revised edition published in Great Britain by Kogan Page Limited in 2002

Kogan Page Limited
120 Pentonville Road
London N1 9JN
UK

Kogan Page US
22 Broad Street
Milford CT 06460
USA

© F Joseph LePla and Lynn M Parker, 1999, 2002

British Library Cataloguing in Publication Data

A CIP record for this book is available from the British Library.

ISBN 0 7494 3720 0

Printed and bound in Great Britain by Biddles Ltd, *www.biddles.co.uk*

Copyright Acknowledgments

The authors and the publisher gratefully acknowledge permission for use of the following material.

Permission to reprint extracts from interviews, testimonials and/or websites is given by:

Deborah Churchill Lister, President, Annie's Homegrown

Peter Challman, President, Arnies Restaurants Northwest, Inc.

Carla Ware, Executive Assistant, Seattle Children's Home

Jean Schnelle, Director, Butterball Turkey Talk-Line, The Butterball Turkey Company

Victor Woodward, Vice President of Business Development, Content Technologies

Eric Berg, President, CimWorks GageTalker

Chris Brandkamp, Cyan

Gene Stabile, President, Data Dimensions Information Services

Amy Kelm, Worldwide Consumer Brand Development Manager, Hewlett-Packard Company

Nora Jaso, Principal, Studio Jaso

Kathy Holm, Marketing Communications Manager, Metapath Software Corporation

Wendy Wheeler, Associate Creative Director, Microsoft Corporation

Wally Smith and Holly Cook, REI

Doss Struse, CEO, Research International USA

Jim Shanklin, Chairman and CEO, Ryan-Shanklin, Ltd.

Joseph J. Kennedy, Vice President of Sales, Service and Marketing, Saturn Corporation

Chris Lyon, Marcomm Manager, Vixel Corporation

Volvo Cars of North America

Kathleen Wilcox, President and Executive Director, WSA

Darcie Wolfe, Director of Marketing Communications, WRQ

Terry Stoeser, Principal, WesDesign

David Reyes-Guerra, Manager, Corporate Identity, Xerox Corporation

Kenneth Zawilinski, Doctor, Emotional Research

John Bukovinsky, Director of Marketing Relations, IBM

Phil Knight, Chairman of the Board and Chief Executive Officer, Nike

David Zierman, Prognostics

Lise Olsen, Director of Public Relations, Beyond.com

Marian Salzman, Director, Young & Rubicam

Patricia Graham, Executive Vice President, Morgage Technology Division, INTERLINQ Software Corporation

Excerpts reprinted with the permission of The Free Press, a Division of Simon & Schuster, Inc. from *Strategic Brand Management: New Approaches to Creating and Evaluating Brand Equity* by Jean-Noel Kapferer. Copyright © 1992 by Les Editions d'Organisation. Translated by Philip Gibbs. First published in the English Language in 1992 by Kogan Page Ltd.

Excerpts reprinted with the permission of Kogan Page Ltd. from *Strategic Brand Management: New Approaches to Creating and Evaluating Brand Equity* by Jean-Noel Kapferer, London, 1992.

Contents

Illustrations

FIGURES

TABLES

Preface

Many studies confirm the benefits of strong brands: a clear companywide focus, higher margins, deep customer loyalty, and a higher success rate with new product launches. While the tangible benefits of a strong brand are obvious, the problem most companies face is, How do I reveal and build a strong brand, one that is integrated throughout my organization? This book answers that question. In the model of branding covered here, *integrated* means that your brand is built on your company's actual strengths and customers' values, and that you implement brand throughout the organization, through both words *and* deeds. An integrated brand, rather than one that is communications-driven only, will provide long-lasting benefits in the areas of market leadership, company focus, and profitability.

It's useful to build a strong brand, no matter what size a company is. Beginning the process of integrating brand when a company is small gives it an immediate market advantage and can save both money and heartache later on. Using integrated branding can help medium-sized companies build market leadership more effectively and at less cost. Large companies can use the integrated branding process to bring to light the practices that have made them successful, and then manage these practices for even greater effectiveness.

You will also find value from this book even if you already have made progress toward building your brand. Because the brand model described here is holistic, rather than a communications-only model, you will learn how to get every employee living and breathing the brand.

We will also cover how to apply brand concepts in specific situations, including developing brand extensions, branding in publicly held companies and high-technology companies, and avoiding brand dilution.

WHY WE CARE ABOUT INTEGRATED BRANDING

We have based this book on work we have done as marketing consultants for the past decade. During that time, we developed and successfully used brand building tools to reveal, integrate, and extend the brands of scores of companies of all types and sizes. We've worked with high-tech giants trying to find one consistent and compelling brand direction, small start-ups trying to carve out their place in evolving service markets, and midsized companies seeking to leverage their product lines and markets in strategic ways.

We have worked with companies in the Pacific Northwest of the United States and California's Silicon Valley to develop integrated brands using a suite of brand-building tools called *organization* and *brand drivers*. These tools allow companies to become brand-driven by elevating brand management to a conscious level, where it can be quantified and managed. Looking at brand in this way takes it out of the cloistered jurisdiction of the marketing department and places it squarely in the executive suite. In order for a brand to be truly integrated, it must be a both a corporate strategy and an organizational development tool.

Since our primary focus as a consulting company is high technology, this book also covers how to apply integrated branding to high-technology companies and how to use electronic media such as the Internet, intranets, shared content, and chat rooms to strengthen your brand experience.

The brand process articulated here is not a "one size fits all" formula. It is a framework for revealing and managing strong brands and will look very different for each brand—even brands in the same business category. This book is a source of brand information to act as a guideline for a successful process. There are places within the process—particularly in research and in brand development facilitation—where we strongly recommend the use of third parties to create an objective atmosphere and introduce an independent perspective necessary for an effective result.

Before you begin, one last point to keep in mind: Becoming a brand-driven company is serious business, but it should also be a creative, satisfying activity. We would love to hear about the creative ways you discover and implement your company's integrated brand—the principles on which you do business, and the promises you want to set forth to customers as the cornerstones of a long-lasting relationship. You can email Joe LePla at jlepla@parkerlepla.com and Lynn Parker at lynnp@parkerlepla.com.

HOW THIS BOOK UNFOLDS

This book will give readers a process for revealing, developing, applying, and managing their company and product brands using the integrated branding process.

The book begins in chapter 1 with a brief explanation of why you should take integrated branding seriously, whether your interest is increasing profitability, gaining market leadership, or serving your customers better:

- Chapters 2 through 6 explain the tools used to develop the core of the integrated brand and how an integrated brand differs from other branding methodologies.

- Chapter 7 gives you a step-by-step blueprint for the integrated branding process.

- Chapter 8 walks you through the possible ways to structure your company's brands and the pros and cons of each.

- Chapter 9 talks about using your new integrated branding approach to attain market leadership.

- Chapter 10 is a detailed case study of a medium-sized company that demonstrates the process in action.

- Chapter 11 shows how to integrate the brand into the fabric of your company, and Chapter 12 tells you how to measure the effectiveness of brand through research and through use of a big-picture perspective in your reports.

- Chapters 13 and 14 focus on communicating your brands through marketing and marketing communications—the places where most traditional branding has focused.

- Chapter 15 takes a look into the impact that new technologies such as the Internet have on the integrated brand experience.

- Chapter 16 talks about the important relationship between brand and going public and some pitfalls to avoid during the process.

- Chapter 17 deals with the unique aspects of high-technology branding; Chapter 18 brings integrated branding versus other branding models into focus.

- The Appendix provides a complete set of questions for getting started in determining your integrated brand—company strengths and what customers value.

ACKNOWLEDGMENTS

Any book is a collaborative effort, with more people involved than is apparent from the outside. Within that collaboration, we'd like to single out some special contributors to our effort. First off, we'd like to thank the entire team at Parker LePla, for making sure we live our brand every-day, and for knowing there was a book locked somewhere inside our practice. They are the finest group of creative professionals that we've had the pleasure to work with. We could not have done without the help of that team, including Sunshine Cronin, Mary Weisnewski, Darcie Wolfe, Lisa Samuelson, Cheryl Stumbo, Scott Carroll, Rhia Siegle, Nancy Robbers, Eric Nobis, Muriel Guilbert, Beth Likens, Diane Murphy, Lisa Geshke, and Susan Majerus, without whom this book would still be just a good idea. Jennifer Haupt was instrumental in getting us started and helped with the infrastructure work of finding and working with a pub-lisher. Sally LePla Perry and Katherine James Schuitemaker brought a customer perspective to the endeavor, making sure what we said made sense to the people we are actually writing for. Katherine James Schui-temaker also helped us in the early days of creating our brand devel-opment tools and ideas. Many clients worked with us to create strong brands and both listened to our counsel and helped us refine our ideas, particularly WRQ, the finest example of a values-driven company we've run across. At WRQ, we'd like to thank specifically Teri Wiegman and Darcie Wolfe, our champions and colleagues in integrated branding. And finally, we'd like to acknowledge our families, for the patience and sup-port they demonstrated daily as we struggled through the challenges of getting thinking onto paper. Thank you for always being there.

INTEGRATED BRANDING

1 Your Company's Most Powerful Weapon: The Brand Within

We've become convinced the most technological piece of machinery a company can employ is the human. The model organization of the 21st century will be the one where the talents and potential of the entire workforce is fully utilized.[1]

—Jack O'Toole, Vice President,
United Automobile Workers, Human Resources

What is this elusive quality, "the brand"? Ask the average person on the street, and he or she may respond with logos, tag lines, or ad campaigns. "It's the Rolls Royce winged Mercury," or "Microsoft's 'Where do you want to go today?'" Move to marketing professionals and ask an advertising executive what a brand is. He or she may respond with a slightly broader definition, saying it is your product's unique selling proposition or a corporate identity. "It's Saturn's down-home friendly service coupled with the consistent use of its logo and other graphics."

In terms of the power of brand, these examples just scratch the surface. In reality, a strong brand has to do with every aspect of a company's relationship with its customers. Since this is true, then developing and using a brand must be a companywide endeavor.

When company and product actions and messages are driven by brand, you experience *integrated branding*. Integrated branding can catapult a company into the realm of category leadership, as defined by customer and employee loyalty, market share, a strong internal focus, product price premiums, repeat purchases, and capacity to be prepared for future market shifts. Not just another new business fad, integrated branding practices have been around for centuries in one form or another, whenever companies have driven actions through stated goals or values. But the Integrated Branding Model described here goes beyond earlier work. It combines these discrete pieces and adds new ones to create a holistic approach to relationships with customers and employees. This book will show you how to reveal your existing brand or brands and will provide a roadmap for practicing integrated branding.

INTEGRATED BRANDING—DEFINITIONS

Integrated branding is *an organizational strategy used to drive company and product direction—where all actions and messages are based on the value the company brings to its line of business*. This value is based both on what the company does well and what customers consider important. By focusing actions and messages on company and product strengths, a company is much more likely to create a deep, long lasting relationship with each of its customers.

To summarize, you could also say *integrated branding is the promise that you keep*. At the heart of any company is the promise that it makes to its customers. Companies keep their promises by understanding their brands and acting on that understanding in every endeavor. That promise is carried out by people at all levels of the company—from the CEO to the line worker—so that integrated branding is much more than a communications strategy or set of messages. It touches the company's organizational structure—the way it makes decisions, its strategic direction, its corporate culture, and its customer relationships. Integrated branding also impacts what has been the traditional area of brand focus—communications. When the brand promise meets customers in an integrated way, through products, services, communications, and culture, it produces unique and valuable customer relationships. These general definitions serve as a yardstick for all aspects of a company's relationship with its customers.

An integrated brand is only as strong as the people who live it. If you have a strong corporate culture, the tools in this book will give you ways to strengthen it. If you don't, these brand tools will help you find the key components to build one.

The other definition is the blueprint for the integrated branding process that the company goes through to reveal its brand or brands: *Brand is the intersection between core company (or product or service) strengths and what customers value* (see figure 1.1). Company strengths are what the

Figure 1.1
A Working Integrated Brand Definition

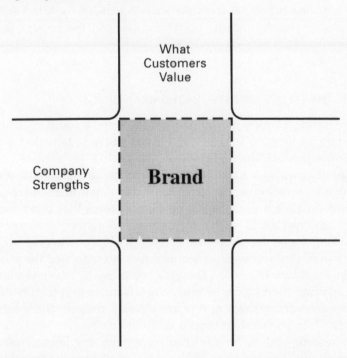

What
Customers
Value

Company
Strengths

Brand

Brand is the intersection of company strengths and what customers value.

company does well. What customers value include the benefits of a product's or service's features, as well as *what customers see as the ongoing worth of a relationship with the company.*

Customers may see value, for instance, in the consistency of your product performance and in the way they feel about your business style or personality. They may also emotionally identify with company actions, goals, and values. Customers may also perceive value from their feelings when in contact with your brand, such as feeling more secure, more comfortable, or more competent. This value adds to relationship depth whether or not customers are aware of their feelings.

WHO NEEDS TO KNOW ABOUT INTEGRATED BRANDING?

Because a strong brand is much more than an image or a logo, brand development should be part of the job description of every CEO, sales associate, product or service development team, human resources person, and marketing executive. In other words, brand is the responsibility of everyone in the company. Integrated branding is typically introduced to companies by either someone in the marketing department or the CEO because a strong brand achieves the shared goals of the CEO and marketing department through its positive impact on the bottom line and the differentiation it affords products.

WHAT IS THE EFFECT OF INTEGRATED BRANDING?

By integrating a brand discipline from the start, a company can effectively retain its focus as it grows and avoid costly pitfalls that a "we're just selling a product" mentality can cause.

For instance, without a strong brand direction, a company that develops software for information technology (IT) department management might end up with a grab bag of product features that don't meet the needs of any specific IT customer segment. Moreover, if a competitor had a strong brand in place that defined its brand direction as *an IT guide*, it would develop product features that strengthened the product's ability to act as an IT guide. The *grab bag of product features* company could easily find itself falling behind on key features as it tried to develop all features equally, or, worse, it might develop features that obstructed the ability of its intended customers to do their job.

When a company is brand-driven from the beginning, integrated branding allows it to leverage all the skills of all workers in a direction that makes best use of its strengths. This process provides immediate strategic direction for product development. A company that builds products that correspond more exactly to its strengths builds value, trust, and loyalty with customers far faster than the competition.

This is particularly important in new product categories. Companies understand the need to educate the marketplace about a new technology—including how it works and why it is beneficial. But they often forget to demonstrate the unique strengths they bring to their product's use of the technology. By focusing only on new category development without differentiating your product within the category, you could lose several years' worth of brand development potential.

For example, early entrants in the high-speed (fifteen to twenty-two pages per minute) desktop laser printer market had several years head start on Hewlett-Packard. Yet none of them was able to claim leadership of the marketplace because they had no way of differentiating themselves beyond having a faster printing technology. HP's first entrant in the category, the LaserJet IIIsi printer, immediately became market leader. HP caught up just by making a product with roughly equivalent

features, because it had fast printing *and* a compelling brand strength—
reliable quality—that corporate users valued.

Consciously managing your brand is extremely important if you are
a small- or medium-sized company. Small companies with inexperienced
management teams tend to want to be all things to all people. They may
emphasize features and benefits that they can't sustain over the long
term. If they are successful, they also tend to grow rapidly and often
lose focus on what made them successful. Instead of trying to be all
things to all people, integrated branding allows you to focus on the needs
of your best customers extremely well. Integrated branding creates a
single focus and direction that allow companies to differentiate around
what their customers value. This focused differentiation turns into higher
margins and market share over the long term.

An integrated brand also results in these benefits:

Internal Benefits

- A consistent and accurate compass for R&D and market and product devel-
  opment
- A clear and defensible strategic direction, regardless of market changes
- Consistent messaging
- High levels of employee loyalty and esprit de corps
- Greater employee initiative

External Benefits

- The ability to charge a 15 to 20 percent price premium above the market av-
  erage for a product and maintain that price delta even as a market matures
- A shorter customer repurchase decision cycle
- Higher levels of customer loyalty
- The right capabilities to capture and retain market share
- Customer evangelists
- A platform for ensuring new product success
- High company financial valuations and less share price volatility

The Relationship Pinnacle: Customer Affinity

Although most product managers wish to create customer preference
for their products, integrated branding goes further. It creates relationships in which customers are able to identify completely with the goals
of the company and translate those goals into personal benefits. Integrated brand managers ask, "What is the entire range of benefits that

Figure 1.2
Self-Indentification Pyramid

the customer gains from brand interactions?" By answering this question, companies can build emotional and intellectual rapport with customers to a very high level.

The goal of integrated branding is to create an authentic experience that allows customers to identify with the brand completely on a rational and emotional level. This is called *customer affinity*. The figure above shows the progressive levels of relationship possible (see figure 1.2), culminating with the customer's saying, "Our goals are the same." This can't be done through manipulation or marketing sleight of hand. It also can't be achieved if your only objective is to get as much money as possible from the customer. It must spring from the company's desire to create a genuine relationship that is built on actual company beliefs backed up by consistent actions.

THE TOOLS OF INTEGRATED BRANDING: ORGANIZATION AND BRAND DRIVERS

Although all companies have brands, most do not consciously manage them. The Integrated Brand Model described in this book includes tools for revealing and building strong brands. These tools, *organization* and *brand drivers*, will allow your company to develop customer relationships

Figure 1.3
Driver Impact on Customers and Employees

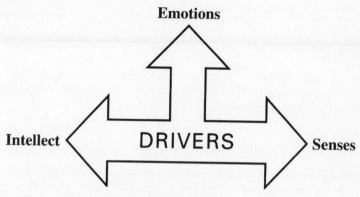

Organization and brand drivers impact all decision making.

and create brand-strengthening customer interactions, one customer at a time (see figure 1.3). These tools will bring your brand or brands to consciousness and then *drive* their development into the future. They apply to what the company and its employees believe, what they choose to focus on, how they act, what products or services they develop, and how they communicate externally.

Organization drivers include the *mission, values,* and *story*—these provide the base for any brand a company creates, from the corporate brand to individual product brands. Brand drivers include *principle, personality,* and *associations*. These often will differ from corporate to product brands and among product brands within an organization.

ORGANIZATION DRIVERS = Mission, Values, Story

BRAND DRIVERS = Principle, Personality, Associations

WHAT ARE THE ESSENTIALS OF SUCCESSFUL INTEGRATED BRANDING?

There are several prerequisites to bringing integrated branding into a company:

- If a brand is to succeed over the long term, that brand must drive *actions* as well as *communications*.
- A company must buy into the premise that retaining existing customers is one of its highest objectives.
- When a company, division, or business unit first moves to a brand-driven

model, company leaders must play a central role in revealing the brand or brands, rather than having their brand handed to them by a committee or consultant.

• The company must also develop a core group of champions who serve on a standing brand team, with a senior manager as a consistent and vocal supporter of that team.

• Finally, in order to stay on track over the long term, integrated brand development requires organization and brand drivers that are both comprehensive and easy for employees to use.

DO ALL PRODUCTS NEED BRANDING?

Whether a company is high-tech or low-tech, small, medium or large, the immense amount of information being thrown at customers has made the battle for their attention—and loyalty—more complex than ever.

Most companies assume that because they were successful in the past, they will continue to be in the future. This is rarely how it works. For companies in technology and other rapidly changing markets the scenario looks like this: Early entrants in a new-but-established market are successful if they offer a product that is reasonably functional and reliable. As the market grows, sales take off. But other companies then enter this growth market, with a rush of lower-cost, "me too" products.

This is the point where many companies falter. When a market becomes highly competitive, a company is faced with two choices: strengthen its brand and become a dominant market leader, or compete on pricing and become a commodity. Companies who see this coming can establish a strong product brand before their product turns into a commodity. They will then be able to maintain their market share and a price premium even in a market where all products are roughly equal.

There is a line of thinking that says that only interesting or exciting products need to pay attention to their brands, that products that are commonplace or border on commodity status have no brand hooks. These might include such products as electricity, salt, personal computers, or voltage meters. But many research studies indicate that any product can benefit from branding. If the research is accurate, and there are literally decades of studies supporting this, products that are treated (and priced) like commodities have become that way as a result of the choices a company makes.

For instance, research shows shoppers will pay 15 percent to 300 percent more for particular brands of salt. Electricians who use digital volt meters to measure electrical current typically buy on the basis of which

Table 1.1
Buying IT in the 90s: The Channels Study

Category	Brands considered prior to purchase	Percent purchasing brand in consideration set
Desktop PCs	2.5	77%
Notebook PCs	2.7	78%
Printers	1.9	83%
Application Software	2.0	81%
LANs	1.9	79%

Notes: PCs=Personal Computers; LANs=Local-Area Networks

Source: IDG (International Data Group)

brand says the most about their professionalism. And as you've noticed when pricing out computer systems lately, people will pay varying premiums for name brand computers, whether for professional or home use.

In terms of high-technology products, between two-thirds and three-quarters of all customers make their brand decisions before entering a computer store and nearly 80 percent purchase a brand that was in their previous consideration set. According to research from IDG (International Data Group) entitled *Buying IT in the 90's: The Channels Study*, 947 corporate buyers of consumer-related products listed the following considerations (see table 1.1). This means that you need to be in the top two brands in any market to be considered. This is relatively easy to do when you are one of the only products in a new market, but what happens when the market begins supporting ten, twenty, or more competitors? Brand provides an answer through encouraging high levels of customer loyalty and market distinction.

With the advent of the electronic age, focusing on the distinctiveness of your brand will become even more important. Integrated branding can help protect you from upstart web-based competitors who make it easier to buy a product or who allow purchases to be made without ever physically coming into contact with the product. In terms of personal computers, we have reached an age when customers can purchase from the manufacturer's or reseller's web site and even configure the product themselves. NEC Computer Systems Division spent $40 million on an advertising campaign for NEW Now, a brand centered on speedy delivery based on build-to-order (BTO) instructions. According to Kathryn Dennis of *Marketing Computers*, "BTO puts a new spin on the age-old question of who owns the customer: so the question du jour is 'Who controls the brand?' "[2]

Within the Integrated Brand Model, the answer to *who controls the brand* is *the brand is controlled mutually by both the company and the customer*. But it is the company's responsibility to provide the place and take the actions necessary for the brand relationship to develop, whether on the retail floor or electronically at the customer's desktop.

DETERMINING WHERE YOU ARE ON THE INTEGRATED BRAND CONTINUUM

Many companies have experienced brand work only as an adjunct to a new corporate identity or advertising campaign. If your company has conducted some branding work in the past or has identified specific brands, the following questions will help you determine how close your brand is to an integrated brand:

- Do all divisions and departments use a common strategy statement as a tool to make decisions? yes/no
- Is there a consistent tone and business style to external communications? yes/no
- Do you have a strong corporate culture? yes/no
- Can employees explain
    - the strategy for each brand? yes/no
    - the brand principle? yes/no
    - the company mission? yes/no
    - the company values? yes/no
    - associations for each brand? yes/no
- Do company actions align with company messages? yes/no
- Are all messages consistent throughout the organization or brand? yes/no
- Would a prospective customer recognize the brand by seeing a number of marketing communications pieces if there were no logo on them? yes/no
- Are product names consistent and understood by the market? yes/no

If you answered yes to two or more of these questions, you have integrated your brand to some extent. If you answered no to any of these questions, you are not yet practicing integrated branding to your greatest advantage. This book will give you the tools to answer yes to all questions on this list.

NOTES

1. Jack O'Toole, "Forming the Future: The Marriage of People and Technology at Saturn," presentation to Stanford University's Industrial Engineering and Engineering Management Departments, March 29, 1990 (available in Saturn's students package).

2. Kathryn Dennis, "The End of Brand Control," *Marketing Computers* (March 1998), p. 10.

2 The Integrated Brand Model: The Basis for Strong Customer Relationships

Fundamentally, a brand is a promise a company makes to consumers.[1]
—Microsoft Corporation

The most important thing to understand about integrated branding is that it is a model for building the most important asset any company has—its *relationship* with its customers. If you understand that your best customer is the one you already have, then creating a rational system for deepening customer relationships is the logical next step.

Basing your product or service offerings on an integrated brand allows your organization to develop more saleable products over the long term by keeping it focused on your strengths as an organization. This focus opens it to new possibilities by broadening the corporate aperture from looking at what you are producing right now to looking at the bigger picture. Seeing the big picture is an essential prerequisite to company longevity. Strategy based solely on current product or service uniqueness ultimately results in decreasing market share, lower margins, missed opportunities, and price wars.

Refined over the past decade, the Integrated Brand Model offers a methodology for differentiating your brands in a significant and lasting manner. Integrated branding helps companies understand *who they are* and how to use that knowledge consistently to create better results. As with all worthwhile change, the process takes some investment in time and elbow grease up front, but results in a huge payoff.

Well-implemented integrated branding can correct and prevent some key problems:

- Loss of focus. Without the conscious management of brand assets, companies can easily go astray over the years. This may happen because a new CEO or executive team takes over and has a different strategic vision from the original team, or because the company has never analyzed what about its original focus made it successful to begin with. This unconsciousness makes it easy for the company to go in new directions on the basis of a mistaken premise.
- Lack of synergy among product line brands. Even if a company has been successful in multiple lines of business, it may have no compass directing additional investment or cross-development of products or services. When brand is unconscious, actions and messages are left at the mercy of company politics and/or the well-intentioned initiatives of those in power. Products that have the most politically astute product managers may receive more investment, or a company might underinvest in places that could ensure future growth.
- Under-valuation in financial markets. Both lack of focus and lack of product brand synergy can result in misunderstandings on Wall Street. Without a simple, appealing, and comprehensive story to tell, companies are left at the mercy of investment bankers to create a story for them. However, when companies have strong brands from the onset, Wall Street rewards them with greater valuations and less share price volatility.[2]

The Integrated Brand Model will give you all of the pieces necessary to reveal, develop, and build an integrated brand. Most of you will have products or services that already have a history and already are a brand or number of brands. This process allows you to *reveal* the drivers of your brands and their business scope. It also shows how to empower employees to use drivers consciously to strengthen the brand in the course of everyday business operations.

THE INTEGRATED BRAND MODEL

The Integrated Brand Model maps out a brand in a way that allows it to be used easily by all employees. The model provides a frame of reference for ongoing brand work and lets you check assumptions for such strategic activities as new product development, mergers, and acquisitions.

The Integrated Brand Model (see figure 2.1) outlines three levels of activity that define all brands. One of the ways the model is different from many other brand approaches is that it provides a clear process for becoming brand-driven that every employee in the company can follow.

Figure 2.1
Integrated Brand Model

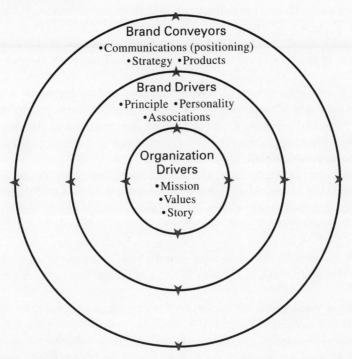

The Integrated Brand Model provides an overview of how to become a brand-driven organization. It outlines the three levels of activity—brand conveyors, brand drivers, and organization drivers—that define brands.

Another way is that it is a process that works just as well for start-ups, small companies, medium-sized companies, and large ones. Perhaps for the first time, it puts effective branding within the reach of many companies that could not have benefited from brand development activities in the past because of high consulting costs.

What does the Integrated Brand Model look like? It is made up of a series of tools, specifically *organization drivers, brand drivers*, and *brand conveyors. Brand conveyors*, the outer ring, describe what happens on the outermost, customer-facing level of your organization, product, or service—it's where day-to-day activities, from product development to communications, happen. Prior to becoming truly brand-driven, most companies spend their time making decisions based on brand conveyors without ever digging deeper. When brand-conveyor-focused companies want to upgrade a product or create an advertising campaign, *rather than working from their brand drivers,* they assemble a team of employees and consultants and ask them to develop the conveyor, such as an advertising campaign. These teams then proceed to create a campaign based on whatever is current company strategy—usually deriving from a short-term analysis of the marketplace. In this outside-in process, companies use brand conveyors without understanding their deeper brand strengths.

This is one reason why you as a customer often experience a disconnection between what a company says and what it offers you in the way of products and services. Or why a brand seemingly has a different message and different personality every year. Lack of consistent direction is why many products fail.

Even companies that have committed to building customer relationships, but don't understand what elements are at the core of their brand, will run into problems. Companies often create products and services without aligning them with brand strengths or thinking about the customer experience. Customer intimacy guru Fred Wiersema says, "Never forget your own identity and what you do best," He goes on to quote John Foster, chairman and CEO of NovaCare, a rehabilitation services provider:

> When you look at them closely, the organizations that survive all stand for something. And it's what they stand for that attracts members, customers, volunteers, contributors, whomever. If you look at your 10 favorite companies, you'll find that in addition to being leaders in their industries, they all have easily identifiable value sets. There's no question in my mind that those values come first, and the results follow in their path.[4]

Most companies only pick up bits and pieces of the two deeper levels of the model—the organization driver and brand driver levels. Therefore, they have relatively shallow and unengaging brand relationships with their customers, which do not harness the true power of their brands.

Brand-driven companies, on the other hand, work the model from the inside out. The organization driver and brand driver levels contain the precepts that allow them to manage each of their brands. Brand-driven companies base all subsequent decisions on their organization drivers— the code for everything they do. This level includes organization drivers of *mission* (what business you are in), *values* (beliefs the company holds important that do not change when situations change), and *story* (what the company tells about itself).

Brand drivers are based on the organization drivers but are different for each brand that your company offers. Brand drivers include the *principle* (the foundation for all actions and messages around the brand), the *personality* (the public face of the brand), and *associations* (mental shortcuts to what is valuable about the brand).

The principle acts like the pointer on a compass, helping employees to make decisions that are *closest* to a company's, product's, or service's primary strengths. It is your company's unique approach to its mission.

The personality is the consistent tone and manner your company uses in all customer interactions and dialogs.

Associations are concepts, visuals, or other parts of your communications that link back to and reinforce key brand messages. They answer the question, "When I say [insert brand name], what comes to mind?"

What's exciting about the Integrated Brand Model is that organization and brand drivers ensure that every employee action builds on company strengths. They are comprehensive, yet very easy to use.

All drivers are important. But the brand drivers, particularly the principle and personality, are what you will spend the most time developing and are the most important tools for integrating brand internally and building customer relationships. Even if you develop and use only these two drivers, you will be on your way to building an effective, integrated brand. And using all six drivers will help you create the most effective long-term results. For more information on how to develop specific drivers, see Chapter 7.

Each brand driver relates to your company's organization drivers. The mission statement defines the boundaries of any brand principle. Company values shape the personality attributes displayed by the brand. And the story acts as the contextual underpinning for all brand drivers.

Here's an example of all six drivers used by the Seattle Children's Home, a not-for-profit agency that is over 115 years old and is dedicated to providing sustained care for at-risk children and their families.

Organization Drivers

Mission—regardless of challenges, we provide sustained care for children and families through partnerships and clinical excellence that help them to live to their unique potential

Values—providing excellent care, achieving results, respect, professionalism

Story—In 1884 the Seattle Children's Home (SCH) was formed by Seattle's founding mothers including Mary Leary, Sarah Yesler, Elizabeth Minor and many others to help orphaned children. SCH acted as the first safety net by offering to house, clean, feed and nurture the poor and homeless. Since then, SCH has continued to adjust to the changing needs of the world around it—through the tremendous growth of the City and the challenges of the Great Fire, the Typhoid and Flu epidemics, World War I, the Great Depression, World War II, up to the modern era. It is one of the first in the U.S. to use trained child care workers in the 1920s and incorporate psychiatric and psycho-dynamic treatment for group care in the mid-1940s.

Today, the reasons for want are different but the need is just as immediate. The need cries out from hundreds of children who are forced to spend each night on the streets of our Northwest cities. The need puts down roots in thousands of abusive homes and flowers in children who can't deal with their frustrations and anger or who simply have problems coping with the difficult demands of today's world.

SCH programs reflect a long-term commitment to each child's future through residential treatment, outpatient services, crisis intervention, outreach for the homeless, school-based, transitional living programs and advocacy. SCH works with children where they are—in homes, schools, on the street, and in shelters—and also takes those that others are unable to. It builds partnerships resulting in a healthy family environment for each child thereby enriching our community.

We know kids.

The Seattle Children's Home has three brand drivers.

Brand Drivers

Principle—building partnerships to improve futures

Personality—respectful, open, focused, nonjudgmental, dedicated

Association—transformation (visually expressed as a butterfly)

These six brand drivers also nurture healthy corporate cultures. Distinctive cultures usually begin with distinctive leaders. But as companies grow, those cultures often lose some of their luster as new voices make themselves heard within a company. The drivers allow companies to stay focused on and even reward culture-enhancing activities.

THE BRAND FILTER—AN EVERYDAY WAY TO LIVE THE BRAND

As stated earlier, one of the definitions of an integrated brand is *the promise that you keep*. An integrated brand promise is the total effect of all its organization and brand drivers. Whether you uphold your promise depends on how well you integrate brand drivers into everyday activities. Drivers result in sophisticated and rich customer relationships, which in turn create greater brand awareness, preference, loyalty, familiarity, affinity, and trust.

Once the drivers are in place, they become the driving force behind all brand decisions, a kind of a brand filter, as it were. The way an employee uses these drivers is simple: when making decisions or interacting with customers, employees ask, Will this decision or action strengthen or negate our promise to our customers?

Every company places a different emphasis on driver usage. But the most important from a day-to-day directional standpoint are the values, principle, and personality. In the case of the Seattle Children's Home an employee may ask, Does this action demonstrate our values of *respect* and *professionalism*? Will it *build a partnership to improve a child's future*? Am I reflecting our personality: *respectful, open, focused, nonjudgmental, and dedicated*?

By asking themselves these questions, they can ensure their activities are "on-brand." This simple test is the key to integrating brand into existing organizations. All employees can be trained to ask these questions and to apply the brand in their job, no matter what role they play in the company.

NOTES

1. Microsoft web site: www.Microsoft.com.
2. David A. Aaker and Robert Jacobson, "The Financial Information Content of Perceived Quality," *Journal of Marketing Research*, 31 (May 1994), pp. 191–201.
3. Fred Wiersema, *Customer Intimacy* (Santa Monica, CA: Knowledge Exchange, 1996), p. 59.
4. Ibid., p. 80.

3 How Integrated Branding Differs from the Alternatives

The requirement of consistent behavior which is needed to establish a brand is what sets branding apart from the rest of marketing and what makes it so difficult to achieve.[1]

—Jacques Chevron, Founding Partner, JRC&A

WHY BRAND IS MORE THAN JUST EFFECTIVE MARKETING COMMUNICATIONS

Although the effects of branding are most obvious in a company's marketing materials, an integrated brand directs message development and action everywhere in the company. Most people know Nipper, the His Master's Voice dog visual symbol used by RCA. But how many are aware of the brand meaning of "sound fidelity" that was one inspiration behind this association? The concept was that the sound from the phonograph was so clear that the dog recognized his master's voice from the record. "Sound fidelity" is a powerful driver of the RCA brand.

How does an integrated brand use its drivers? If one of a brand's associations is sound fidelity, then it must manifest sound fidelity holistically, throughout the company. That means engineers, marketers, human resource professionals, service personnel, salespeople, accounting, and upper management must all ensure their decisions, actions, and communications further the impression of sound fidelity with customers. For instance, if RCA didn't produce products with high sound fidelity, then an association like Nipper would not seem true to customers. In fact, it might breed customer cynicism, reduce customer loyalty, and cloud the company's true strengths. The consequence of communication not backed up by actions is devaluing of the customer relationship. This mismatch of promise with reality is one reason why some brands lose value over time.

You might say that the basis for the customer relationship is the same as it is for personal relationships. Relationships built through interactions that reinforce trust and common goals create an emotional and intellectual bond between the customer and the brand. Relationships that don't, weaken the brand.

How can you start down the road to a strong brand? Begin by redefining what the concept of brand means to you. Contrary to popular understanding, brand is not simply a corporate identity, an advertising campaign, a name, or a logo. Although these parts are all facets of a brand, they are only small pieces of a much larger whole. They are supporting players to the main attraction: the customer's experience of a company's strengths and value. Nipper is only a holder of brand meaning, not the brand itself. An integrated brand lives deep within a company or product line, within the minds, the creativity, and the skills of every employee, and shows itself through advertising, logos, and the like, not the other way around.

This point must be made very clearly because all too often, companies confuse advertising campaigns with the brand. But that's the tail wagging the dog. Advertising is an effective way to communicate brands, but it is not the basis for communication. Advertising cannot facilitate the integration of action and message. It is the integrated brand that creates a unity of direction among employees by allowing everyone to focus on core strengths and reinforcing a distinctive personality within the customer relationship.

A company's *organization* and *brand drivers* are used to develop *brand conveyors*—tools to convey brand meaning—such as positioning, advertising campaigns, products, and features. These drivers also determine other conveyors, such as levels of product customization, educating/mentoring, partnering, services, and customer support—rather than the other way around.

The following is an excerpt from a Zona Research report that outlines the difference between branding and advertising.

The Netscape Story—Building the Brand

Netscape announced plans to launch an aggressive $10 million marketing campaign to promote its redesigned and expanded Netcen-

ter web site and drive membership growth....From a 20,000-foot
perspective, this scenario holds an enterprise software company—
that used to be a browser company—spending $10 million dol-
lars—after a quarter in which it generated zero profit—to promote,
of all products, its web site. Closer in, we find a company with a
popular Internet brand trying to contend for the portal site title....
Is Netscape a content company? Or is it an enterprise software company? Or a browser company? Or an e-commerce company? Or
next month's flavor-of-the-month company? We have yet to see a
unifying vision from Netscape that encompasses all of its interests,
and in the interim, the company has pursued each interest more
aggressively. Perhaps there is no umbrella strategy and the company is simply looking to leverage the hell out of its brand name
across as many Internet interests as possible.[2]

The point of the Zona report is that a company can spend a lot of
money on advertising various services such as becoming a portal site. But
spending all that money on advertising will not help you if you haven't
first defined your business as one of *content, portal, enterprise software,* or
browser, or something else, and your unique approach to that business.
This is the same pitfall that many dot com companies fell into—they spent
a huge portion of their budgets on advertising to buy market share
without understanding what, if any, value they were offering to potential
customers.

Although advertising is an excellent brand conveyor, it cannot determine an overall brand direction or set the parameters for the customer
experience. These must come from inside the company. Any brand con-
veyance medium is brand-neutral. It can convey brand only if it is supplied with the right direction from deep within the genetic code of the
company. In the case of Netscape, at least from this report's point of
view, the company must first determine who it wants to be (its mission)
and its unique approach to the business (its principle) before it will be
able to use advertising effectively.

Approaching brand as just a communications strategy is flawed for
three reasons. First, marketing communications campaigns not tied to
organization and brand drivers run the danger of not reflecting company
values and actions. They may weaken the relationship with customers
by setting expectations that the company as a whole is not designed to
meet on a complete and consistent basis.

Integrated brands match actions and messages. RCA's "sound fidelity"
could give the company's product developers direction to guide their
actions. The automaker Volvo's "safety" focus tells company engineers

to build safer cars and marketers to advertise the safety of Volvo products. If advertising is a brand conveyor, it stands to reason that all advertising campaigns have brand elements in them—from the tone of the ad to its perspective on the market. But are they the right brand elements? And if they are, why build brand elements in an unplanned, unconscious way, tearing down in the next campaign what you built up in the last? Brands based on advertising typically last only the life of the campaign. And the scary part is that company management tires of an ad campaign long before customers have figured out how what you're saying fits into their existing perceptions of your company. Then you see a new message, a new direction, and perhaps even a new company image. No one knows who the company really is, and without that knowledge, *no relationship can exist*, except as a shallow, short-term transaction.

Second, marketing communications may not be in synch with brand actions. An integrated brand creates differentiation (and deepens customer relationships) at all levels of an organization and puts everyone on the same page regarding the actions and messages being presented to customers. Integrated branding creates a consistent, powerful experience each time a customer interacts with the brand. By relegating brand to the marketing side of a company, product, or service, the organization may end up developing products or new product features based solely on the beliefs of a product manager or VP of development. Often, these people have little contact with the marketing department, the customer base, or the shared brand knowledge of the rest of the work force. In this case, the product brand could be and often is entirely different from the brand being communicated. No wonder customers are so often confused and cynical!

A large bank in the Northwest once designed its ads around the message "Don't use credit unwisely." On the face of it, this is a great message from a bank, one that will differentiate it, set it up as the customer's friend and ally, and ultimately result in longer-term, more profitable relationships. But in this instance, the advertising was the *only* part of the company communicating this message. Branch managers, compensated on loan volume, ignored the message and continued to sell every customer who came in the door. The cognitive dissonance set up between the customer's real experience and the messages received through the media left customers strongly dissatisfied—not exactly the best way to encourage long-term relationships.

Compare this with REI, the outdoor equipment co-op, whose employees send their customers to other retailers when they don't have the right equipment. By doing this, REI builds customer trust and becomes a resource for all outdoor needs.

If the bank had used brand drivers as the basis for the advertising campaign, then employees would have *lived* the brand, creating consistency between the message and the employee/customer interaction. If the bank had been brand-driven and used the same advertising campaign, branch managers would have been compensated by measures other than loan volumes and would have made decisions about whether credit was wise for a particular customer. Customers would come to trust the brand, would recommend the bank to others, and would stay loyal to the bank for all their financial needs. This is the road to strong brands and, ultimately, market leadership.

Third, without brand drivers to point the way, the company is less likely to leverage all of its strengths through its products and services. This directional aspect of an integrated brand is one of its most powerful benefits.

A company may be trying to make its brand be all things to all people. This lack of direction will leave product designers in the dark about what features to emphasize or new products to develop.

Consistent, valued experiences are the basis of brand/customer relationships and customer loyalty. Without customer loyalty, market leadership is an unrealizable goal. Whether prospective customers will sit up and notice and whether the experience will cause them to buy are determined by what is driving your brand: true brand strengths or simply the latest communications strategy.

AVOIDING A SHALLOW BRAND

If all products would greatly benefit from integrated branding, can we assume that most companies are engaged in some sort of ongoing brand development process? In most cases the answer is no.

The road from successful brand introduction to commodity product is well traveled in the business world. It stems from a reasonable assumption—that people buy products or services primarily on the basis of their features, specifications, and price. The problem with acting upon this assumption is that it ultimately forces all products and services into competitive and margin-destroying price wars as a market matures. As products (or services) achieve a level of parity over time, without other reasons for loyalty, the most common way to retain or increase market share is through lowering price, illustrated in the following diagram (see figure 3.1).

Commodity brands typically stem from shallow brands. It's valuable to contrast a shallow brand with a strong brand in order to get a clear

Figure 3.1
Integrated versus Shallow Brands

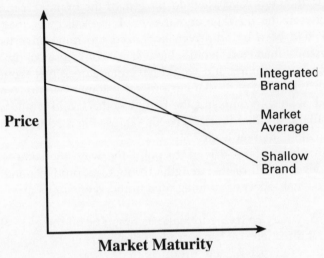

Over time, integrated brands command higher than average market prices and significantly higher prices than shallow brands.

mental picture of integrated branding. A shallow brand:

- impacts a customer's thoughts and emotions in only a limited way.
- focuses on the offering, not on a solution or relationship.
- communicates very few ideas or traits, like a one-dimensional person.
- does not create a consistent and distinctive experience with each customer interaction.

You can recognize the qualities of a shallow brand on your first one or two interactions with a company. Ask yourself, "Is my interaction with the brand just a transaction?" If you answer, "I could take it or leave it," you probably are looking at a shallow brand. A shallow brand reduces your relationship with the product to a monetary transaction that you are happy to be done with.

You can look at the difference between a shallow brand and a strong brand as the *level of depth of the customer experience*. Strong brands treat each customer as a relationship they can improve. Shallow brands are there to take orders (see table 3.1).

Starbucks, the coffee company, is the perfect example of a product that could have gone the route of a shallow brand. After all, what is so special

Table 3.1
How to Recognize a Shallow Brand

Focuses on the transaction

Low customer emotional involvement

Sells on features or price

Unclear promise

Low customer loyalty

Provides few possibilities for relationship building

about serving coffee? As the Starbucks brand proves, this is a question that other retailers would have benefited from asking.

Think about your last experience inside a Starbucks store. What did you notice first? Starbucks is full of warm, rich colors and shapes and is set up so customers have a lot to look at while waiting for their order. It is visually stimulating in a way that is pleasant to most people. Compare this to a typical coffee shop, where the customer is often subjected to bright, harsh lighting and is often in the way of traffic flow, making him or her feel vaguely uncomfortable.

What does Starbucks smell like? For centuries, bakeries have devised ways of getting the smell of freshly baked bread out onto the street to evoke a pleasant memory in passers-by. Starbucks has adopted this principle for distinction. Even before entering, you experience the intricate and complex smell of brewed coffee.

Have you ever noticed that the way the servers (called *boristos*) fill orders is not necessarily the most efficient? The filling of orders is done in a dramatic and entertaining way, with the order taker calling out the order and having it repeated by the order fulfiller. This theater approach encourages high customer involvement in the experience. Compare this to places where the same person who takes the order fills it, or, even worse, where you take a number when you enter. In those situations the act of giving you the coffee is more likely to be just a transaction and you are literally just a number.

A shallow brand is like flat beer—the unfocused idea of something rather than a clearly defined reality. If a beer is sold on a quality message but is priced at the low end and tastes like carbonated bath water, then the brand promise is diluted by the product and prospective customers will turn away from the brand. Customers become confused by the difference between the promise and the reality—a brand message not backed by substantive actions will not last long. Alternatively, a beer with a great taste but low brand interaction will lose out in the marketing wars, even if it wins the blind taste tests. For example, Old Milwaukee beer, a low-price-based brand, consistently wins the blind taste tests. In spite of this, in taste tests in which customers can see the brands, they typically choose Budweiser.[3]

A shallow brand opens the doors to competitors. If a company doesn't know what it stands for, other companies who have strong brand promises and act on them will move in. Owning a brand promise requires living the brand everywhere. If Volvo cars weren't really safe, and if safety weren't the basis of every Volvo action, then another car manufacturer could steal that position over time.

Finally, a shallow brand gives existing customers and prospective customers fewer places to interact with and feel good about the brand. Coca-Cola has deepened its brand throughout the long life of the product with such brand elements as polar bears, Always, the contour bottle shape, the cursive spencerian script and block letter logos of "Coca-Cola" and "Coke," and the color red. Coca-Cola has built many associations over time that engage a customer's emotions and memories. RC Cola, on the other hand, has always been more limited in its branding efforts, and, as such, has fewer loyal adherents.

How can a less than exciting or unglamorous brand become a customer favorite? The answer lies in creating a special experience for customers that adds value to their life, from either a rational or an emotional standpoint. Integrated branding allows you to free your products from a commodity death sentence and can even take currently flat brands and help them escape death row.

Integrated versus Shallow Brands—Some True Stories

One basic tenet of this book is that a truly integrated brand creates strong, almost unbreakable relationships with customers. When communications are used only as a facade to gloss over a company's problems, the product or company will lose out. In the following case histories, one company attempted to cover up its real essence with an advertising-based branding program. In the second story, a company took steps to reflect its brand further in everything it did. The name of the first company has been changed, for obvious reasons.

COMPANY XYZ—NOT STAYING TRUE TO ONE'S BRAND

West Coast–based Company XYZ, Inc., was in a quandary. The company's market leadership in transceivers (a small computer network component) wasn't building brand equity for the company's high-end hub products. Keeping up with the larger market leaders in high-end hubs required substantial R&D that the firm, as low-cost producer, couldn't afford to spend. Price-message ads weren't generating any appreciable sales, because information technology (IT) managers were afraid low-cost hubs would be a source of problems for their mission-critical networks.

After examining its brand, Company XYZ came to a conclusion—it had to compete on a different plane, not just on price. Market research suggested that the company could built its brand around "cost of ownership," both a key customer value and a key company strength, yet one that changed the conversation from one of price to the stronger one of long-term value. Company XYZ, however, wanted something more exciting, more leading-edge, for its brand and rejected its own market data.

Because Company XYZ was planning on launching a higher-end product using next-generation technology, it wanted, despite its market research, to base its brand on being an "industry innovator." A series of ads based on this message were developed and placed in the media, but sales didn't follow. Without enough R&D to back it up, and with no existing brand equity around innovation, no one trusted the company enough to buy its higher-end products. There was no reality under the mask of innovation, a truth easily perceived by a sophisticated market. Instead of building from strength, Company XYZ threw away its main price-versus-performance advantage, and ultimately its chances in the market.

ARNIES RESTAURANTS—REVISITING A BRAND FOR A NEW ERA

Like the hub manufacturer, Arnies Restaurants, a small group of fine-dining seafood restaurants in the Northwest, was losing market share. In this case, however, the aging population of customers for this seafood-based chain were literally dying off. The challenge was to find a way to appeal to a younger demographic, while still catering to the needs of its valued, older customers.

The restaurant chain had a lot going for it: a loyal customer base, great locations with water views, and personal, caring service. The food preparation, however, was old-fashioned, with a menu that desperately required updating.

After conducting research on attitudes of both existing customers and

Figure 3.2
The Arnies Logo

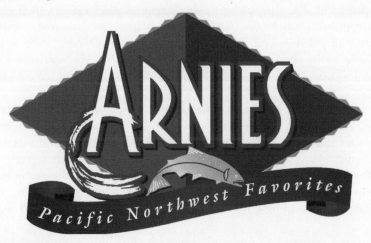

Source: Reprinted with the permission of Arnies Restaurants Northwest, Inc.

prospects in the desired age group, Arnies determined its brand principle focused on the idea of *Pacific Northwest favorites*. Its brand incorporated the best things about the Northwest—the hospitality, events, water, salmon, mountains, and food indigenous to the area. *Pacific Northwest favorites* allowed Arnies to span the generations by focusing its brand on what all its customer segments valued about the restaurant. This is illustrated in Arnies Pacific Northwest Favorites logo (see figure 3.2). *Pacific Northwest favorites* could also be extended to include the restaurant chain itself. Arnies could be promoted as a *Pacific Northwest favorite*, a tourist destination for Pacific Northwest residents and their out-of-town guests.

Then came the implementation of its brand. The company put up new signage, redecorated the restaurants so they appeared more friendly and casual to capture the younger generation, and revamped both the cooking techniques and the menu to reflect Pacific Northwest foods, but with a younger bent. However, it was careful to keep things that were favorites of its older clientele, such as early-evening specials and the wait staff's gregarious attitude and willingness to accommodate special requests. In this case, the brand was integrated into all company actions, from food preparation to waiting tables, and the result has been an increase in revenues at all three locations, with people below the age of forty now accounting for 40 percent of all guests.

INTEGRATED BRANDS = RELATIONSHIPS = PROFITABILITY

Arnies prospered while Company XYZ faltered as a result of how closely each company mapped its brand back to its strengths and what customers valued. Whereas Arnies listened to what current and potential customers were looking for and discovered that customer needs intersected the company's strengths at *Pacific Northwest favorites,* Company XYZ completely ignored both sides of the brand equation.

Brand management such as that practiced by Arnies has been a cornerstone of the biggest success stories in this century—from Coca-Cola to Proctor & Gamble. These companies have used their resources to build *brand equity*—the value customers give to a brand that keeps its promises.

The reason brand has such a strong impact on human behavior is that it mirrors human nature and the way human beings interact with the world. It fits into the places where we define our hopes, beliefs, aspirations, and friendships. We are relationship-oriented animals and seek to create relationships with almost anything we come in contact with, from people to companies to cars. In the Integrated Branding Model, *buying a product becomes a relationship-building activity*, often with a profound impact on our self-image, rather than merely a utilitarian way to meet our needs.

Companies that understand this and are willing to be consistent and committed partners with their customers, naturally develop long-term customer relationships. Those who choose to view their products as only part of a needs-fulfillment transaction will tend to turn their products into commodities.

Defining and managing relationships with customers are what strong brands are all about. People purchase products from those brands that reflect their views, goals, and emotional temperaments. We want to be with people who reflect our values and our interests. We want to buy brands that do that, too. You may drink Starbucks because you think of yourself as sophisticated in terms of coffee taste and selection; someone else drives a Saab because of his self-image as an independent thinker, and yet another shops at Nordstrom because she believes she deserves a high level of service when buying clothes.

The more a company's actions and communications reflect its underlying brand strengths, the more integrated the brand. Integrated means that everything is in line: a product's industrial design, the way the phone is answered or email responded to, the quality of paper of a direct mail piece, and even the not-for-profit organizations to which it donates. All actions deepen the relationship with the customer.

Figure 3.3
The PhotoDisc Logo

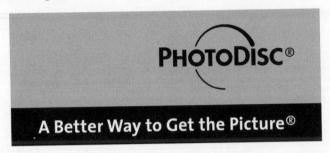

Source: Reprinted with the permission of PhotoDisc.

Many companies don't understand the integrated brand concept. This means that they may place more emphasis on their graphic identity or name than they do on relating to customers. *Working Woman* magazine, for instance, decided that it needed to protect its trademark vigorously from Lisa Kohl, a small business owner who promotes women's and other selected businesses in the Sacramento, California, area. Ms. Kohl had been operating a web site with the domain name *workingwoman.com* for two years. From Kohl's point of view, *Working Woman* "isn't living up to its ideals," because the magazine's actions had made her feel that "she and other women are an expendable portion of the magazine's business." *Working Woman* editor Bernadette Grey argued that the company had to protect its trademarked name, stating, "The brand we built is everything."[4] Although this situation put the magazine in a very tough position—brand trademarks are one of the most valuable brand assets—the brand should never be a detriment to the customer.

INTEGRATED BRANDING: THE PHOTODISC EXAMPLE

Companies in any industry can build brand, including those who are exclusively on the Web. One successful example of integrated branding in the cyberspace market is PhotoDisc (now Getty Images), a supplier of stock photography content, supplied both online and on CD-ROM. See the PhotoDisc logo (see figure 3.3).

PhotoDisc was founded by Mark Torrance, Tom Hughes, and Sally von Bargen. Torrance had been a successful entrepreneur in the music business. He served as president of Muzak and was founder of Yesco, where he pioneered the distribution and licensing of foreground music.

After leaving Muzak, Torrance, along with von Bargen and Hughes, applied technology to high-quality creative content in a way that made it easy to use and license. PhotoDisc had one goal, to make it easy to access and use high-quality stock photos.

PhotoDisc went through an integrated branding process and developed three principles that support its goals:

- *High quality*: All photos must be distinguishable as high quality by customers and must be skillfully edited.
- *Hassle-free*: The process for finding, purchasing, and using the photo must work the way it is supposed to, and employees must provide outrageously good customer service.
- *Value added*: Photos must be delivered in the right file formats and must work with all customer software and browsers; both human and online research services and help must be effective; and customers must be able to obtain whatever they need from PhotoDisc twenty-four hours a day, seven days a week.

PhotoDisc pays attention to building each customer relationship through a specific loyalty program. Besides using a relational database to track customer preferences, PhotoDisc also ensures that each customer benefits from the experience. "From the beginning, we work to deliver outrageously good customer service," explains Katherine James Schuitemaker, vice president of marketing at PhotoDisc. "This has to do with everything from how quickly we answer the phone, to whether the customer can get the right image, at the right time, in the right format, at the right price.

"Brand is being driven by people on every level of the company," explains Schuitemaker.

> Our entire senior management team, as well as our directors, managers and front line employees, spread brand thinking and action throughout the company. This is built through regular PhotoDisc brand classes—required for new employees and attended by folks from all departments—to our brand champions site on our corporate intranet. In addition, our brand handbook provides brand guidelines in virtually every area, from employee actions to message development. Every employee in the company can speak on, from memory, our three brand principles.

To reinforce its fun, cutting-edge personality, PhotoDisc occasionally includes wild and wacky gifts in its shipping boxes and mailings to customers.

Has integrated branding helped the company stay focused and capture and retain customers? TrendWatch, a research service that tracks and rates the U.S. creative professional market, shows PhotoDisc skyrocketing. TrendWatch rates the top thirty stock photography companies in terms of those that have been most important for the last three years and those that will be most important over the next three years.

In 1996, PhotoDisc was a distant fifth on the list. In 1997, it was listed first among the most important in the next three years in 80 percent of the market segments TrendWatch tracks. In 1998, the company was listed first in all categories for both the past three years and the next three years.

THE LONG-TERM BENEFITS OF INTEGRATED BRANDING

As the PhotoDisc example demonstrates, over time integrated branding creates tangible value for a company far beyond the sum total of its products. PhotoDisc is selling more than high-quality photos. It is also selling ease of use, innovation, and fun. The result of integrated branding is that people are willing to pay more for a product just because of its brand name. For example, people will pay more for Morton's Salt than store-labeled brands—even though NaCl is NaCl—because the brand has a value tied to its blue cylindrical box and the little girl with the umbrella. In fact in a recent survey of Seattle-area grocery chains, Morton commanded prices from 10 to 15 percent higher than those of store-labeled brands. For Morton, brand clearly contributes to market leadership.

Besides adding to margin, brand impacts a company's bottom line through increased sales. Integrated brands have created a promise that customers believe from past experience around particular aspects of quality, service, and commitment to the category. Brand name then becomes shorthand for *a good buy*. According to Peter H. Farquhar, director, Center for Product Research, Carnegie Mellon University, "Marriott estimated that adding its name to Fairfield Inn increased occupancy rates by 15 percent. In the breakfast cereal category. . .[testing different brands of] corn flakes cereal, choice increased from 47 percent when the brand name was not known to 59 percent when the Kellogg's brand name was identified."[5]

In an annual study done by McKinsey & Co. for Intelliquest on personal computers, results show a consistent willingness to pay more for certain brands—such as IBM, Compaq, and HP—even when all products have exactly the same specifications.[6]

BRINGING BRAND TO CONSCIOUSNESS

There is one more concept that is crucial to practicing integrated branding—*conscious brand action*. Using marketing communications to drive brand is a type of unconscious branding because it is not based on underlying brand strengths. However, using the integrated branding tools of organization and brand drivers to direct the brand brings branding up to a conscious level.

In the Integrated Brand Model, brand drives company actions. Company actions are then communicated to customers. Understanding and using company, product, or service drivers throughout the organization focus employees on brand strengths.

When executed properly, brand can be transformational—permanently enhancing the way each employee represents a company and its products. The result of this transformation is a long-term series of consistent, high-quality brand experiences with each customer or prospect.

An integrated approach to branding that focuses on both internal strengths and customer beliefs unearths the core of what makes a company and product unique and translates those strengths to employees and customers in an honest and consistent manner. The clarity of purpose this approach brings to management teams also allows companies to shift gears to meet the needs of rapidly changing markets.

NOTES

1. JRC&A Main Page: http://www.cl.ais.net/jchevron/art_sausage.html.
2. Zona Research
3. "Can You Judge a Beer by Its Label?," *Consumer Reports* (June 1996), pp. 10–15.
4. Heather McCabe, "Battle over a Woman's Place on the Web," *Wired Magazine* (May 18, 1998), http://www.wired.com.
5. Peter H. Farquhar, "Managing Brand Equity," *Journal of Advertising Research* 30, no. 4 (August–September 1990), pp. 7–12.
6. Intelliquest Brand Tech Forum Three.

4 A Blueprint for Creating Organization Drivers

> Every company needs to identify "the things that it is particularly good at" and build its strategy around them.[1]
> —Dr. Michael Hammer, President, Hammer and Company

Organization drivers determine the form and direction your brands will take. These drivers are the genetic code of the brand. Will your brand focus on integrated customer solutions (such as IBM) or will it be an emotionally appealing brand, as is the case with Southwest Airlines? Will it be embodied by the CEO (such as Berkshire Hathaway's Warren Buffett), or will it be a multifaced brand exemplified by Nike, in which many branded products are tied to specific people? What the company brings to the brand is based on *how* it defines its business, *which* concepts it cherishes, and *what* story it has to tell.

The six drivers described in Chapters 4–6 will give you the operating instructions for your company's integrated brand.

THE MISSION STATEMENT: SETTING THE BOUNDARIES OF YOUR BRAND UNIVERSE

The first organization driver (see figure 4.1) is the mission statement. Before you say, "We've got a mission statement," please consider two questions: What is the purpose of a mission statement? What does one look like?

Figure 4.1
Integrated Brand Model: Mission Statement

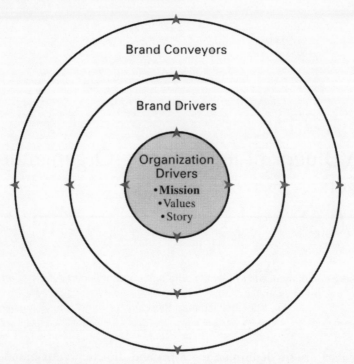

A mission statement outlines what business a company is in. Mission definition drives all corporate brand development.

How you've answered these questions determines how effective your mission statement is. In a nutshell—if a mission statement isn't memorable and doesn't inspire and motivate employees, it isn't doing its job.

Most companies create a mission because business theory tells them that all successful businesses have them. This statement then goes on the desks of upper management, is passed around to department heads, and occasionally, is framed under glass in the front lobby. And that is the first and last time most people in the company pay any attention to it.

Ask someone in your company to recite your mission statement from memory. How many people can say even part of it? Can you remember it? If you are in upper management, how often have you heard it used in strategy discussions? The mission statement is one of the most undervalued and underused organization driver. The following table shows the three questions used to create an effective mission statement (see table 4.1).

Table 4.1
Three Questions to Determine an Effective Mission Statement

Does it help you to get up in the morning?

Is it easy to understand?

Can you remember it?

The following discussion will help you bring the mission back into its rightful place in the company.

The mission statement describes what your business does. It is future-oriented while addressing current activities. Future-oriented means it provides an essential function—giving management a perspective on trends by allowing them to see a bigger picture. In the case of Fortune 500 giant Xerox, it's the difference between being in *copying* or *document management*. This big picture *document* focus allows Xerox to step back from its current product offerings and plan for future market shifts before they occur.

A mission provides boundaries for all brands. Because a mission answers "What is our business?" it defines the direction and messages for your company brand while acting as a "citizenship test" for potential product brands. Therefore, the mission statement has to address the needs your business fulfills in the most basic and comprehensive way possible. If it is too specific, it will put blinders on the company that cause it to miss major market shifts. Ironically, building in the ability to adapt to market changes is one of the stated reasons companies create missions in the first place.

As an example, suppose you define your mission as *delivering messages cost-effectively.* If new technology allows customers to deliver affordable messages for themselves you might miss a major market shift—even if you were the one who developed the technology that allowed the shift. This happened to Western Union, who developed faxing in the 1930s and then watched fax machines take away a good portion of its market in the 1970s and 1980s.

In another example, Digital Equipment Corporation focused on selling reliable, *complete* computer systems in the 1980s with its very successful and high-quality line of VAX minicomputers. This worked very well until the market began looking for systems that allowed customers to pick and choose components from multiple companies. Then, Digital discovered that customers were less inclined to purchase proprietary systems and watched its market share shrink.

Does this mean that CEOs and other upper management leaders need to be clairvoyant? Only partially: you need to stay on top of all trends that impact your business so that you aren't caught standing still while your market passes you by. This means wording the mission statement in a way that will allow employees to focus on the big picture. So instead of *delivering messages cost-effectively*, perhaps you should be *helping customers communicate*, or instead of *selling complete computer systems*, maybe you should be *selling best-of-breed computer components*.

When should you change your mission? You should revisit your mission statement every year. If a brief review indicates that the mission still accurately defines the marketplace and accounts for new market directions, then leave it alone. If your mission is an integrated part of your business operations, this review will happen in the normal course of doing business.

THE MISSION STATEMENT REVIEW PROCESS

To begin, ask yourself, "Are there new trends that impact our markets not addressed by our mission? Are we developing products and services based on our mission, or are we acting partially outside its scope?"

If new products are outside the mission's scope, determine whether the mission should be broader than you have defined it. Or are you making products that may harm the company over the long term through a resulting loss of focus? If you find the mission to be outdated, then launch into a review process.

Reach consensus through facilitated meetings. It's a good idea to use a third party to gather together the thoughts of internal opinion makers independently and then facilitate mission development meetings. Facilitated meetings in which all team members have a voice are the most effective way to create a sound mission statement, as well as critical upper management buy-in. A professional third party will keep outside the political fray. He or she may also be more respected than someone who is considered an insider. This will allow your team to focus on the issues and more easily create a real consensus. It's a good idea to create a brand team that includes upper management and members from each department. For more information on how to create a brand team see Chapter 7.

In this process, a preliminary mission statement, based on the input gathered from company opinion leaders before the meeting by the third party, is presented. The purpose of this preliminary statement is to create a lightning rod for discussion. Each idea and word is analyzed and reconstructed by the group until all parties agree on its final form. Often, because of differing personality types, one or two members of a mission

team will buy in but not consider the outcome to be the very best solution. Going for a solution everyone thinks is perfect often results in a
hung process. Therefore, the definition of consensus is *everyone's agreeing
to support the final statement wholeheartedly* even if it is some team member's second choice for the outcome. For more specific information on
the development process for all organization and brand drivers, see
Chapter 8.

CRITERIA FOR SUCCESSFUL MISSION STATEMENTS

One characteristic all effective mission statements have in common is
that they capture the excitement and vision of the company founder(s)
or current upper management team. Without an inspirational foundation, the mission will not capture the imagination of employees. This
means that the mission needs to be *forward looking*. Don't create an additional vision statement beyond the mission. It becomes too much for
everyone to remember. The word *mission* is defined as "a special vocation." If you have more than one vocation (such as both a mission and
a vision), then they probably both aren't special. Companies who have
both mission and vision statements often focus on one and ignore the
other. The Integrated Brand Model gives you the opportunity to explain
company vision within the *story* organization driver.

The best mission statements are motivators—they give everyone a reason to be excited about getting up in the morning and going to work.
That's the first criterion for a good mission: *Does it get you excited about
getting up in the morning?* If your mission statement falls short in motivational power, ask your team to ask themselves, *What would get you
excited?* Sometimes the magic of a mission statement reveals itself in the
answer to this more emotional, rather than analytical, question.

The second criterion is *clarity*. Often, mission statements are followed
by long, wordy explanations. If employees can't understand your mission without explanation (because the language is unclear or uses internal jargon that only your executive committee understands), then your
mission is not going to help focus, motivate, or define future direction
for employees. Also, once your team moves on to other tasks, you may
forget the meaning behind something that is too complex.

One of the jargon phrases you may see pop up in mission statements
is *maximizing shareholder value*. Maximizing shareholder value should be
a check-off-the-list item for all publicly held companies, not an explicit
part of the mission statement. It does nothing to provide strategic direction or motivate employees.

The third criterion for a good mission statement *is brevity*. Missions that go into too much detail are the most common mistake that companies make. Conduct this test—try reciting your mission from memory. If you can't, then it's too long. If your intent in creating a mission is for all employees to use it, then brevity is one of your most important allies.

A fourth mission statement criterion is that it must focus on *the most basic, most foundational aspects of the business* that you can think of. What is it you are trying to do for your customers? This can save you from basing company direction on product direction. Focusing too closely on existing products is like trying to fly a plane through mountains at an altitude of only five hundred feet. You'll never know what will be around the next turn. Conversely, if you aren't on top of trends, you won't notice that your customers are about to go somewhere else.

A CRITIQUE OF MISSIONS BY COMPANY

Included here are missions from different industries and company sizes to help you evaluate your own company mission. When reading the following missions, ask yourself: "How well do these mission statements meet the criteria mentioned? Do they match my experience with each of these companies? What would I change, if anything? Do these companies take actions that support their missions?"

For companies that don't use integrated branding, the mission is often made to do double duty, with aspects of other organizational and brand drivers included in it. This makes the mission more nebulous and less useful as a boundary setter and motivator, and it makes the overall brand promise less clear. The result is that employees will not know what actions will help the company stay on brand or how doing their job builds the brand.

The following are several missions, rated by how well they perform on the criteria given.

Microsoft: "To create software for the personal computer that empowers and enriches people in the workplace, at school and at home." Microsoft's mission statement is exciting, clear, and memorable but may be too specific. The personal computer might go the way of the adding machine in the not-too-distant future. It could be dropped from the statement.

Xerox: "Our strategic intent is to be the leader in the global document market, providing document solutions that enhance business productivity." This mission statement has it all—inspiration, brevity, clarity, and breadth.

IBM: "We create, develop and manufacture the industry's most advanced information technologies, including computer systems, software, networking systems, storage devices and microelectronics. We have two fundamental missions:

• We strive to lead in the creation, development and manufacture of the most advanced information technologies.

• We translate advanced technologies into value for our customers as the world's largest information services company. Our professionals worldwide provide expertise within specific industries, consulting services, systems integration and solution development and technical support.

This statement does well in inspiration and breadth. But it sounds as if there are two different companies here—one a technology company and one a services company. You could leave off everything but the first sentence with the following addition: We create, develop, manufacture, and support the industry's most advanced information technologies, including computer systems, software, networking systems, storage devices, and microelectronics.

Saturn: "To market vehicles developed and manufactured in the United States that are world leaders in quality, cost and customer enthusiasm through the integration of people, technology and business systems, and to exchange knowledge, technology and experience through General Motors." This statement fails on brevity but focuses on the key brand elements of quality, cost, and customer enthusiasm. Instead, you could say: Market U.S.-made vehicles that are world leaders in quality, cost and customer enthusiasm.

Annie's Homegrown: "The mission of Annie's Homegrown, Inc. is to produce high-quality natural food products for our customers, and to serve as an ethically, socially, and environmentally conscious business model for customers, other companies, and the food industry." Annie's Homegrown has a unique approach to product sales—word of mouth. Customers like the taste of its pasta products and its donations to scores of charitable organizations. This mission does a good job of describing that model. The mission would be clearer if it explained the term *high-quality*.

VALUES AND YOUR BRAND

After the mission, the second organization driver is your company *values* (see figure 4.2). The definition of *values* is beliefs that a company prizes above all else. Values drive employee and company actions. For instance, if a company values a balanced work life for its employees, it

Figure 4.2
Integrated Brand Model: Values

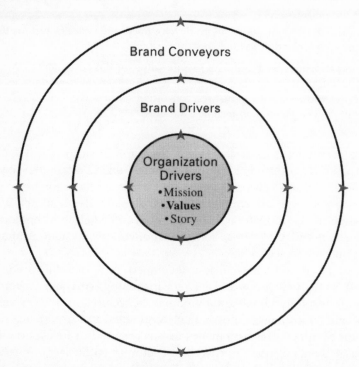

Values can help drive company actions, ensure continuity of corporate culture and help employees live the brand.

may measure its actions by whether they add to or take away from its commitment to balance. A company value is something that a company holds onto, even at the expense of short-term profitability. It is considered so important that the company will not give it up at almost any cost.

It's important to state your company's core values, whatever they are, explicitly. By doing so, your employees will *know* what commitments are driving the company, and be able to use values effectively to deepen your culture and customer experiences. But as with all brand tools, if you talk the talk you must walk the walk. Anyone who has been in the business world for a period of time has experienced a company that claims its primary value is "customer satisfaction" or says that "people are its greatest asset," yet does not support these stated values with its actions.

Companies that state one set of values and live another sow employee confusion and dissension. When company values are not followed, employees justifiably cry, "Unfair!" When values are clear and employees know what those are, they have the choice to buy into these basic tenets of company action. Clear values ensure continuity of corporate culture and help employees live the brand.

Values, like a company's mission or brand principle, also provide positive brand benefits. According to James Collins, author *of Built to Last: Successful Habits of Visionary Companies*, "Companies like Hewlett-Packard, Disney, and Boeing, which as a group have outpaced the stock market averages some 15-fold since the 1920s, have one thing in common. They have successfully adapted over the decades to a changing world without losing their core values."[2] This emphasis on core values, in turn, has helped them keep their brands consistent over time.

REI, the national outdoor clothing and sports equipment retailer, has kept the same values for the sixty plus years of its existence. The customer-owned co-op was formed to be a buying club for climbers looking for better quality and value and has expanded its original 7 members into more than 1.5 million members. Its values are *quality, service, assortment, good value, and an annual dividend to members.*

To REI, *quality* means creating the best product attributes and features possible. "The product is a means to our customer's end of enjoying the wilderness experience," explains Wally Smith, president. "It must last, endure tough conditions and perform correctly. We make a quality promise to our customers and they trust us."

Customers come to REI for its *service.* REI employees are very knowledgeable about all equipment within the store and are active in the outdoors—they share the interests of their customers. According to REI's director of brand management, Holly Cook, "Customers often seek out the same employees time after time when they come in one of our stores. We give our employees standard customer training, but our big focus is on continual new product training." REI also focuses on *good value* for products that carry its brand name. Value means that the company uses the best possible materials, pays close attention to all details, extensively product tests its goods, and runs them through a customer product test committee. The company also uses email feedback to improve its product lines continuously.

PhotoDisc (now Getty Images), a company that specializes in royalty-free digital stock photography, believes that its values are one of the strongest parts of its culture. In fact the company gives awards to *culturekeepers*—those people who do the best job of demonstrating company values in action. The company's five values are *creativity, communication, teamwork, initiative, and customer service*.

- *Communication*: PhotoDisc measures all communication by whether it is "truthful, fair and constructive." The company has a saying, "Send your mail to the right mailbox," that helps prevent unproductive back-channel communications.
- *Teamwork*: The company performs annual 360-degree reviews. Each employee picks out six to ten people above, below, and beside him or her in rank and asks these people for an evaluation, in writing, of his or her performance and values. The employee then works with his or her supervisor to create an action plan to improve.
- *Initiative, productivity, and follow-through*: These values mean *roll up your sleeves and make it happen. Do what you say you are going to do.*
- *Customer service*: Employees ask the question "Have we given this person a PhotoDisc experience?" Their definition of *customers* includes both internal employees and anyone who contacts the company.

At PhotoDisc, values provide direction for decisions and are an effective organization driver because they provide a framework that encourages *trust* both among employees and with customers.

A company's values can work in concert with other brand drivers to empower great decisions, creativity, and quality. They can free employees from the need to follow rigid rules. They offer flexible guidelines that allow employees to make decisions for the company through fully using all of their talents. Finally, a company with clearly practiced values will attract employees with those same values. If one of the values that the company demonstrates is innovation, this will attract and encourage employees who are innovative.

Xerox believes that following its values is a key reason for its success. "In our annual corporate direction release from chairman Paul Allaire last year (1998), he mandated the following four points: (1) Keep customers first; (2) grow our revenues; (3) become more productive; and (4) live our values. Values are the bedrock on which the company is built," explains David Reyes-Guerra, manager of corporate identity.

Xerox's values are as follows—"Since our inception, we have operated under the guidance of six core values:

- "We succeed through satisfied customers." Xerox sends out forty thousand surveys each month to understand how satisfied customers are. Studies indicate that highly satisfied customers are seven times more likely to become repeat customers.

- "We aspire to deliver quality and excellence in all that we do." Xerox is the only company to win the Grand Slam of quality awards: the Deming Prize in Japan, The Malcom Baldridge National Quality Award in the United States, and the European Quality Award.
- "We require a premium return on assets." Xerox rewarded its shareholders with continuing price gains and three consecutive years of dividend increases. (Adjusted for a three-for-one stock split in 1996, Xerox stock rose steadily from $31 in August 1994 to a fifty-two-week trading high of $116.5 in July 1998.)
- "We use technology to deliver market leadership." Xerox spends over $1 billion on research and development every year.
- "We value our employees." An annual employee satisfaction survey helps to determine corporatewide satisfaction and motivation down to small "family" groups, where each employee can rate his or her manager. "We strive to create an environment where people enjoy what they are doing," explains Reyes-Guerra.
- "We behave responsibly as a corporate citizen."[3] Xerox boasts the highest copier and printer cartridge recycle rate in the industry, issues an annual report on its environmental track record, and builds new and remanufactured products on the same assembly line. "We have a unique social service leave program, where we pay selected employees a year's salary and allow them to go out into the community to help in an initiative of their own choosing, such as raising awareness for AIDS centers or helping hurricane victims," adds Reyes-Guerra.

Like Xerox, many companies practice values dealing with concerns outside making a profit, such as international human rights, conservation, and community action. By challenging employees to rise above their own personal agendas, these altruistic values can serve to build cohesive internal teams, indirectly strengthening company brands.

It's no secret to anyone that employees watch management closely and pattern behavior after theirs. The most important place to begin understanding and practicing values is in upper management. As with all other brand drivers, if upper management does not live the company values, few below them will (or they may practice their personal values with their feet—by leaving the company). That's why stated values are not important unless they are practiced. If a company has a stated value of a socially flat organization, and the CEO's office is five times the size of all others, you will create a cynical atmosphere within the company. Or if you say you value open communications yet people in upper management not only don't encourage it, but even punish such openness, employees will do as you do, not as you say. That's why it's important to discover what a company's real values are, before stating them to employees. You should also consider giving employees a safe mechanism for telling you that they don't think a particular value is being followed.

Do values evolve with the business? Yes and no. Although core values never change, many businesses find that new values appear as they mature. For instance, Seattle software firm WRQ has added a value of *business success* that focuses employees more on measurements such as market share, revenue growth, and profitability over both the short and the long term. This is being called out by top management as an additional value to make sure that the high-quality, entrepreneurial work environment of the company continues to generate productive action as the company grows.

How many values does a company need? The number of values you practice should be kept to a very short list. One way to do this is for one value to hold many others. *Personal responsibility* could also hold values of *innovation* and *caring*, for instance. Try to find the handful of values on which the company bases its decisions. A long list of values is like no values at all, because they are too numerous to follow. Nike, for example, has just five values: *performance, authenticity, commitment, innovation, and teamwork.*[4]

VALUES IN ACTION: BRANDING AND ITS ROLE IN SOCIETY

Values also speak to the commitment a brand makes to the society at large. Since a brand and its customers operate within society, what values a brand uses in its societal interactions will also have an impact on its customer relationships. In fact, these values may strongly influence customer preference and loyalty.

How does the brand participate in the societies of the countries it does business in? Does it address social issues such as unemployment, social security, equal opportunity, health, safety, human rights, and environmental protection in its dialogue? What does society expect and what builds an integrated brand in these areas?

As the world gets smaller, society will demand companies and their brands respond to issues that once were thought to be outside the corporate landscape. For example, every U.S. company is now expected by the populace to work toward environmental sustainability, or, at a minimum, to do nothing that would harm the environment. Going back to the test of whether each brand action weakens or strengthens the customer relationship, U.S. companies that do not clearly state and acknowledge environmental responsibility will weaken their brands. This weakening may result from negative articles on their environmental position in the press, or criticism from shareholders, employees, and customers for not having or not stating their environmental policies. Alternatively, the general public tends to lump most companies into the "big business" category, which commonly assumes that corporations are out to get the most gain with no thought for the impact of their actions. All these situations will have a negative impact on the brand. By stating and acting on an environmental policy, companies create positive customer experience and limit vulnerability from surprise attacks by the media and others.

Beyond the environment, one of the responsibilities of a brand-aware company is to keep watch on societal issues and determine what, if any, issues the brand needs to address. Although this activity also falls under proactive crisis management, it is also a key area of brand management.

Since globalization began, brands have been vulnerable to allowing practices that are legal in one country that aren't acceptable in another. This includes such things as child labor, or dumping products that do not meet U.S. standards because of health risks, yet are allowed elsewhere in the world. Although this behavior may make good short-term business sense, customers may see it as antibrand, thus potentially risking a brand's leadership position.

Nike has run into such a problem as U.S. critics have claimed it isn't paying a living wage in countries where its shoes are assembled. This has resulted in a backlash against the Nike "swoosh" visual and caused Nike to reduce the visibility of this very popular association. "The 'Just Do It' era has given way to a 'Just Cool It' philosophy. Nike is toning down the swoosh, removing it from its corporate letterhead and most advertising nowadays, replacing it with an understated, lowercase 'nike.' "[5]

Changing an image in response to criticism makes sense. Dropping or reducing the visibility of a highly successful association does not. It is like shooting the messenger for delivering an unwanted message. The swoosh symbolizes Nike. If those practices change, the swoosh will again be looked on favorably. Deliberately toning down the swoosh cachet will result in only a loss in Nike brand equity.

Although many companies feel that their job is strictly to maximize profits, others have a commitment to give back to the communities in which they work. Giving back helps to deepen the brand's relationship with its customers and others in the community.

If you look at the brand as you would look at a person, then what kind of actions befit your brand? People who give back to their communities are typically thought of as *community leaders*. They are also looked at more favorably than people who live solely for their own gain. In fact, this is a very strong value in the United States, where the media and citizens will criticize billionaires who do not give back to their communities. Many Fortune 500 companies look at community "give backs" as a part of doing business, and they expect their suppliers to do the same.

Lucent has a highly developed giving program.

One of the core values of Lucent Technologies is a strong sense of social responsibility. It is a commitment to help people—and to help communities.

LUCENT TECHNOLOGIES FOUNDATION

In 1997 we announced the Lucent Technologies Foundation and a corporate contributions program, through which we plan to award about $20 million annually. We're focusing on education, community outreach, and support of our employees' volunteerism and giving.

Education

At the heart of our effort will be a long-term, comprehensive program to improve education from prekindergarten through high school. Focused on inner-city schools, the program will aim to improve reading and math skills and encourage students to graduate from high school and attend college.

In the area of higher education, we support science and engineering programs.

Through the Manufacturing Workforce Collaborative, a three-year, $3 million program, Lucent works with community colleges to address knowledge needed by today's manufacturing workers.

In partnership with the National Science Foundation, Lucent has contributed $500,000 for fellowships in the emerging field of industrial ecology.

Lucent also supports programs for top women and minority students in science and engineering.

Community Outreach

Lucent reaches out to communities through organizations such as United Way, to which we contributed $2.7 million in 1997, and the American Red Cross, which used our $50,000 grant to help communities devastated by flooding in 1997. We also made over $2.5 million in corporate contributions to community projects around the world.

Support of Employee Volunteerism and Giving

Through our Matching Gifts program, we matched close to $3 million in employee and retiree gifts to educational institutions and cultural organizations.

Lucent employees have a long history of volunteerism, which we support through Lucent CARES, a program that provides small seed grants based on hours volunteered.[6]

What you decide to do in the area of giving back may depend on the personality of your brand and the type of product or service it offers. For instance, technology-based Lucent particularly focuses on higher education, and that focus makes sense given that better higher education is necessary to keep technology companies successful. As shown in the following Nike-created manifesto, Nike focuses on kids for similar reasons; its success is dependent on the success of this target market:

Revolutionary Manifesto

Preamble

All kids deserve and demand an escape from the daily pressures facing us in our society: somewhere to go, something to do, someone to be. A kid's movement is awakening. Kids are taking the initiative and responsibility for positive, energetic actions charged with fun and free motion. These are our inalienable rights: Active life, sport and the pursuit of fun.

It's tough being a kid. So many distractions. So many temptations and obligations. So much growing and learning. Play gives kids the chance to put those challenges aside and just be kids. It's a way for them to build confidence and develop critical life skills. Play provides kids a jump start on the road to a healthier and more productive life.

That's why in 1994, Nike launched the P.L.A.Y. initiative.

NIKE, INC. One Bowerman Drive, Beaverton OR 97005–6453. Telephone: 1–800–929-PLAY.[7]

Values and Crisis Communications

In times of crisis, the brands that go above and beyond the call of duty are valued by their customers. Those that don't, lose equity and market share. An example of a company that went above and beyond was McDonald's after the terrible shooting that took place in its San Ysidro restaurant in 1984. McDonald's paid for psychiatric counseling for the survivors and razed its building to build a memorial park on the spot.

On the other side, many people remember the *Exxon Valdez* oil spill incident, a disaster that resulted in lost sales for the Exxon brand. Although these are extreme examples of actions based on strong community values, they demonstrate the power values have to build or tear down a brand.

Although good works may not seem directly related to a company's brand, because they reflect values—an organization driver—and because they communicate a company's brand to a wide set of audiences, no company should neglect charitable acts when expressing its values to the world.

CONVEYING MEANING THROUGH THE STORY: A POWERFUL CONTEXT GENERATOR

The final organization driver is the *story* (see figure 4.3). The story is the least understood and most powerful of organization drivers in its ability to deepen the customer relationship. For tens of thousands of years, human beings have been using stories to *convey meaning* to each other. Stories teach us about behavior. They inspire and provide insight. They are a guide to social, moral, work, and ethical actions and were used before writing to preserve the collective memories of the tribe. Human beings seem to be hard-wired to share their own experiences in story form and listen to others' tales.

Even the modern world bases much of its communication and entertainment on stories. Movies and television are all about stories that teach behavior, from the evening news to the latest sitcom. Words and phrases from these stories become part of our everyday vocabulary. The Internet provides a new style of storytelling that is more like the traditional form than you would expect—at its best, Internet storytelling can be an active collaboration between teller and listener. In the new century, as ideas become more of the currency for creating value, storytelling will take on even greater importance. The structure of a story has the ability to break through the noise of daily life and create memorable impressions in customers.

Figure 4.3
Integrated Brand Model: Story

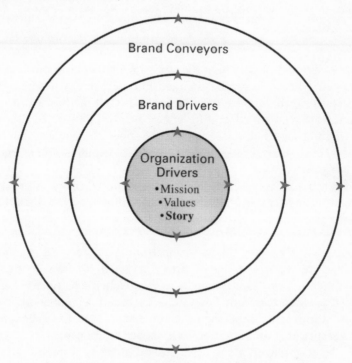

The company story is a powerful tool for building understanding and trust among all audiences.

Jennifer James, a columnist for the *Seattle Times*, talks about the power of stories within the context of teaching reform.

My belief is that the profession of teaching is in great need of a new story—that is, a new way of thinking about itself.. . .I would like to concentrate on a new education story. If such a story is to carry significant influence for our culture, it requires three things:

- Ideas that fit the marketplace;
- Values that resonate deeply with the existing culture;
- Individuals who can tell the story by the way they conduct themselves.

The theme of the old story is that teaching is an undervalued, underpaid and overworked profession. The theme I would offer is that teachers should be well-trained, well-paid, full-time intelligent professionals capable of running their own education systems, public or private.[8]

James believes, as do many, that the stories we tell about ourselves affect our behavior. They also can be changed to reflect new ways of acting.

Effective salespeople are typically those who tell the best stories. "Stories about how we arrived at different designs may be entertaining, but the storytelling also helps us explain the shoes to retailers, sales reps, consumers, and other people in the company," explains Tinker Hatfield, creative director, Nike.[9]

Customers rank storytelling, in the form of word of mouth and magazine case studies, as one of the highest influencers on their buying habits.

When you look specifically at brand, the story answers the questions "Who are we?" "Where did we come from?" "Where are we going?" and "What are we doing here?" The story is thus showing the other organization and brand drivers in action. When customers hear the brand's story, they take a first step into the brand relationship.

In most cultures, to be the one to whom a story is told is to be honored. In brand terms, it is an invitation to a deeper relationship.

The basic formula of a successful brand story is dramatic and even heroic. It is about how the protagonist beat the odds and became greater than he or she was previously. In business terms, it's frequently about the aspirations of a company's founders, seizing opportunities and successfully overcoming obstacles. And the stories of strong brands are a never-ending tale. The story will continue to grow and be even more attractive to customers as long as there are new challenges for the company to overcome.

The story also serves as a way to reinforce employee beliefs and direction. It allows them to experience the mission and other brand drivers in a contextual way, helping them to map their actions in line with brand direction. At a basic level, getting every employee to use the same story elements, brings clarity to your message as their stories get repeated in the marketplace.

Brand stories reflect what each company views as important. Although most are a literal rendition of the facts, some companies move comfortably to the metaphorical or even visual. The brand team of one award-winning Seattle-based architectural and design firm, Jaso Ludviksen, made the leap from a verbal story into two drawings of its story. The story is now hanging in the company's offices (see figure 4.4) and is used by employees to determine whether each client relationship is on track.

The first drawing is the path, Jaso Ludviksen's history of individuals coming together as the studio grows. The firm's projects result from interactions with its clients' own paths, where both partners work together to create a meaningful environment; then the detail is the activity of meeting and doing a project. This begins with a release of individual ego by both Jaso Ludviksen and the customer. They join into *a merged project ego* that both parties build, fight for, defend, and preserve. The physical evidence of this struggle is the work. In this example, the visual story helps Jaso Ludviksen to define its approach to customers while communicating to employees and customers how to get the best results from the process.

The second picture is in effect a detail of an interaction along the path. Like a compass, the diagram demonstrates the elements that need to be present in successful customer projects. These include both concrete and spiritual things that result in a meeting of the minds, hearts, and souls of both the client and Jaso Ludviksen in partnership. This meeting results in the growth of awareness for both parties and creates new meaning through the public face of each resulting building or interior. When there is no meeting on all levels, including minds, hearts, and souls, the relationship will bear no fruit or be stunted. The firm's business is a series of such intersections with clients, represented by the crossroads on the picture.

This visual story also acts as a filter—prospective customers who are not interested in instilling meaning in their projects will not be a good fit for Jaso Ludviksen. Nora Jaso, owner, explains, "The story continues to give us a lot to think about and we always refer to the story when considering new clients."

WHAT MAKES A MEANINGFUL STORY?

You begin the process of story creation by asking a group of employees from all parts of the company to tell you the company story. This is usually done in tandem with other brand research. Step two is to take these many renditions and boil them down to one. The final step is to bring this synthesized version to your brand team for verification and change. See Chapter 7 for more information on the facilitation process.

The following are criteria for creating a story that will have the most impact on your customers, prospective customers, and other interested parties.

The first criterion is *passion*. Does the story capture the heart of the brand in a way that evokes strong emotion? Most entrepreneurs believe

Figure 4.4
The Jaso Ludviksen Story

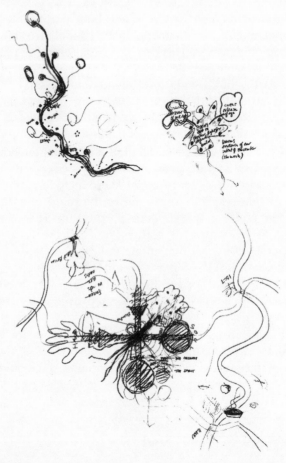

Innovative architectural and design firm Jaso Ludviksen uses a visual story to provide context
  to their customers and employees.

Source: Reprinted with the permission of Jaso Ludviksen.

passionately in a new or better way of doing something. That passion
helps them build reality around their vision and, if they are lucky, carries
others along with them. That passion, when integrated by employees, is
one of the elements that separate highly successful organizations from
all others.

The second criterion is *values*. Does the story reflect company values? Values are the method great companies use to guide employee behavior. They promote personal responsibility and initiative, as opposed to rules-based behavior, which tends to be top-down and bureaucratic. Fast-paced markets, such as high technology, require employees who are dynamic decision makers, who don't have time to wait for approval, who understand the fine nuances of a situation, who know when to step over a line and when to hold back. Values guide behavior and build customer loyalty by creating a framework for customer trust.

The third criterion is *vision*. Does the story capture the company's vision? Vision is about a company's unique market perspective. What do you see that others don't? How does that affect the company's product and service offerings? Can the company vision be stated in the story in a way that allows others to *envision* the future of your company with you?

Another criterion is *audience reaction*. Once you have a story created on paper, you have completed half of the job. For a story to work, it needs to be a shared experience with the listener. So, tell the story to a variety of people inside and outside the company. Gauge their emotional reaction and analyze the questions asked. Were listeners attentive? Excited? Engaged? Can you enhance the story on the basis of the questions they asked? A story is one of the most "organic" elements of the brand, because it changes over time and varies according to both who tells the story and who is listening to it. If a listener's questions were about clarification of either the facts or the reasons for doing something, the story needs to change. If the questions demonstrated an understanding of what you were trying to convey, and were further explorations into the company brand, congratulations; your story is working for you!

However, there are several points to avoid. One is *industry speak*. Since the story is a way of reaching out to all of your audiences, don't load it with phrases that only people in your industry, or even in your company, will understand. Be sure that outsiders understand it without further explanation.

Jargon unfortunately is a term that applies to more words in our language every year. Jargon is the result of using words without backing them up with meaning—the antithesis of what you want to do with your brand! For example, when a company tells you it does quality work, do you believe it? Do you know what *quality* means in that context, or do you just skip over that sentence altogether and continue looking for something more meaningful in way of explanation? A story needs to speak in terms that can't be glossed over, that convey something tangible to the reader or listener.

Also avoid *passive voice*. For those of you who hated English class growing up, don't worry. This is the only grammar discussion in the entire book. Passive voice may rob your sentence of strength and clarity by hiding the subject or doer. Therefore, understanding and generally avoiding passive voice are worth the effort, especially in a company brand story, which should be a clear, strong invitation to buy into an approach and vision. The following is passive voice: "Switches are used to create enterprisewide networks." One active version of the same sentence is "Network managers use switches to create enterprisewide networks." Notice that passive voice always has the verb *to be* (*are*) and another verb (*use*) and you can't find the subject. By adding the subject (*network managers*), the sentence becomes both stronger and easier to read.

HOW DO COMPANIES USE STORIES?

Companies use stories as a way to communicate context and meaning to outsiders. By using one story as a foundation, all employees will speak consistently about company history, current actions, and vision. This does not mean that employees will memorize the story and repeat it verbatim. Instead, they will tend to use it as source material for their own personalized story about the company.

The story is also used in written form to talk about the company— such as the annual report, the corporate section of the web site, and newsletters. In very large companies with many brands and product lines, the story ties all company activities together in one neat bundle.

Finally, the story is used as input to the creation of your *principle, personality*, and *association* brand drivers.

Making the Story Personal through Story Training Sessions

For a story to be powerful, employees must put it in their own words. You can help this process along through story training. Questions to get employees thinking about include "What is the most important part of the story to you?" and "What gets you excited about the brand?" You can help employees discover and elaborate on the story for themselves. One way to do this is by using a structured session in which you instruct employees to role-play telling the story to a larger group and then critiquing the rendition. See Chapter 11 for more information about integrating brand action throughout the company.

SELECTED STORIES BY COMPANY

Most companies have not fully embraced the potential of their stories for brand building. The following corporate stories will give you insight on how to evaluate your own:

Xerox

No longer just a copier company, Xerox has successfully recreated itself as The Document Company, which means unrivaled expertise in the production and management of documents: color and black-and-white, paper and digital, across networks, for the small office/home office or the global enterprise.

Xerox and its partner, Fuji Xerox Co., Ltd. of Japan, offer the broadest array of document products and services in the industry: copiers, printers, fax machines, scanners, desktop software, digital printing and publishing systems, supplies, and comprehensive document-management services, from the operation of in-house production centers to the creation of networks. (From the Xerox web site)

Xerox's story focuses on transformation and the impact of that transformation on its customers. This story successfully conveys the breadth of its product line and the huge shift in the boundaries of its brand. It also communicates Xerox's brand principle, *The Document Company*, which is what drives the brand forward and provides vision for the future.

Coca-Cola

The Coca-Cola Company is the global soft drink industry leader. In 1998, consumers enjoyed an average of one billion servings of Coca-Cola (known as Coca-Cola classic in the U.S. and Canada), diet Coke (known as Coca-Cola light in some countries), Sprite, Fanta and other products of The Coca-Cola Company daily.

Syrups, concentrates and beverage bases for Coca-Cola, the Company's flagship brand, and other Company soft drinks are manufactured and sold by The Coca-Cola Company and its subsidiaries in nearly 200 countries around the world.

By contract with The Coca-Cola Company or its local subsidiaries, local businesses are authorized to bottle and sell Company soft drinks within certain territorial boundaries and under conditions that ensure the highest standards of quality and uniformity.

The Company takes pride in being a worldwide business that is always local. Bottling plants are, with some exceptions, locally owned and operated by independent business people who are native to the nations in which they are located.

Bottlers provide the required capital for investments in land, buildings, machinery, equipment, trucks, bottles and cases. Most supplies are purchased from local sources, often creating new supply industries and areas of employment within local economies.

The Company supplies the concentrates and beverage bases used to make its products and provides management assistance to help its bottlers ensure the profitable growth of their businesses. Product manufacturing, quality control, plant and equipment design, marketing, and personnel training are just a few of the areas in which the Company shares its expertise. (from the Coca-Cola web site)

Coca-Cola's story does a very good job of making the brand's values real by sharing them within the context of the story. These values include high quality, profitability, consistency, partnership, universal inclusiveness, and support for local businesses around the world.

Cyan (Makers of *Myst* and *Riven*)

Before 1987, brothers Rand and Robyn Miller were leading very separate lives. Rand was a computer programmer at a bank in Texas while Robyn was studying anthropology in Washington State.

Being a programmer and a father, Rand had an interest in developing high quality children's software. After sharing this vision (and some software) with Robyn, they both began work on their first collaboration: *The Manhole*.

When it was released in 1988, *The Manhole* stood out in terms of its unique and playful graphics and sound. But more importantly, it forged new ground in the area of interactive worlds. *The Manhole* was a nonthreatening, fully navigable environment to explore on a desktop. You couldn't push the wrong button; you couldn't lose.

The Manhole was awarded *Best New Use of a Computer* by the Software Publishers Association in 1988. It was quickly followed by a CD-ROM version, the first entertainment CD-ROM ever released.

Excited by their first success and the potential of an entirely new medium, the brothers Miller went on to create *Cosmic Osmo and the Worlds Beyond the Mackerel*. "Our goal was to create something not only our kids would like, we wanted adults to enjoy the world as well," explains Rand. *Cosmic Osmo* won numerous awards and industry kudos for the Millers.

After working within the realm of children's software for a few more years, the Millers were ready to start a project that would put all of their acquired skills to the test. "The time we spent working on the early children's projects was mostly a time of exploration and experimentation for us. We had stumbled across a new medium and we wanted to see what it could do," says Robyn. "But finally, we were ready to meet the challenge of creating a world that appealed to 'grown-ups'—we were ready to make the player the main character of an interactive story."

So Cyan began work on *Myst*.

"*Myst* was by far the largest project we had attempted, and it presented some unique challenges," said Rand. "We spent a lot of time planning the story and design. When you're working on children's software, you can draw the door first without knowing what goes behind it. But with *Myst*, there was an enormous amount of planning to ensure that everything was tight and consistent."

A team was assembled and headquarters established in the proverbial garage to get started with the monumental task. Although the original plans were for the vast number of images to be hand-painted much like their earlier worlds, plans quickly changed when 3D modeling and rendering tools became readily available on low cost computers. It became immediately apparent that there would be advantages to building 3D models of the new world they were creating. "We could build a wireframe model of a tree, scan in a piece of bark and set various parameters which include lighting, fog, reflectivity, and texture," explained Robyn. "It was a tedious process for a single tree, but that single tree could become an entire forest, and we could generate images from anywhere in the forest!"

In the years since September 1993, *Myst* has sold approximately 5 million copies worldwide, making it the best selling CD-ROM game of all time. It has received awards too numerous to mention.

The October, 1997 release of the long-awaited *Myst* sequel, *Riven*, marked the end of three and a half years of intense labor by the

Cyan team. The effort and resources put into *Riven* dwarf the production of *Myst*, but it was worth the wait and the long hours put in by so many talented people, as *Riven's* public reception proves. *Riven* reached the "one million units sold" mark faster than any other package in software history, with the exception of *Windows95*, and continues to stay in the "top ten" lists of software sold. It has already won several awards, and has raised interest in the world of D'ni to new levels. (From the Cyan web site)

This example meets all the criteria of a strong story. It holds forth on a theme of exploration—two brothers, Rand and Robyn Miller, set out on a quest to explore a new realm: the interactive world. It tells a story of hard work, innovation, and success. The brothers approach this quest with unique vision and the discipline to plan each new venture in ways that bring customers deeper into their realm with each new purchase. As you read the story, you can relate to their passion to discover new worlds, to find new realms, a deeply rooted human motivation that computer games both recognize and cater to. It also feels like a very comfortable and personable brand, one that you would trust to give you more high-quality experiences in the future.

Microsoft

Since its inception in 1975, Microsoft's mission has been to create software for the personal computer that empowers and enriches people in the workplace, at school and at home. Microsoft's early vision of a computer on every desk and in every home is coupled today with a strong commitment to Internet-related technologies that expand the power and reach of the PC and its users. As the world's leading software provider, Microsoft strives to produce innovative products that meet customers' evolving needs.

Microsoft® products include operating systems for personal computers, server applications for client/server environments, business and consumer productivity applications, and interactive media programs, and Internet platform and development tools. Microsoft also offers online services, sells personal computer books and input devices, and researches and develops advanced technology software products. Microsoft products, available in more than 30 languages and sold in more than 50 countries, are available for most PCs, including Intel microprocessor-based computers and Apple computers. (From the Microsoft web site)

Microsoft's story is well rounded and heavily visionary but is perhaps too focused on tangible product. On the plus side, what could be more in line with the American myth of plenty than "a computer on every desk and in every home"? The story also inspires us with promises to "expand the power and reach of the PC and its users," and that is very close to Microsoft's brand principle of *access*, although the term *users* unnecessarily distances the brand from its customers. The story also communicates strong values around innovation and commitment to the future. This story contains many of the criteria for success: it is values-based, it drives the brand principle, and it inspires and is visionary.

IBM

Louis V. Gerstner Jr. arrived as IBM's chairman and CEO on April 1, 1993. For the first time in the company's history IBM had found a leader from outside its ranks. Gerstner had been chairman and CEO of RJR Nabisco for four years, and had previously spent 11 years as a top executive at American Express.

Gerstner brought with him a customer-oriented sensibility and the strategic-thinking expertise that he had honed through years as a management consultant at McKinsey & Co. Soon after he arrived, he had to take dramatic action to stabilize the company. These steps included rebuilding IBM's product line, continuing to shrink the workforce and making significant cost reductions.

Despite mounting pressure to split IBM into separate, independent companies, Gerstner decided to keep the company together. He recognized that one of IBM's enduring strengths was its ability to provide integrated solutions for customers—someone to represent more than piece parts or components. Splitting the company would have destroyed a unique IBM advantage.

With the rise of the Internet and network computing the company experienced another dramatic shift in the industry. But this time IBM was better prepared. All the hard work IBM had done to catch up in the client/server field served the company well in the network computing era. Once again, customers were focused on integrated business solutions—a key IBM strength that combined the company's expertise in solutions, services, products and technologies. In the fall of 1995, delivering the keynote address at the

COMDEX computer industry trade show in Las Vegas, Gerstner articulated IBM's new vision—that network computing would drive the next phase of industry growth and would be the company's overarching strategy.

That year, IBM acquired Lotus Development Corp., and the next year acquired Tivoli Systems Inc. Services became the fastest growing segment of the company, with growth at more than 20 percent per year. From 1993 to 1996, the market value of the company increased by more than $50 billion.

In May 1997, IBM dramatically demonstrated computing's potential with Deep Blue, a 32-node IBM RS/6000 SP computer programmed to play chess on a world class level. In a six-game match in New York, Deep Blue defeated World Chess Champion Garry Kasparov. It was the first time a computer had beaten a top-ranked chess player in tournament play, and it ignited a public debate on how close computers could come to approximating human intelligence. The scientists behind Deep Blue, however, preferred to stress more practical concerns. Deep Blue's calculating power—it could assess 200 million chess moves per second—had a wide range of applications in fields calling for the systematic exploration of a vast number of variables, among them forecasting weather, modeling financial data and developing new drug therapies. (From the IBM web site)

The IBM story is derivative of many classic tales in which the land had been laid waste and the people cried out for a champion to save them. Just such a champion comes in the form of Louis V. Gerstner, an outsider, who brings the talents of a customer-oriented sensibility, strategic thinking, and a penchant for dramatic action. He holds the company together against the forces of darkness, brings stability, rebuilds, and reduces the brand's vulnerability to cost. He also recognizes the power of the core brand—*integrated business solutions*—and brings out the vision of a network computing future at the most sacred of all technology conferences, COMDEX. He then demonstrates his prowess through conquering other rivals, Lotus and Tivoli. The end of the story presents Gerstner's technological counterpoint, Deep Blue (the color blue is an IBM visual association), which promises additional riches for IBM customers.

This is an excellent example of a well-told brand story, offering a richness of experience to the customer that goes far beyond specific products or features. In fact, if measured on a hypothetical brand maturity continuum, it is much more well developed than many other technology company stories, which barely scratch the surface of brand and dwell mostly on specific product offerings.

THE ELEVATOR STATEMENT: A SHORTENED STORY

An elevator statement is a pared-down version of the story. You can think of the elevator statement as the introduction to the story—something you tell when you don't have time to go into great detail. It's called an elevator statement because you should be able to say it while going up (or down) five floors in an elevator. The elevator statement needs to tell in everyday language understandable by all:

- What you do, and
- Why you are different

The elevator statement gives prospective customers a quick take on the company and/or brand.

NOTES

1. Dr. Michael Hammer, *Beyond Reengineering: How the Process-Centered Organization Is Changing Our Work and Our Lives* (New York, NY: HarperCollins, 1997).

2. James C. Collins, "Change Is Good—but First, Know What Should Never Change," *Fortune* (May 29, 1995), p. 141.

3. Xerox web site: http://www.xerox.com.

4. Nike web site: http://www.nike.com.

5. William McCall, "There's Mud on Nike's Swoosh," *The Seattle Post-Intelligencer* (October 9, 1998).

6. Lucent web site: http://www.lucent.com.

7. Nike web site: http://www.nike.com.

8. Jennifer James, "Self-Help Books: From Daydreams to Depression," *Seattle Times* (September 6, 1998).

9. Geraldine E. Willigan, "High-Performance Marketing: An Interview with Nike's Phil Knight," *Harvard Business Review* (July–August 1992).

5 The Role of the Brand Principle

An automobile is made by and for people. The basic principle for all manufacturing is and must remain: safety.[1]
—Gustaf Larson and Assar Gabrielsson,
Founders of Volvo, 1927

A CENTRAL BRAND DRIVER: THE BRAND PRINCIPLE

Of all the brand drivers in the Integrated Brand Model, the most important is usually the *brand principle*—it's the foundation for differentiating the brand in all areas (see figure 5.1). Think about everything you've ever heard about branding—such as that brand is about consistently communicating one message, or that creating a differentiator is important to brand, and so on. Putting all of these ideas into action is possible with a brand principle. Without this critical brand driver, companies squander brand assets by not remaining focused on them, overlooking them, or inadvertently discarding them.

The principle impacts all activities of the brand.

The principle is a decision-making tool that creates a unified direction for all employees regardless of department or title. For example, Volvo's *safety* principle encourages all employees to ask themselves, "Is this action contributing to safety?"

The principle directs new product and new feature development. If I am working in product development at Xerox, *the document company*, I will focus on products and features that allow for the more effective

Figure 5.1
Integrated Brand Model: Principle

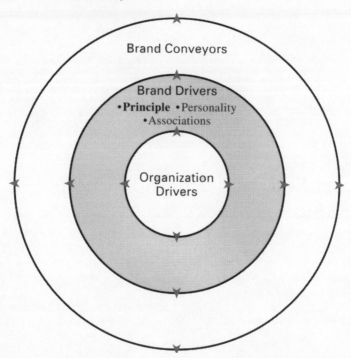

The brand principle is the foundation of a successful brand. It helps drive all activities of the brand such as strategic and product direction and communications. It is the compass for employee actions.

creation and use of documents.

The principle has the power to differentiate the brand everywhere it interacts with the customer. It is the foundation for developing a unique and consistent customer experience. It enables employees to reinforce the brand with each customer interaction. In the Microsoft example of *access*, customers' experiences will be centered around having access to the information they need to be more effective in their professional and personal lives.

What is the definition of a brand principle? If your mission is *what you do*, your principle is *your unique approach* to what you do. In a company with multiple brands, it is limited to each brand's specific business category. So if Volvo's mission is to *make great cars*, its unique approach to this mission is through being the *safety choice*. Many companies attempt to include both of these functions in the mission. By separating what you do from the approach you take, you can make both drivers more effective and focused. The principle then becomes the foundation for all actions and messages.

The principle uncouples product, service, and brand message development from the individual beliefs of product managers, marketing managers, or whoever wins the latest round of internal politics. Instead, it bases messages solidly on the brand promise—the intersection of company strengths and what customers value. Because of this, the brand principle takes the brand to a new level of sophistication beyond just consistent message creation. It provides the brand with a versatile, differentiated platform for employee actions and message development both now and in the future. When employees follow the principle, it shapes the customer experience and strengthens customer loyalty along lines that emphasize a brand's points of difference from all other competitors in the market. And it does it in a way that is defensible over the entire product cycle.

The principle (and all drivers) takes the differentiation process and matches it to valued company strengths, while providing each member of the company with an easy-to-use tool for implementation. If your company has multiple brands, each brand has its own principle, with all principles being complementary to the umbrella corporate brand principle. So Dockers and 501 jeans would each have their own principle, and both would map back to the corporate brand of Levis.

The principle guides all decisions and actions around a brand. It is an *explicit agreement* by all employees about how to build the brand. This means employees use the corporate brand principle as a compass for every decision that has a significant impact on the company. Hence, the power of a principle to align every employee of a company in the direction that creates the most impact for the brand is enormous.

What form does a principle take? It is usually one word or a short phrase based on your promise as a brand. It is written in a way that focuses on the unique strengths of the brand. You can think of it as both a brand focusing and a brand differentiating mechanism. The principle is designed for internal use—it is rarely repeated word for word with customers. It is not a slogan or tag line. Think of it as the foundation of a house. The foundation cannot be seen without going under the house, yet it is totally necessary for a stable, lasting structure.

The principle is a balancing act between forward-looking and current actions; it is both broad and specific. If it is too specific, it won't be sufficiently flexible to adapt to marketplace changes. If it is too broad, it will not be something that employees can easily act upon.

Depending on how your company is structured, you may have one principle for all products. In this case, the company is the brand. A good example of this is Volvo. All Volvo products feature the company name followed by a number, such as the Volvo 850, and are based on the principle *safety*.

You might have different principles for some or all product groups. A good example of this is Proctor & Gamble, which is the umbrella brand for a variety of product brands, such as Tide and Pampers. In general, the more similar the product lines, the easier and more cost-effective it is to group them under one brand name, promise, and experience.

VOLVO AUTOMOBILES AND SAFETY

Volvo has a very strong brand principle, first outlined by its founders, Gustaf Larson and Assar Gabrielsson, in the late 1920s. Volvo is credited with inventing the automobile seatbelt, which it introduced first to front seats and then to rear seats, in 1957 and 1958, respectively.[2] The company also made shoulder harnesses part of the basic car package, while other companies were still arguing that they could be dangerous.

What do you think of when you think of Volvo? Most people would answer *safety*. Volvo fulfills this promise in how its customers experience the company. This experience begins long before customers ever get into their first Volvo automobile. For instance, Volvo lives safety on the factory floor and assembly line. Volvo designers seek out new ways to bring safety to their customers and Volvo owns safety in its communications.

When a company truly integrates a brand principle, the principle drives it to new investments that it might not otherwise make. For example, since 1970, Volvo has used an internal Traffic Accident Research Team to analyze tens of thousands of accidents to get a better understanding of how to protect its customers. The company continually wins top honors in safety worldwide and, on many of its innovations, has been ten-plus years ahead of meeting local governments' safety legislation. Volvo invests 10 percent of its revenues in R&D annually and is spending $84 million on a new accident laboratory to be opened in the year 2000.

The list of safety innovations in the following table demonstrates Volvo's commitment to safety (see table 5.1).[3]

The process of investing in brand-related actions, in turn, widens the differentiation gap between the company and its competitors. Since brand-driven companies are clear on what their brand is, it is easier for them to integrate feedback from customers on how to improve the customer experience. These are fundamental branding processes that act as "anticommodity insurance" for a brand's products.

Does this mean that Volvo cars are the safest on the road? Not necessarily,

Table 5.1
Volvo Safety Innovations

Volvo Safety Innovations 1944 to the Present

- **1944**
  Safety cage around the passenger compartment
  Laminated windshields

- **1956**
  Split steering column
  Safety-padded dashboard

- **1957**
  Attachments for 2-point belts at the front

- **1958**
  Attachments for rear safety belts
  Three-point shoulder/lap seat belts patented

- **1965**
  Brake servo and pressure-sensitive relief valves
  Volvo's child safety research begins

- **1966**
  Disc brakes all round
  Safety door locks
  Crumple zones front and rear
  Collapse function in the split steering column

- **1967**
  Safety belts on the rear seat

- **1968**
  Head restraints front

- **1969**
  Inertia reel belts
  Heated rear screen

- **1970**
  Industries first auto investigation team established

- **1972**
  Child seat
  Childproof locks on rear doors

- **1973**
  Side collision protection
  Collapse function in the steering wheel

- **1974**
  Energy-absorbing shock absorbers
  Energy-absorbing steering column
  Isolated fuel tank and protection in a rear-end collision

- **1975**
  Day running lamps
  Warning lamps

- **1979**
  Headlamp washers/wipers
  Wide angle rear view mirror

- **1982**
  Safety belts combined with anti-submarining guard
  Fog lamps rear-front
  Warning lamps on open doors
  Fuel tank in front of the rear axle

- **1984**
  ABS-anti-locking brakes

- **1985**
  ETC-electronic wheel spin control

- **1986**
  New child safety program
  Brake lights in rear screen
  Three-point belt on the center rear seat

- **1987**
  Airbag

- **1989**
  Mechanical seat belt pretensioner

- **1990**
  Integrated child safety seat in the rear seat

Table 5.1 (continued)

Volvo Safety Innovations 1944 to the Present

• **1991**
  SIPS-side impact protection system
  The self-adjusting safety belt
  Integrated booster cushion for
    children 50 to 80 pounds

• **1992**
  New safety improvements in rear seats

Source: Reprinted with the permission of Volvo Cars of North America from http://www.volvo.com.

or, at least, not every year. But they are always ranked highly and customers have the assurance that Volvo is committed to backing up its safety experience with yet more safety innovations. So although safety may be the hot button for another carmaker for a year or two, customers can be assured that it will *always* be at the center of the Volvo experience.

With the proliferation of cars throughout the world, safety and the number of automobile-related deaths are becoming more of an issue, thus increasing Volvo's potential customer base. If you travel to Volvo's web site, you can also read about the *Volvo Saved My Life Club* (see figure 5.2),[4] which gives the stories of customers who have written to Volvo to say that because of the way it builds its cars, they, their spouse, or their children are alive today. "The truck spun out of control, hydroplaning across the center divider and crashing into us—ultimately we were hit in the rear by a semi trailer truck....I feel I owe my life and my husband's life to the fact we owned a Volvo and we will be Volvo owners forever" (Helen and Ralph Capo, January 3, 1989).

Defining your brand to the degree that Volvo has allows you not only to focus your internal resources on what you do best, but also to attract like-minded customers. The clearer you are about who you are, the easier it will be to attract customers who have the same values and goals. Safety is something that a large segment of the car-buying public puts as their first or second priority. But a principle of safety doesn't restrict you to people who buy solely on safety—so you can build models for people who buy on safety and then secondarily want performance or styling. Also, your market may expand as people change their buying habits with changes in their life. For instance, many non-safety-oriented car buyers become safety-oriented buyers when they have their first child.

Figure 5.2
The Volvo Saved My Life Club

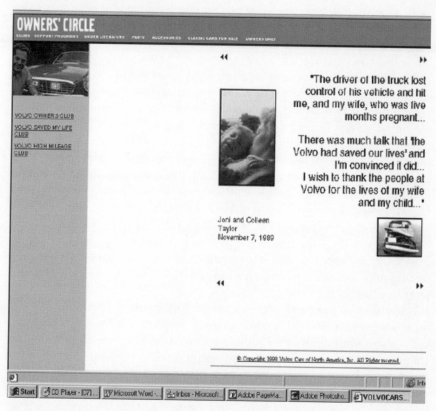

Source: Reprinted with the permission of Volvo Cars of North America from http://www.volvo.com.

CRITERIA FOR AN EFFECTIVE BRAND PRINCIPLE

An effective brand principle shares some of the same criteria as a company's mission statement. Remember the difference—the mission is about what business you are in: the principle is your unique approach to that business. For example, your mission might be to build vehicles for transporting people from place to place (currently automobiles), but your principle could be anything from safety, to luxury, to leading-edge engineering.

What are the qualities of an effective principle? They include being *true, useful for focusing actions, and close to the buying decision; providing emotional resonance;* and *being not too narrow, not too broad.* Other criteria for a brand principle include *ownability, clarity, and brevity.*

The brand principle must be *true*. Matching your principle with the way you really act is critical to brand success. The principle can be partially aspirational, but it must be largely based on the real customer value that you provide. For example, if your brand is based on innovation, then you need to be spending enough on R&D so that you can claim innovation as your own.

It should also *focus actions*. The principle must not just be a quick read; employees must be able to see easily how it applies to the decisions they are making. Where brand has become second nature, employees will use the brand principle yardstick to measure all decisions. INTERLINQ Software Corporation, a leading provider of PC-based business solutions for the residential mortgage and construction lending industry, has a principle of *partner*. The company has used this principle to help channel employees into taking actions that are *proactive, insightful, innovative, and responsive*—all activities that would characterize a partner.

The brand principle is *close to the buying decision*. The principle is the active force within the brand that works the magic of differentiation. Its goal is to make each customer interaction one that differentiates and strengthens the relationship, and to do that it needs to be of high value to the customer.

It should also have *emotional resonance*. Your brand principle must strike an emotional chord with people in your company. It must get them excited about your company's unique approach to your business and allow them to see the possibilities for enhancing your product or service. West Stock Photography, a national stock photography service, has a brand principle of *image guide*, because it helps people solve the frustrating hassle of wading through hundreds of inappropriate photos. This principle was the driving force in designing the company's e-commerce web site.

The brand should *not be too broad*. The principle must be sufficiently narrow so that employees can take action based on it. When they are faced with important decisions, they must be able to understand how they can use the principle to direct the decision. A principle that is about *creating value for our customers and shareholders* does not give any direction on decision making, whereas *safety* does.

Nor should it be *too narrow*: If a principle is *too narrow*, it won't be able to adapt to the changing needs of the market. Remember, the principle remains the same for the life of the brand. So if Volvo had stated its principle as, *We develop cars that exceed European safety standards*, it would have been too narrow, because the company branched out into other markets.

The brand principle should have *ownability*. Whatever you decide for a principle, it needs to be ownable by the brand and company. This does not mean that it has to be unique. Many companies claim that their cars are safe, but Volvo owns the principle. A company obtains ownership through a long-term focus on the brand and long-term communication of that focus. If the principle is the right match for the brand, and if it has been successful, chances are that the brand is already on the road to owning this area. Once a company uses a principle for a length of time, no one else can own it anyway because the principle will be integrated into all layers of company action. Talk is cheap, but unless it's backed up by action, customers don't believe it.

Another attribute of the brand principle should be *clarity*. The brand principle is a basis of all decisions. If the principle needs further explanation or is not a quick read, it will not be used by most people in the company.

Brevity is also necessary for a brand principle. If it is to be used, people must be able to remember it without having to refer to a piece of paper.

Most companies also create *supporting statements* that elaborate on the principle. They explain many of the things that the original brand team implied in the principle, and they are added to as needed, to adapt to changing market circumstances. Specific supporting statements may be used as short-term positioning for the brand—see the discussion of positioning later in this chapter—but are not substitutes for a clear, concise brand principle.

If you feel that the principle your team has crafted does not convey the full meaning of the organization, yet you can't see any way to change it, don't despair. You may discover that this meaning can be captured in one of the other brand drivers—the *personality* or *associations*. Develop all three drivers before returning to the drawing board.

SELECTED PRINCIPLES

Put yourself in the shoes of an employee at each one of these companies. Can you see how the principle might help you design new product features? Talk to customers and prospects? Determine new product directions?

Principle Descriptions by Company

Microsoft emphasizes access to the power and information you need in your personal and professional life. The company states this as "Microsoft is the leader in providing technology that helps people do exciting things today and in the future." This principle works very well with a company that has as broad a line of products as does Microsoft. *Access* is reinforced by the company slogan "Where do you want to go today?"

Jaso Ludviksen focuses on meaning. As an architectural and interior design firm, Jaso Ludviksen makes spaces that are a meaningful extension of the businesses and people they are designed for. A space designed with meaning creates more richness, differentiation, and effectiveness for the people living in such an environment. Jaso Ludviksen brings brand meaning into building and space design.

Pivot & Levy is a high-tech design firm with the brand principle of *engaging experience*. This is exactly what its customers look for from it—an engaging process in which both the path to product completion and the result engage both Pivot & Levy's customer and the customer's customers.

Seattle Children's Home (SCH), a not-for-profit agency that is more than 110 years old, is dedicated to providing sustained care for at-risk children and their families. The organization's principle, *building partnerships to improve futures*, demonstrates what is unique and exciting about SCH. No one else in this sector comes from the position of providing sustained, holistic care for children with emotional and psychological problems from infancy to adulthood. *Building partnerships* also implies working with children to help them help themselves, rather than doing everything for them. By partnering among SCH employees, with at-risk children and their families and the community and with other institutions, SCH is able to provide the sustained support each child and family needs for an improved future. Says its president, R. David Cousineau, "You can sum up our brand difference as follows: our entire staff cares deeply about all at-risk children; therefore improving each child's ability to find a better life is at the heart of what we do."

HOW TO USE THE PRINCIPLE

The brand principle is a relatively simple idea, yet is all-encompassing and powerful when executed well. Use the brand principle as part of the brand filter that you apply to any decision, project, or communication. When employees are making a decision related to the company, they ask, *"Will this decision strengthen our focus on [insert your brand principle]? Or will it at least be complementary to the principle?"* So in the case of Jaso Ludviksen, the test was "Will this decision add meaning in my client's environment?" "Will it make the setting for their work and life more meaningful?"

Is the principle the full promise of the brand talked about in the definition, *Brand is the promise that you keep*? No. The promise is about the complete relationship you create with your customers, which includes all organization and brand drivers, and brand conveyors. The promise includes all aspects of what you do as a company and how you act in the customer relationship. The other brand drivers that impact creating a strong customer relationship include the *personality* and *associations*. These drivers will be covered in the next chapter.

Figure 5.3
Integrated Brand Model: Positioning, a Brand Conveyor

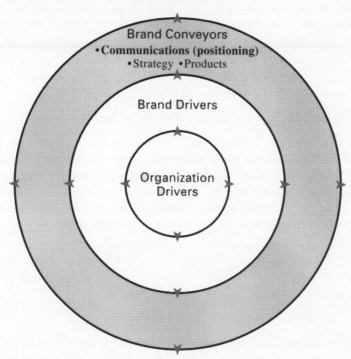

Company or product positioning conveys brand actions and messages in a way that answers current market needs.

POSITIONING AND THE PRINCIPLE

Those of you reading this book who hail from the marketing side of business will probably be familiar with the process of positioning a company or product. Positioning is a method for showing how your company and/or products relate to others in the marketplace. One definition of positioning is *what currently distinguishes you in your customers', prospects', and other audiences' mind from your competition*. Two experts in this area, Al Ries and Jack Trout, have published the defining book on the subject, *Positioning: The Battle for Your Mind*,[5] and Trout has published a follow-up, *The New Positioning: The Latest on the World's #1 Business Strategy.*[6]

In the context of brand, positions are a *brand conveyor* and/or a supporting statement of your brand principle (see figure 5.3). You can determine your position in the marketplace on the basis of what business or category you use to define your position, your primary short-term benefit, and how you are better than your competitors. These elaborations on the brand principle are used as the basis for current communications until elements in the marketplace cause you to revise your position. Depending on the marketplace and your approach to it, some brand positions end up looking very much like the brand principles upon which they are based.

Positioning: Differentiating Your Product in the Short Term

Whereas the brand principle is a brand driver, positioning is a *brand conveyor*. It is a vehicle for conveying brand actions and messages. Positioning allows marketing communications to focus on differentiating brand messages that relate to the immediate competitive environment. Differentiation is central to the branding process. Once you have developed your organization and brand drivers, you also need to develop what the brand should say in the current competitive landscape.

There are two types of differentiation in positioning: differentiating by category and differentiating by product.

Differentiating through New Category Creation

In new category positioning, positioning statements focus on selling the category rather than unique product benefits, such as *e-commerce* versus *easy to use*. In the short term, building a new category through positioning can be a highly effective road to getting your product out the door. However, long term, it can be a trap. As the category matures, a company may find that it has done a great job of selling the category but has not communicated its uniqueness to its customers. This may allow other companies to steal market share or force the company to discount its offerings. It's important to build brand-specific benefits and differentiators into the equation as early as possible in the market cycle. The results will be increased customer awareness and preference and a defensible position against competitors.

To understand category versus product positioning, let's look at examples from the software industry. As software became more complex, new categories emerged to help classify and define product types. Personal computer software categories started out as operating systems and word processing and spreadsheet applications. Now there are categories for desktop publishing, personal information management, scheduling, email, personal firewalls, browsers, server consolidation, and presentation software, just to name a few.

If your software has applications across several existing product category lines, is a totally new application, or is a subset of an existing application, you might consider creating a new category. Prior to trying to develop a new category, conduct online research to see whether a new or emerging category that fits your software's description already exists.

If you decide to lead the market into a new category, the upside is that you could be viewed as the expert or leader with the resultant market share and margin advantages. The downside is the obligation of a leader to educate its audiences—very few categories take off on their own, so you will need to support the category with educational pieces, speeches, and analyst and editor meetings until it attracts a critical mass of users. This takes time, money, and personnel—precious assets for small- to medium-sized companies.

This process of establishing a beachhead with a new category is described by Geoffrey Moore in *Crossing the Chasm* and *Inside the Tornado*.[7] He has taken the classic business adoption curve and separated the area of *early adopter* from *early majority* with a chasm. This chasm is the distance—the leap of faith, as it were—between early adopters and the rest of the market. It represents the leap your product or service needs to make to be accepted by the early majority. Both positioning and branding can help you cross the chasm and help you remain a market-share and margin leader once you get across.

The downside is the risk of not making it across the chasm.

Differentiating at the Product Level

The second area where positioning is possible is at the product level. Even if you are in a field where a category exists, communicating how your product is different from all others in the current market can be a very powerful way to generate market interest and sales. There are two ways to differentiate a product or service: one is around its features and the other is around the support you provide for it. By creating product differentiation, the customer will see a clear choice among product possibilities.

Defining Features, Benefits, and Differentiators

When you create a position, one of the first things that you need to do is distinguish among *features, benefits*, and *differentiators*. By doing this exercise, you will have a better idea of what your prospective customer will respond to positively. *Features* are aspects of the product that are useful to the customer. They help the customer do the job your product was designed for. *Benefits* are how doing the job translates into an advantage for the customer. And *differentiators* are unique features or benefits that make your product stand out from its competitors.

If a feature helps your customer to do a job—such as the spell checker in a word processing program—then the benefit would be how the spell checker improves the job, such as enabling you to produce a more professional finished document. Your spell checker could also differentiate your word processing product if it were the only spell checker that automatically corrected misspelled words as you type. The benefit of automatic correction would be *faster*, professional documents.

The most beneficial features are the simple, obvious ones. Because you spend so much time with your product, you will assume that everyone will want to understand its abilities to the same depth that you do. The truth is that most customers learn only what they need to know to do the work that is right in front of them. Therefore, features that impact everyday activities are most valued. The benefits of those features are where you should focus your messaging.

Similarly, the most important benefits are those that are specific and simple. Benefits that are highly specific, like *makes it easier to create professional documents,* are most valued. If you have to go into a detailed explanation of a benefit, you will lose the attention of the marketplace. Benefits such as cost of ownership and productivity aren't good sales motivators in most cases. These benefits are typically too general, too difficult to understand, and too difficult to prove.

When you haven't marketed a product before, it's easy to assume that prospective customers will be much more interested in your product than they really are. You've probably poured your heart and soul into the product and lack the objectivity to determine to what degree it is important to the marketplace. Unless you match the description of a typical user of the product, you will not have the same responses to it as the marketplace will.

The first step in understanding what features your market values, what benefits they are looking for, and what differentiates your product in a way that will increase the number of people who buy it is to conduct research with potential customers. The most effective positioning research digs deeply into customers' motivations. For best results, use telephone interviews, one-on-one interviews or focus groups, where you get a number of potential customers in a room to react while a moderator walks them through a product demonstration. You can include positioning research questions with other brand research.

Once the research is in, you can begin the process of creating a positioning statement. At this point consider the following questions.

- Is the difference significant from the customer's point of view? For instance, *a better quality product* is not a customer differentiator; neither is *leading technology*. Customers expect companies to say things like this and ignore them.

- Is the point of difference something you can defend for as long as possible? Focus your messaging on those differentiators that are both closest to the purchase decision and the most defensible.

- Are there other nonproduct differences that customers might value? For instance, is the way you distribute the product a differentiator? For example, if you distribute your software in a way that allows automatic upgrades, that can be a differentiator and as such, is a possible way to position in the marketplace.

- Is your support different from the competition's in quality or cost? Free support may be a strong differentiator in a product category where a lot of support is required.

Differentiating in a Mature Market

If you are a leader in a mature market, chances are you have a strong brand, even if you haven't been managing it. Your job is to go through the branding process and determine your brand principle. Your position will be the same as the principle in many mature markets.

Positioning a new product in a mature market is a very difficult task. For instance, in the software market, longtime users are not willing to switch products without a very good reason. This is especially true with large enterprises, where switching means changing thousands of installations and training thousands of users with the resulting costs and disruption to companywide productivity. This is a headache that information technology departments will go out of their way to avoid. Software users in a mature market will not switch without either a major product or service misstep from their current vendor or a significant technology breakthrough in the marketplace.

Therefore, if you are introducing a product into a mature market, you must bring a differentiator that adds a whole new twist to the technology if you expect to gain significant market share. One example of this was the change from DOS to Windows operating systems. This allowed new companies to launch products into mature markets when older companies with established products failed to move quickly to the Windows environment.

The Internet space has allowed new companies to enter into mature categories. For instance, Amazon.com has dominated the Internet book business even though it didn't exist in the previous, nonwired world. Amazon.com offers tools to make buying on the Internet easier than ever before. It allows one-click shopping for both its book and music selections. Repeat customers simply need to click one button to have the sale go through. Amazon.com also takes advantage of another asset of electronic shopping—the ability to have a massive selection of titles because you don't need to display or inventory them. Finally, the company provides something called *collaborative filtering*. This process looks at a customer's purchases and makes recommendations for other titles the customer would probably like. Because it has made book buying easier, Amazon.com is continuing to dominate this space despite the entrance of market leader Barnes & Noble. For information on low-cost methods for small companies to break into a mature market see Chapters 8 and 15.

Positioning for the Current Market

Your goals are to create a defensible position that is not easily copied—at least not until you've built a market share lead or developed other differentiators—and to build awareness for your brand principle in the process.

You can position both your company and individual products, although most companies focus on product positioning. One advantage to company positioning is that it tends to change less often and is more focused on responding to broader market or technology trends. For example, Xerox Corporation used to position itself around copiers; now it positions itself around documents. This expands its competitive group to include desktop printer companies such as Hewlett-Packard and Tektronix.

If the brand principle is a building's foundation, a position is the steel rebar for the building's message wing. Typically companies don't use positioning word for word, but use the concepts to focus and prioritize their communications.

A simple way to critique a positioning statement is the 4B test:

- *Does it state your business?* This answers the question of what business you are in from a customer/prospect point of view.
- *Does it state your primary benefit?* The position should state your primary benefit from the customer/prospect point of view. *Primary* means the overriding single reason people will buy your product right now.
- *Does the position state why you are better?* Although the reason people buy you right now may change, your point of difference will tend to be more defensible and more closely tied to your underlying brand strengths.
- *Does it state your brand?* Your benefit or differentiator needs to express your brand in at least a complementary way.

As with other building blocks such as the mission and the brand principle, a position needs to be stated clearly and concisely. Because of this,
company or product management teams typically go through a facilitated, iterative process for developing and refining their positions.

If you already have a position in place, one way to determine whether
it's doing its job is to compare it with you competitors.' You can usually
deduce their positioning (or lack thereof) through looking at the first few
pages of their Web sites. What are they trying to communicate? Is it different from other market players? Often you will find few competitive differences and no priority given to messages that could differentiate them. This
allows you to take market leadership by standing out from the crowd.

SAMPLE POSITIONING STATEMENT

Company X develops Internet-based business solutions that automate
legal billing, resulting in faster revenue capture.

In this statement:

- business = Internet-based business solutions
- benefit = faster revenue capture
- better = automate legal billing
- brand = automate process

All companies are tempted to add multiple benefits and differentiators
to their positioning. In the case of positioning, *less is more*. Think of your
position as the one message you always need to communicate to any
audience. List supporting points with other benefits below the main
statement for reference.

NOTES

1. Volvowebsite:http://www.volvo.se/corevalues/SafetyPhilosophy.shtml.
2. Volvo web site: http://www.volvo.com.
3. Ibid.
4. Ibid.
5. Al Ries and Jack Trout, *Positioning: The Battle for Your Mind* (New York:
Warner Books, 1993).
6. Jack Trout and Steve Rivkin (contributor), *The New Positioning: The Latest on
the World's #1 Business Strategy* (New York: McGraw-Hill, 1997).
7. Geoffrey Moore, *Crossing the Chasm* (New York: HarperCollins, 1998); Geoffrey Moore, *Inside the Tornado* (New York: HarperCollins, 1997).

6 Other Core Brand Drivers: Personalities and Associations

We are a company. . .that is based on a brand, one with a genuine and distinct personality, and tangible, emotional connections to consumers the world over.

—Phil Knight, Chairman of the Board and Chief Executive Officer, Nike Corporation

The second brand driver is the brand personality (see figure 6.1). Personality is *an emotional compact with your customers*. It complements the principle, which acts primarily as a *rational agreement* with customers. The personality steers employees' action in each customer interaction. The need for a personality driver in brand is based on the concept that we all treat companies and products as if they were *other people*. We imbue them with human attributes, from likes and dislikes to a complete personality.

Some companies use personality as the leading brand driver in their relationship with customers, employees, and stakeholders. These personality-driven companies, such as Saturn Corporation, attract customers who are seeking to identify strongly with the companies whose products they use.

The Integrated Brand Model says that your company, division, business unit, or product line has a unique way of acting that is predictable. If this idea of giving a company a personality sounds too fantastic, think of a company with which you have had multiple interactions. If they

Figure 6.1
Integrated Brand Model: Brand Personality

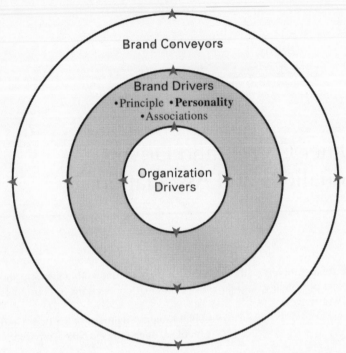

A company's personality is the foundation for each customer's emotional relationship with the company.

were all pleasant, did you come away from those experiences with a positive feeling for the company? If so, why do you think you had an emotional response to their actions? You may have even told someone, "I really like that company because everyone there is so *pleasant* and *helpful*."

In this hypothetical case, you were attributing personality traits to the company *and then reacting to it as you would another person*. If you had another set of experiences with the company and one was positive and the other negative, you might say, "I wish that company would get its act together." This is exactly the same comment you might have about a friend's actions that you weren't happy with.

Personality influences how the brand and the company make the customer feel. The personality also determines whether a brand furthers the customer's emotional understanding of a company. If the brand personality is *open* and *accepting*, it can make customers feel secure and comfortable. If a brand is about *respect*, it can make customers feel important.

Personality is the emotional component of building customer affinity. Developing an emotional relationship with the customer is the only way to create an unbreakable relationship.

In their book *The Media Equation*, Byron Reeves and Clifford Nass analyze individuals' relationships with their personal computers. They discovered that people trust the information received from their own computer more than they do that from other people's computers. Research participants didn't believe they did this, until shown the results. The authors state, "People are not evolved to twentieth century technology. The human brain evolved in a world in which *only* humans exhibited rich social behaviors, and a world in which *all* perceived objects were real physical objects. Anything that *seemed* to be a real person or place *was* real."[1]

The personality aspect of the brand admits that there are a strong emotional component and a strong relationship element to every decision that we make. If you don't think your brand is interesting enough to have personality, go ask your sales department about how they sell. Most will tell you that the selling process is all about creating a relationship with the customer. The customer will see the salesperson as the company in sales situations and will extend the personality traits they witness to the entire company, unless shown differently. This holds true for any company representative with whom the customer interacts!

Amy Miller, president of Amy's Ice Creams, uses traits such as *fun* and *vivacious* to differentiate her superpremium ice cream stores from all other competitors. The rapidly growing Texas-based company sells entertainment with every scoop of ice cream. Visit any of her stores and you'll see all types of performances. "They juggle with their serving spades, toss scoops of ice cream to one another behind the counter, and break-dance on the freezer top. If there's a line out the door, they might pass out samples—or offer free ice cream to any customer who'll sing or dance or recite a poem or mimic a barnyard animal, or who wins a 60-second cone-eating contest," reports *Business Week*.[2]

Microsoft calls its personality its *brand character*. The company says that brand is like a conversation, and it's the way for employees to talk to people all over the world about the possibilities of technology. The company's brand character includes the traits *approachable, trustworthy, quality-driven, interested in who you are and what you want to do,* and *passionate about the future of technology.*

HOW TO REVEAL A BRAND PERSONALITY

You discover the personality through asking employees and customers indirect, metaphorical questions. Because most customers relate to brand personality on a subconscious level, most will not understand a question like "What is the company's personality?" Instead, it's important to ask questions such as *What is the company's business style?* and *If the company died tomorrow, what would be written on its gravestone?* For complete question templates, see the Appendix, Conducting Organization and Brand Driver Interviews.

These questions will provide the interviewer with a series of personality traits with which to describe the company. Since some traits may be more important than others, you may wish to focus on one or two particularly apt traits. Alternatively, you can create a longer list, if that seems appropriate for your company.

This set of traits, once implemented by employees, will shape what customers take away from interactions with the brand on an emotional level. They will describe the voice that the company or product brand uses in its communications and guide how the brand will act with customers and other publics. This does not mean that employees need to make their personality conform to the company's—that is not possible or desirable. Rather, the company personality is something that will guide the company's public voice and ways of acting.

Is it important for a brand to have a consistent personality? An inconsistent personality weakens the customer experience. According to Nass and Reeves, "People *like* identifiable personalities....Quick assessments are valued, and undiluted personalities are more quickly and accurately considered....Even though personality can be assessed with limited information, inconsistencies in the presentation of characters will diminish the purity of personality, and thereby contribute to confusion, and even dislike."

Other brand experts have suggested that there are only a few types of possible personalities and that all brands fit into one of just a few general categories. This concept is needlessly limiting. Forcing a brand's personality into a box is a way of generalizing the personality—therefore making it less effective. It also depersonalizes the uniqueness of the brand/customer experience.

LEADING WITH PERSONALITY: THE SATURN STORY

A good example of a personality-driven company is Saturn Corporation. Saturn has taken the traditional automotive business and stood it on its head. Whereas many automotive companies are faceless giants, Saturn has made itself down to earth, real—the people at the corner diner or Mr. Smith down the road. If you look at the company's communications, you rarely see a close-up of its cars. It's as if the cars are an afterthought. What Saturn really tries to get across to customers are who the company is and the quality of the relationship it forms with customers. Saturn creates a community of customers and builds the best cars out there. The company takes middle America folksiness to its highest level, as a value that can become a shared experience with Saturn and other customers.

Saturn's web site includes snapshots of Saturn owners in front of their cars (called the CarClub), and a database on Saturn owners and their cars. In the future, the company plans to hold Internet chats on various Saturn-related subjects. The web site also includes unsolicited letters from happy owners like the one that follows.

Saturn Sonnet

Well, I've had my new Saturn a week to the day,
The whole deal was different, just like they say.
The sales staff was helpful and courteous, too—
Not like some who are pushy and rude.
Wayne is a wizard with the numbers and loot,
But Jeff's the man—that guy's a hoot!
Thanks, everyone, for being so nice,
I guess you could say
I've been SATURNIZED!
Just one more thing,
Jeff, could you help me see?
Why my wife got the candy
But you sent the payments to me!!
Thanks for everything,
Larry and Sharon Hensle[3]

What are Saturn's personality traits? If Saturn were a person, it would be a down-to-earth, genuine, friendly, people-centered person who also supports the community. The Saturn personality drives its brand development and deepens customer relationships. In Saturn's case this includes everything from giving potential customers the best price to begin with to keeping fresh doughnuts at every service center.

CHANGING A BRAND PERSONALITY

Integrated branding focuses on specific traits, rather than generalized personality types. This allows a company to add to or subtract from its personality as appropriate to its situation. For instance, one company had the trait *quiet* but wanted to be known for leadership in its category.

To do this it decided to add the trait *confident* and drop *quiet*.

Changing a company's personality traits is not any easier than changing an individual's. Remember that the act of adding traits does not change employee actions. But companies *have* successfully changed their personality through a carefully orchestrated plan. The company in the case described plans for and encourages activities that will demonstrate confidence and leadership, while eliminating situations that portray it as quiet.

Be prepared for walking the talk for quite a while—it can take one or more years to change specific traits. Departments that are most radically affected by personality changes are those that have a high level of front-line interaction with customers, such as corporate, sales, product support, and marketing. Your new trait adoption plan needs to include a timeline with measurable milestones. It should also not exceed two years, as organizational development experts have determined that two years is the upper limit for making a lasting change. If a change is not in place by then, the company will revert to its former practice.[4]

THE SYBIL EFFECT—CAN A COMPANY HAVE MULTIPLE PERSONALITIES?

The answer to this question depends on the company's brand structure. In general, the stronger the company or parent brand, the more difficult and counterproductive it is to have more than one personality. When subbrands act as complete brands in their own right, such as when a manufacturer uses a completely different name and a small corporate brand signature, an additional personality may be appropriate. This is particularly true if the company is trying to appeal to a market that is very different from that of its current best customers.

PERSONALITY CRITERIA

The following criteria are critical for the creation of an effective personality.

- *Does the personality reflect the brand?* The personality that a brand projects to the marketplace must reflect the way that the company really acts. For example, the Seattle Children's Home personality, *respectful, open, focused, nonjudgmental, and dedicated*, provides the right attitude tools for fulfilling its brand principle of *building partnerships to improve futures.* You may add aspirational traits to the brand. But for each trait added, you will need to create an implementation plan.

- *Is the personality one that customers will like?* What do customers say about your current business style? What kind of emotion will each personality trait create in your customers? This will help you to determine what they like and dislike.

- *Does it meet customers' needs for self-expression?* A brand that has a personality attribute of *thoughtful* may play well with customers who want to be perceived as careful and discriminating, for example.

- *Is the personality consistent with customer expectations of the brand?* The personality must reinforce how customers experience your products and services. This is particularly important in service-based companies where there are no tangible products involved.

- *Does the personality help define the spirit with which you will approach future actions?* Can it help guide you in decision making? For instance, if the basis of your personality is *respect*, you can use this trait to define how you will work with business alliances.

One way of getting employees to understand the brand personality is to create a personification of the brand. This brand persona exhibits the brand's personality traits and demonstrates its principle. Companies often chose well known people either real or fictional—one company chose Steven Spielberg to represent their personality due to his creativity and inquisitiveness.

For more information about integrating personality into the work force, see Chapter 11.

USING ASSOCIATIONS TO UNLOCK MEANING

Associations are the final brand driver (see figure 6.2). They are the *meaning* you associate with the brand when you see its name or logo, see a related visual, hear a company jingle, see a color, and so on. Anything that the brand does or says or looks like that's made an impression on you that you *link with the brand* is an association. Although this could include virtually everything a brand does, there are specific categories of associations that will enhance customer relationships.

Why are associations considered a brand driver? Associations are *a mental shortcut to the brand promise*. As with other areas of the brand, associations exist whether a company manages them or not. Ones that grow up without company cultivation are called *organic associations*. If positive, these can be very valuable to the brand building process. If negative, they are things that you will want your company, product, or service to stop doing. An example of an organic association is *cows* for a milk brand.

Figure 6.2
Integrated Brand Model: Associations

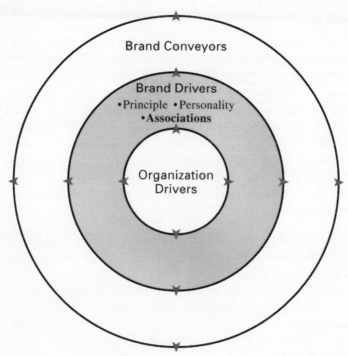

Associations are a mental shortcut to what customers value about the brand.

Created Associations

The other category of associations are *created associations*—ones that brand teams select to represent the brand. Typically, companies come away from an initial integrated branding process committed to building a new association about 50 percent of the time. One reason is that organic associations do not necessarily have the distinctiveness to hold customer interest.

Left to their own devices, customers create organic associations that "gravitate to the more obvious, functional and transient attributes, such as features and price,"[5] which unfortunately is the gateway to commodity country.

That's why it's often important to build your own. Do not try to make an indefensible or transitory feature into an association; rather, look for an association that stands for a basic customer benefit such as security, professionalism, control, or power.

Associations allow customers to access memories of valuable experiences they have had with your company directly. Associations are also a way to develop a deeper relationship with customers by getting more of their senses involved in the experience. Therefore, the more valuable associations are those that are less abstract. Associations that stimulate your senses, including sight, sound, and smell, are particularly powerful. Folgers invokes smell by emphasizing the word *aromatic*—even though you can't smell its coffee through a television. McDonald's signals that readily available food is close by through its golden arches. General Electric uses an eight-note jingle to increase the memorability of its slogan "GE: We bring good things to life."[6] Can you hear the tune in your mind? That's an association.

Companies can use an element as basic as color to create positive associations with their brands. Color psychologists point to a close tie between a product's color (or a service's perceived color) and customer preference. Although individuals react differently to a specific color, once a color becomes associated with a brand, it can become an important part of that brand's equity. "Red is so closely associated with the Coca-Cola Co. that sales would plummet if it dared to change the color of its cans," explains David Masten, of Cheskin+Masten ImageNet, a San Francisco color-research firm.[7] Other companies that have used color to good effect include Kodak, IBM, Symantec, Healthy Choice, and Tide.

For more information on developing associations see Chapter 14.

Even brands that are transparent to customers can successfully use associations to build relationships. A good example of this is the "Intel Inside" visual that is plastered on computer manufacturers' advertisements and products. In the case of an ingredient brand (a brand that is used as a component of another company's products) such as Intel Inside, in which value behind the visual is not obvious, companies build meaning through education.

Intel has accomplished this through several years (and millions of dollars) of print and television advertisements. The company has done a great job of making Intel Inside stand for *power, ability to do what you want to do with your computer*, and *cutting edge technology*. This not only helps Intel, but also boosts the sales of manufacturers who use its microprocessors. If you have gone out shopping for a computer recently, isn't Intel Inside (or the lack thereof) one of the first things you look for on the computer casing?

Although other original equipment manufacturers (OEMs) have tried to follow in Intel's footsteps, they haven't supported their associations with meaning-building communications. This has resulted in a string of icons being run across the bottom of the page of most computer makers' advertisements, with little or no value being gained by either the OEM or the manufacturer. Ingredient brands typically work only if they are the first to a market (à la Dolby for stereos) and/or are substantially promoted through educational campaigns.

WHEN DO BRANDS NEED ASSOCIATIONS?

All brands can benefit from associations, particularly visual associations. Since our world is highly visual and symbolic, associations can be powerful tools for helping a company further develop and refine its customer relationships. Associations can be considered as important to customer dialogue as how the company speaks. They also play a part in creating brand equity.

For example, Coca-Cola's distinctive contoured bottle is part of the customer experience. It adds to the enjoyment of the beverage by eliciting memories of other bottles enjoyed in the past. This visual and tactile dialogue may bring up specific past experiences, such as fun picnics or heartwarming family gatherings. It may elicit memories of car trips to Florida: how exciting it was to be on the road and how refreshing it was to have an ice cold Coke from a roadside vending machine after being in a car for several hours.

Apart from the initial expense of creating them, visual associations can add a lot of leverage to the brand for very little cost. If you do choose to create a visual association, be prepared to stick with it for the long term. Many experts estimate that it takes three to five years to build a created association to the point where most customers can retrieve it from their memory without aid.

While many companies are associated with their logos, having a visual association that is additional to the logo gives you more mind share in the marketplace. Think of an association as a visual tagline that you can use in conjunction with all of the other elements of your corporate identity.

CRITERIA FOR VALUE-BUILDING ASSOCIATIONS

Even small companies can and should create and build associations. They are cost-effective because they typically ride piggyback on other marketing materials. The following discussion will help you to decide whether your brand's associations are working hard enough for you.

Associations must be "in your face." Most companies don't have the dollars to do expensive promotions for their associations, so good associations should be obvious. They must be so obvious that anyone looking at them for three seconds will understand the value they represent. Alternatively, like Intel, you can spend millions to educate people about an association's meaning, but that is not an option for many organizations.

Here's a test. Pretend that your association is on a billboard and your customer is passing by in a fast car. There isn't much room for contem-plation. Imagine having three seconds to figure out what it means. Could you?

Associations must tie back to the brand principle or personality. Early on, RCA developed an association of a dog (Nipper) listening attentively to a phonograph with a caption underneath, "His master's voice." One idea behind this concept, as mentioned earlier, was that the dog could identify his master's voice on the phonograph. The benefit? *Sound fidelity.* Thomson Consumer Electronics, Inc., the U.S. manufacturer of RCA brand consumer electronics, recently updated this association with a second, smaller dog sitting next to the first. Thomson held a contest to name the second dog (Chipper) and received over 100,000 entries.

Subsequently, the company has run several commercial campaigns, spending about $20 million per year, which imply fidelity of both sound and picture. Both the association and the new campaigns have been extremely popular. According to *USA Today*'s Ad Track Poll, RCA ad campaigns rank as the eight most popular of those tracked,[8] and the dogs have spawned a new category of collectible items.

"It's one of the oldest trademarks still in use. And probably the third most recognizable animal in the world—after Mickey Mouse and Donald Duck," explains Neil Maken, whose Huntington Beach, California, antiques store is also a network for Nipper memorabilia.[9] Licensed or authorized replicas of Nipper and, with increasing frequency, Chipper have been made out of papier-mâché, rubber, plastic, and cloth. There are posters, lighters, glassware, salt and pepper shakers, and neckties all sporting likenesses of one or both of the dogs.[10] The RCA MasterCard from MBNA America Bank, N.A. is graced by Nipper and Chipper (see figure 6.3). "Every time you dig that out of your wallet, no matter what you purchase, you get an advertising reminder....It also tells people immediately that you're talking about RCA consumer electronics products," explained James Harper, a spokesperson for Thomson Consumer Electronics.[11]

Nipper and Chipper have also become a way for Thomson to build its relationships with customers further, by putting a friendly face on an otherwise impersonal corporate entity.

Associations must tie back to the company or product. The bunny used in the commercials for Energizer batteries was very memorable in tests, but viewers couldn't remember what product it represented. The bunny was then clearly named the Energizer bunny and gives a picture of an Energizer battery on its drum.

Figure 6.3
Nipper and Chipper

The RCA dogs reinforce "sound fidelity" with every purchase a cardholder makes.

Source: Reprinted with permission of Thomas Consumer Electronics.

Associations must be used for the life of the brand. It takes effort to build associations. Companies may get tired of their own associations and be tempted to get rid of them. This is a costly mistake. It hurts customer loyalty and makes it more difficult to sell subsequent branded products because the customer has lost his or her emotional link to the brand. This is true whether an association was deliberately created, as in the case of the Jolly Green Giant, or accidental, such as the Marlboro Man.

Local schoolchildren in Boise, Idaho, were asked to do advertisements for Hewlett-Packard's LaserJet printers as a school project. Even though it had been several years since HP LaserJet brand had featured Dalmatian dogs in its advertising campaign, most of the kids drew Dalmatians in their ads. Dalmatians had obviously become a valuable association for HP that implied professional-quality printing. However, that value was never leveraged as a lasting part of the customer experience.

Many companies are currently discovering the value of their old associations. Hamm's Beer, for example, once famous for its bear-based ads, recently reintroduced the bear in communications, to great effect.

SELECTED COMPANY ASSOCIATIONS

The Xerox Digital X

Xerox created the *digital X* graphic with Landor Associates in the early 1990s and elevated a former advertising tag line—*The Document Com-*

Figure 6.4
The Xerox Digital X

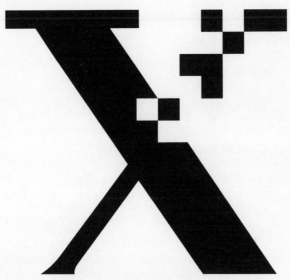

The Digital X reinforces Xerox's expertise as The Document Company.

Source: Reprinted with the permission of Xerox Corporation.

pany—to prominence in its corporate signature logo to communicate its expertise in the complete range of hard copy and electronic documents.

"We track the association of 'The Document Company' phrase, the digital X [see figure 6.4] and the word 'document' to Xerox. It is running at about 90% awareness among our customers and about 75% awareness among the general public. Our ability to get this much acceptance so quickly after our August '94 launch of the new identity validates that a total document solutions focus is both the heritage and current strength of Xerox," explains David Reyes-Guerra, Xerox's manager of corporate identity.

Cape Cod Potato Chips

On the East Coast, a brand called Cape Cod Potato Chips uses associations to evoke strong, positive emotions in its customers. For many in the Northeast, Cape Cod means vacation, fun, an overall good feeling. Cape Cod Potato Chips takes advantage of this fact. Every aspect of the product, from the bag illustration of a chip by Cape Cod artist Elizabeth

Figure 6.5
PhotoDisc Photographs

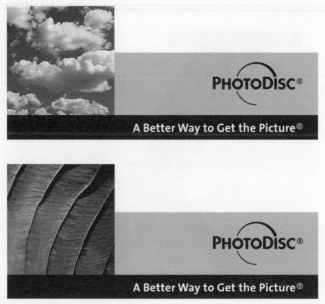

PhotoDisc's association is its photographs.

Source: Reprinted with the permission of PhotoDisc.

Mumford, to the lighthouse visual association, to letters on the bag that describe how the great life on the Cape contributes to a tasty chip, attempts to pluck the chord of fond memories of this quaint locale.

PhotoDisc

PhotoDisc uses photographic images as its association (see figure 6.5). The photographs *are* its product. So it is able to associate the brand directly with product while evoking many different customer responses, depending on the photo used.

Annie's Homegrown

Annie's Homegrown is a national food company that specializes in pasta dinners. Its brand is known for being natural and committed to the betterment of women, children, and the environment. It uses a visual association (see figure 6.6) of a cheerful looking rabbit with the words

Figure 6.6
The Rabbit of Approval

The rabbit of approval provides Annie's Homegrown with a memorable and versatile association.

Source: Reprinted with the permission of Annie's Homegrown.

"Rabbit of Approval" encircling it on its product boxes. The rabbit reinforces organic and children-friendly associations.

A SUMMARY OF BRAND DRIVERS

These chapters have provided you with an overview *of organization* and *brand drivers*. The role of drivers is to create an easy-to-follow structure for leveraging and focusing employee potential. The result? Customers share a high degree of affinity with the brand, based on sustainable points of difference and emotional attachment. Drivers generate category-leading customer loyalty and consistent price premiums, even in mature markets.

Your mission *tells you where to build value.*

Your values *show you what foundation to build on.*

Your story *provides shared context for the value you bring.*

Your principle, your personality, and associations *drive home the brand promise.*

NOTES

1. Byron Reeves and Clifford Nass, *The Media Equation: How People Treat Computers, Television and New Media Like Real People and Places* (Cambridge, England: Cambridge University Press, 1998), pp. 101–108.

2. John Case, Inc., "Corporate Culture," *Business Week* (November 1996), p. 43.

3. Saturn web site: http://www.saturn.com.

4. John P. Kotter, "Leading the Change: Why Transformation Efforts Fail," *Harvard Business Review* (March–April 1995), pp. 59–67.

5. Marty Brandt and Grant Johnson, *Powerbranding* (San Francisco, CA: International Data Group, 1997), p. 107.

6. GE web site: http://www.ge.com.

7. Meera Somasundaram, "Red Packages Lure Shoppers Like Capes Flourished at Bulls," *The Wall Street Journal* (September 18, 1995), p. B-7D.

8. Dottie Enrico, "Marketers Learn to Teach Old Ad New Tricks," *USA Today* (November 4, 1996), p. 4-B.

9. Kate Gurnett, "New Owner Pressured to Keep 4-Ton Dog," *Albany Times Union* (September 21, 1997), p. 51.

10. Nipperscape web site: http://www.ais.org/lsa.

11. Chris O'Malley, "RCA Seeks to Collar the Affinity Credit Card Market," *The Indianapolis Star* (March 3, 1997), p. F01.

7 How to Reveal Your Brand: Seven Steps to Integrated Branding

There is no one giant step that does it. It's a lot of little steps.[1]

—Peter A. Cohen

The following chapter will lead you through the integrated branding process in a step-by-step commonsense manner. Whether you do this process yourself, or work with a consultant, use this chapter as a reference point. The following diagram provides an overview of each step (see figure 7.1).

STEP ONE: HOW TO SELL YOUR COMPANY ON THE INTEGRATED BRAND MODEL

If the world were a logical place, the company with the best products, and the products with the best specifications, would be market leaders. But logic is not the main driver of most decisions, even those made on behalf of a business. If logic prevailed, we'd all buy products on the basis of how well they fit our functional needs. We wouldn't be swayed by cars that appealed to our egos—we'd all drive stripped-down Honda Civics. But we don't, because we feel and believe, at a deep level, that certain products and companies speak to us. They provide us with an experience that meets other needs beyond the obvious product function.

Even if your company and your products are the best, you still need to do the work of integrated brand development. But how do you get

Figure 7.1
Seven Steps to Integrated Branding

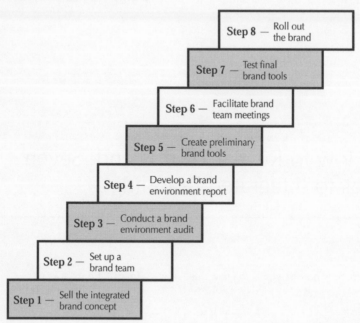

the rest of the team on the brand wagon? What if you could convince senior management that the branding effort would pay off on the bottom line, and do so with a superior ROI (return on investment) and stock price? The facts indicate that you can.

Fact: Of Americans 66 percent make purchase decisions based on brand.

Fact: Companies with strong brands can charge price premiums of up to 15 to 20 percent.

Fact: In the area of technology brands, most customers go to a computer store with fewer than two brands in mind.

Fact: Companies with strong brands have higher customer retention rates and lower employee turnover.

Fact: Even so-called commodity products, such as computers, will sell at a premium if they carry one or more strong brand names.

Fact: The goodwill component of a strong brand's valuation is often greater than its tangible assets.

Fact: An integrated brand increases a company's share value while reducing volatility.

The Benefits of Integrated Branding by Department

Besides all of these reasons why senior management would be interested in becoming brand-driven there are others that appeal to each company department.

Product Development

An integrated brand provides strong product direction. Brand drivers are a compass for developing product, product feature, and service direction. Remember this compass is based on company strengths and customer values—increasing the likelihood of product success and market share gains.

This focus can streamline the development process as product managers and developers make fewer mistakes in product direction. An integrated brand therefore reduces money spent on new product failures. If you understand the boundaries of your brands, you will not spend R&D dollars on products that are off-brand or on features that your customers don't want. Levis won't go into formal wear; Lexus will avoid an economy model.

Service and Support

An integrated brand makes the job of service and support people easier, while typically requiring less expenditure in this area. The reason? Strong brands have the highest loyalty ratings in their categories and therefore have stronger customer relationships in general. Because an integrated brand responds to its customers with products they want and the quality they are looking for, there are fewer complaints. Because customers tend to be more loyal, they are also less likely to complain. In brand-driven companies, support people have the ability to strengthen the customer relationship further, increasing the likelihood of additional sales.

Human Resources

Human resource staff use organization and brand drivers—particularly mission, values, and personality—as a way to find the best employees for the company. Using these drivers, human resources can match job candidates with the company culture more easily and more accurately. This does not mean that every employee will have the same personality. It does mean all will share a direction, values, and certain personality traits. By using drivers and conveyors, the human resource department can also begin the process of getting new employees to use the brand during their orientation period. This helps companies preserve their culture, particularly in times of high growth.

Marketing

Even with a healthy marketing budget, how are you going to break through the clutter that bombards your prospective customers? Brand was an important factor in the early 1900s, when media were relatively few and almost quiet by comparison. Today it is a necessity. Brands fight it out at the speed of light over the Internet, through hundreds of cable TV channels, and in thousands of magazines. The average person is exposed to many thousands of messages per day.

Branding Hewlett-Packard's Home and Small Business divisions grew from the need to have a centralized direction and a consistent brand face across divisions. This consistent face included guidelines for packaging, web activities, public relations, and advertising—all activities that touched the customer. The company wanted to build on its historic equity around quality and reliability while adding a third element of *practical enabling innovation*.

HP conducted research around the world, talking to customers about what the company stood for. Customers said quality, reliability, and practicality were the consistent threads of the HP brand. HP also discovered that it was not perceived as innovative or inspirational, despite its long track record of innovation. "Our job was to make those brand assets more relevant and differentiated. We wanted to marry that to our future direction," explains Brian Burch, worldwide consumer brand manager for HP's Consumer Products Group, "and empower our customers." The HP brand team, facilitated by the St. James Group, met many times to enhance the practicality of its brand with the concepts of enablement and innovation.

"We are focusing heavily from a message perspective on making exciting things possible," adds Burch. The result was a consumer brand logo that includes the HP logo with the words *expanding possibilities* below it (see figure 7.2). "This also resulted in the first non-product brand advertising in HP's history," says Burch. "Working with our agency Goodby Silverstein & Partners, we created a series of television commercials whose focus was to sell solutions and show people the ability HP has to harness technology and do exciting things through the power of imaging."

One commercial shows John "Buck" O'Neil, one of the players from the Negro Baseball League, who created baseball cards of Negro League players using an HP PC, scanner, and printer (see figure 7.3). The com-

Figure 7.2
HP's "Expanding Possibilities" Consumer Brand Logo

Source: Reprinted with the permission of Hewlett-Packard.

mercial does a great job of communicating the richness of this man's life and how HP helps enhance it.

Integrated Brand Selling Strategies

The following are some of the most effective arguments for creating an integrated brand.

Reason 1: An integrated brand aligns company actions and messages with its greatest strengths.

Reason 2: A brand-driven organization allows a company to create a direction for launching new products and features that are in synch with customer needs.

Reason 3: An integrated brand leverages marketing dollars to their best and highest use. This is because, in brand-driven companies, all aspects of the marketing mix work together to produce impressions and reinforce messages that have most impact.

Reason 4: Because brand drivers don't change, the advertising and other communications that are derived from them will have a cumulative effect on the customer relationship, rather than the typical stop-and-begin-again process caused by the twelve- to sixteen-month advertising campaign focus of many companies.

Reason 5: An integrated brand will produce a high level of customer affinity. It will attract customers who demonstrate very high loyalty and tell others why they feel this way. This word of mouth is incredibly valuable. In study after study, business people say that peers are the key reason they consider a product.

When customers encounter distinctive brands that they like, they become brand loyalists and champions, recommending them to friends and peers. Starbucks coffee drinkers will do Starbucks' marketing for it. In Starbucks' case, this word of mouth helped creating an awareness and brand interest before stores were opened in new areas—decreasing the time it took for each new store to become profitable.

Figure 7.3
HP's Nonproduct Brand Commercials

HP adds the concept of practical enabling innovation and a rich customer brand experience to its commercials.

Source: Reprinted with the permission of Hewlett-Packard.

Taken together, a brand's positive impact on the company organization becomes visible. But giving lip service to the concept of brand will not produce these results. The brand must be developed into a rich, deep experience. Therefore you must have buy-in from upper management and employees from the start, and that is what Step 2 is all about.

If an integrated brand can do all of that, why isn't every company brand-driven? There are four reasons: First, being brand driven is not taught in business schools as a basic business fundamental; companies must discover it in some other fashion. Second, creating a brand-driven culture requires that the people at the top of the organization buy into and understand branding. So most brand-driven companies become that way because upper management has learned how to do it somewhere else. Third, many practitioners of brand mistakenly limit its scope to creating brand conveyors, such as positioning, advertising, and creation of graphic identities. Finally, building an integrated brand is hard work. It takes discipline over the long term and forces people to manage a process that previously they weren't even aware of. Therefore, companies that embrace integrated branding are typically experiencing some pain—such as increased competition or inability to create a strong, uniform direction.

Integrated branding is typically initiated by the head of marketing, the head of a division, or the CEO of the company. David Reyes-Guerra, manager of corporate identity at Xerox Corporation, says, "You always need a champion for these types of major changes. At Xerox, our champions included the Senior Vice President of Strategic Development & Communications and the Chairman of the Board."

When the CEO and the upper management team are committed to becoming brand-driven, you will have passed the first milestone in the process.

STEP TWO: HOW TO SET UP A BRAND TEAM AND DETERMINE WHO SHOULD BE ON IT

Now that your management team has bought in, the next step is to appoint a brand manager and create the team that will be responsible for revealing your brand.

Both steps are critical. The brand manager is someone who will have responsibility for oversight of all brands within a company. He or she must be a good strategist, be adept at managing and working with people, and have the ear of the CEO and other top officers. The brand manager also needs to be a generalist—a person who understands in some detail how various company operations work—so that he or she can help build brand in each area of the company.

It's a good idea for your brand manager to go through brand training at the outset. In this way, the manager will be several steps ahead of everyone else on the brand team and will be able to manage each brand proactively. This is especially important when a company is just beginning to use its brand or brands. Early on, the process for using brand drivers to guide decisions will not be automatic for most employees and they will have a lot of questions for the brand manager to answer.

The brand team is the group that will demonstrate branding to the rest of the employees, a necessary step for incorporating lasting change into any company. This is the group that, along with the brand manager, will assure quality control for the brand, ensuring all actions and communications strengthen the brand.

Deciding on organization and brand drivers via a brand team is essential for the brand to be effective. Without an honest consensus of key company influencers and managers including the CEO, your branding efforts will most likely fail or be very limited in their effectiveness.

Criteria for the brand team include:

• Senior management, including the CEO. Branding must be bought into at the highest levels, or lower level employees won't embrace and live it.

• A matrixed group. Representatives from many departments will provide the different perspectives needed, and will be influential in then selling the brand to their departments or divisions.

• People closest to the customers. The customer viewpoint is critical in the branding process. As a result, the sales and marketing departments should have a disproportionate number of representatives on the team.

• One or two troublemakers/naysayers/political operatives. You want even the major troublemakers at a company, if they have following or power, to be part of branding. Often, their issues disappear as they see how branding works and as they take part in decision making.

The best size for a brand development team is between eight and fifteen people, although you can produce good results with teams of up to twenty-five. The rule is to assemble a group small enough to get work done and make scheduling meetings possible, but large enough that the company trusts its outcomes. A caveat: It is important that every team member commit to attending all brand development meetings or review with another team member and agree to the results of a meeting they don't attend. Otherwise, a single participant can undermine the consensus reached by all the others because he or she did not walk the same path as the rest.

Once you assemble the brand team you will need to do two other things. The first is have team members attend an *Introduction to Brand Management* seminar. The second is to give them an outline of brand team duties. The seminar will provide context for brand development, as well as get them on board the brand bandwagon. The outline of team duties will give them an understanding of the extent of the commitment they are making.

STEP THREE: CONDUCTING A SUCCESSFUL BRAND ENVIRONMENT AUDIT

This is the research phase, where you will discover the raw material for your brand promise through matching company strengths with what customers value. The quality of the results of the revealed brand is dependent on the quality of research. No existing company creates a brand out of nothing; its fundamental elements already exist in the interactions between you and your customers.

Although companies may believe they understand and can predict their market's actions, this is almost never the case. There's nothing like objective information to tell you what customers really feel, rather than what you think they feel.

This research will allow you to paint an accurate picture of the company, each of its brands, and their brand environments. The research answers several questions:

Who is buying your products?

Why are they buying them?

Why aren't they buying them?

What do customers think of competitors?

How are customers solving the problem without your products?

What do customers want from the product but aren't getting?

What category do customers put your products in?

What's your brand personality?

What do customers associate with you?

What concepts don't customers link to your company?

That's all from the external perspective, talking to both customers and prospects. Internally, you must reveal company strengths and weaknesses, values and landmines, visions and realities. What are the company's chief differentiators? Benefits? Where do you lead the market? Where would you like to lead? What is the company's self-image? Its business style?

A brand environment audit can be as simple as talking to a few people inside and outside the company. Alternatively, it can be as extensive as conducting worldwide focus groups and carrying out quantitative research. It all depends on the size of the company, the size of the customer base, and the timeline. But for any brand research project, no matter the scope, there are a few rules to keep in mind.

For an internal audit you should

- interview both brand team members and employees not on the team.
- ask the same questions of every employee.
- expect to spend between forty-five minutes and an hour on each interview.
- have an independent third party ask the questions so answers are not biased.
- provide confidentiality of individual answers.

For an external audit, you should

- work from a randomized customer/prospect list that is five times larger than the number of completed surveys you require.
- protect the confidentiality of individual answers.
- keep the company name hidden until the end of the interview.
- make sure the research is completely separated from sales efforts.
- if using phone interviews, expect to have a maximum of twenty minutes with each customer.

For a complete list of suggested interview questions, please see the Appendix.

When reporting the results, use quotes liberally, as these most closely capture the sense of the interviews. Use both quantitative and qualitative approaches; that is, tally up responses and their percentages of total responses. Report particularly telling responses, even if only one or two people gave them. This way, you can report on both factual experience and what your intuition is telling you.

When reporting the results, simple slides with two or three ideas on each are the most effective way to present information. A quote, followed by the percentages of responses for a question, followed by salient points, will give the brand team the clearest picture of the overall responses. Always present all the results before making recommendations. Everyone needs to be on the same page before conclusions will make sense. Fewer summary slides are better than an exhaustive list of everything that was said. However, make sure that you anticipate your brand team's questions and have your verbatim results with you in case you need to access it.

If a third party is conducting the research, start with defining what you want to get out of the research and work backward from this. Let the consultant write the questions. Once he or she has, read each question carefully and make sure it will get you to the anticipated result. If something looks as if it won't work, make sure that the research consultant demonstrates to you why it will.

STEP FOUR: DEVELOPING A BRAND ENVIRONMENT REPORT YOU CAN ACT ON

The key deliverable from the research process is a brand environment report that maps out the brand's marketplace. This report outlines the boundaries of the brand, the current state of market trends, the competition, brand strengths, brand weaknesses, opportunities and threats, and customer preferences, and provides context for integrated branding efforts.

As the Cheshire Cat said to Alice when she asked which way she should walk from here, "That depends a good deal on where you want to get to." You can't know whether they got the information they were after unless you know what you're looking for first. Only by having objectives for the research, and stating outcomes prior to asking questions can you know what direction to go with the audit.

One outcome might be a picture of the current brand and a direction to move in for the future. Another might be deciding whether a new product fits under an existing brand or requires the creation of a new one. Typically, when a company is first revealing its brand, the brand environment report will be designed to provide all of the information to define the common ground between company strengths and what customers value. This will help the company understand what it is promising. It will give it the raw material from which to create the organization drivers of mission, values, and story and the brand drivers of principle, personality, and associations.

When writing a brand environment report, first summarize the results of your internal audit and qualitative or quantitative external research. Organize the results by general area such as strengths, personality traits, or associations, then create conclusions and recommendations based upon this information.

It's helpful to summarize brand results from the first audit in a way that produces a quick read. A single report that can track category trends and awareness (both aided and unaided), provide two years of bench-making figures at a glance (where available), and track loyalty and repeat purchase likelihood at a glance is your best way to summarize brand results. You may wish to create this type of report in order to track brand results and communicate those to the rest of the company.

STEP FIVE: CREATING PRELIMINARY BRAND TOOLS THAT STIMULATE TEAM THINKING

After the report comes the fun part: revealing or enhancing the brand. If you are revealing the brand, you're coming up with first stabs at the brand drivers of principle, personality, and associations—preliminary versions that the team can accept, refine, or reject. You may also be working on preliminary versions of the organization drivers of mission, values, and story.

This preliminary work is best done in a small group of three to five people. This could be an executive committee of the brand team, as long as it includes the brand manager. Or this could be done by an outside consultancy, which then gives the information to the brand team. You don't need a large group, because you don't need buy-in yet; that happens later. But you don't want to do it by yourself, because you need a variety of perspectives that only a team can bring. You probably won't challenge any muddy thinking that occurs if you try to do it by yourself. It is also a difficult activity to undertake if you have never done it before. That's why brand development training is recommended for your brand manager and/or other team members prior to beginning the process or using an outside consultancy to handle this step.

There are two goals for coming up with preliminary drivers. The smaller committee first needs to think through all the branding issues prior to getting together with the entire brand team. By developing preliminary drivers, you address and work through many issues that may come up with the larger group. This will help the group to avoid dead ends. In addition, you are giving the larger group a way to start, rather than trying to create each driver from ground zero. This will save several hours of fumbling around simply to reach a starting point. Good preliminary drivers will encapsulate much of the information derived from the brand environment report.

The development of the preliminary tools is a gathering and synthesizing activity, one in which you sift through the research to see what's relevant from both a rational and an intuitive point of view. If you are working only on brand drivers, begin with the brand principle, since this typically guides the direction of both your personality and associations. If you are doing organization drivers as well, begin with the mission statement since this determines the overall business of the company.

Preliminary Principle Brainstorming

Before starting work on the principle, set up a war room where you surround yourself with key data and competitive information from your research. Many people like to use large whiteboards and Post-It note tablets, so that they can rearrange and reorder ideas as necessary. Remember, in a principle you are looking for key benefits/differentiators for your company that customers value and that are also internal company strengths. Because in this example you would be revealing an existing brand, rather than creating one from scratch, the research will typically show patterns of agreement from customers and internal respondents. For example, a very strong focus on customer needs may be a consistent theme of the research (Nordstrom's brand), or it may reveal a number of people who believe your key value to them is your product's reliability (HP LaserJet printers), or customers may really value their relationship with individual people within the company (INTER-LINQ Software).

Once you have a list of customer values and company strengths (see figure 7.4), you need to decide which ones optimize both values.

It's important not to discount customer *or* company input—brand teams tend to place more weight on one or the other. There have been examples in which one or more members of the brand team chose to deny customer views simply because they had a strong emotional attachment to contradictory views. And vice versa.

The brand principle is typically a word, a phrase, or a sentence. A shorter principle is almost always better. An effective principle needs both to be usable by employees and to have a visionary, emotional element to it. Remember, you don't have to create the final principle here; you just need to find something that your smaller group feels is in the neighborhood.

Once the group has agreed on a direction for the brand principle, it's time to wordsmith. The principle will typically never be used with outside audiences—it is an internal compass for effective day-to-day brand management. Don't worry about its translating to the outside world. Do worry whether employees will understand it quickly and easily.

Often, customers articulate benefits of *productivity* or *quality* as the rea-

Figure 7.4
A Working Integrated Brand Definition

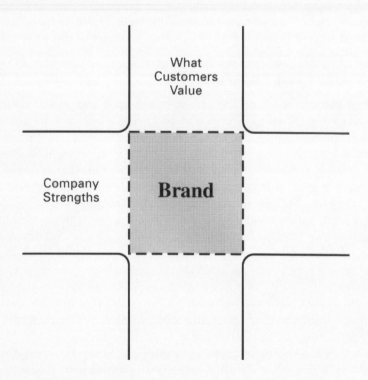

Brand is the intersection of company strengths and what customers value.

son they value the brand. Although these ideas are close to the buying decision, they are too vague, nondifferentiating, and lacking in direction to be used as a brand principle. A brand principle must drive actions and decisions. If you can't answer the question—How can I do this [insert action/communication] with [insert brand principle]?—then you do not have a useful brand principle and need to keep trying.

For example, Data Dimensions Information Services, an outsource systems manager and testing lab for Year 2000 compliance, has a brand principle of *empowering trustworthy relationships*. So they would answer these questions "Does this new service or action empower our customers? Does it build trust? Does it strengthen our relationship with customers?"

The Washington Software Alliance (WSA), a not-for-profit organization, is tasked to help organizations and people in software and digital

Figure 7.5
The Washington Software Alliance Logo

Source: Reprinted with the permission of WSA.

media companies succeed and make Washington state the information technologies center of the world. The WSA's brand principle of *sharing expertise, resources, and insight* speaks to the heart of the way it helps companies succeed. Member research indicated that WSA members, who include over one thousand software and associate-member companies and seventy thousand people, found the primary benefits of the WSA to be *education* and *networking*. The brand principle goes to the foundation of the organization's promise to be a resource for its members. It has focused the organization on finding new ways for staff and member companies to share information and form alliances. The WSA logo (see figure 7.5) was changed on the basis of this brand work to demonstrate the idea of sharing bits of information and opening doors of opportunity.

If something generic like productivity or quality show up as both a company strength and a customer value, you need to make sure that your researchers drill down deeper and find what specific aspect of productivity or quality is unique to your brand. Is it making a certain subset of your audience more productive? Is it helping people by reducing training requirements, or by allowing them to complete certain tasks faster? These kinds of questions can help you get closer to a brand principle that can drive actions.

Ask yourself the following questions when evaluating a preliminary brand principle:

Is it true?

Does a competitor own it?

Is it defensible over the long run?

Does it drive actions?

Is it close to a buying decision?

Is it broad enough to allow for future growth?

Is it narrow enough to base actions on?

Is it brief and clear for easy usage?

Will employees relate to it on an emotional level?

Once you've developed a principle that answers these questions, you'll know you have thought through your initial choice to reach a useful place to start in the larger group meeting.

For more examples of principles see Chapter 5.

Preliminary Personality Brainstorming

Next develop a preliminary brand personality. In your research, you should ask questions that reveal personality traits.

If the company were a famous person, fictional or real, who would that be?

What is the business style of the company?

How would you characterize people you have dealt with at the company?

For a complete list of personality questions see the Appendix.

In most cases, and particularly in technology companies, a company will have only one personality, regardless of the number of subbrands it has. Customers demand a consistent experience from each company interaction. It is also very difficult and undesirable for one company to manifest multiple personalities. The only time multiple personalities work is when the product connection to the company is very weak. You may choose to create multiple personalities if you are offering two competitive products designed to give you more of the total category market share.

The only other exception is that a company has acquired other brands that it keeps as wholly owned subsidiaries. In those cases there is value in keeping discrete brand personality traits that customers value. However, if a company brings an acquired brand inside its corporate structure, it's often easier to meld the two personalities as quickly as possible.

The answers to the questions will start to reveal the personality traits of your brand. Oftentimes, a company's internal view of this is extremely biased. You may need to give more weight to external views if the two are in conflict. For instance, some companies are much harder on themselves than their customers are. Many companies have emphasized personality traits that were irrelevant to what customers value.

Look for patterns, emotion-laden words, and anecdotes that reflect personality traits in the research. List all the ones you find. Let's say the research indicates that your company is *flexible, friendly, abrasive, brash, in-your-face, creative,* and *prone to exaggeration.* Determine among your smaller group whether you want all of these traits to reflect the brand. Once you have a list that includes all of the important traits, brainstorm people who embody these characteristics.

There's no shame in being aspirational about your brand personality, as long as you have a plan for how to incorporate currently underdeveloped aspects of that personality.

The following are tests to help you evaluate a preliminary brand personality.

- *Does it reflect the brand?* The personality that a brand projects to the marketplace must reflect the way that the company really acts. You may add aspirational traits to the brand, but for each trait added, you will need to create an implementation plan. It can take two years or longer, depending on company size and its motivation, to integrate a new trait.
- *Is it one that customers will like?* What do customers say about your existing business style? This will help you to determine what they like and dislike.
- *Is it consistent with customer expectations of the brand?* The personality must reinforce how customers experience your products and services. This is particularly important in service-based companies.
- *Does it help define the spirit with which you will approach future actions?* Can it help guide you in decision making? For instance, if the basis of your personality is respect, you can use this trait to define how you will work with business alliances.
- *Is it consistent with the brand principle?* The personality must be complementary to your principle. If you have a principle of "collaboration," a personality trait like "independent" would be contraindicated.

Preliminary Association Brainstorming

Now that you finished the preliminary principle and personality, it's time to move on to the preliminary association. Creating a preliminary association is a different process from creating the other two brand drivers. Effective associations are usually visual or auditory. What you will do with the group is take the first step toward a final association by determining the *concept* you want the association to project. You will leave the final creative process to other creative teams such as designers and creative directors. Because most companies already have several existing and potential associations available to them, selecting among them is a more arbitrary process than is following the revealing process for the principle and personality.

That said, there are several ways to get to a preliminary association. One way is through listing all the company's or brand's associations (for example, ask the question, What do you think of when I say [company name]?) and choosing the one that is most representative. Another is to decide on your top three associations and then discuss the pros and cons of each before coming to a consensus. A brand can grow more than one association at a time, but most don't in the short term because of the need to stay focused. Brand guru David Aaker estimates that it takes three to five years to build an association to the point where customers play it back.[2] In any event, associations should be obvious, be memorable, and tie back to the brand principle, personality, and company or product.

When you select the preliminary association to present to the larger group, ask yourself the following questions:

- *Is it "in your face" obvious?* A good example of an obvious association is Allstate's good hands. It means the company will take care of you in times of trouble.

- *Is it memorable?* People and animals tend to be more memorable than inanimate objects, such as geometric shapes. Shapes can, however, be very powerful if customers are given a clear understanding of their meaning. The Nike swoosh is one of these.

- *Does the association tie back to the brand principle or personality?*

- *Does it tie back to the company or product?*

Although logos are considered associations, companies usually need at least one additional association, which may sit anywhere in an ad or brochure or may be the subject of the communication.

The preliminary brand development process ends when the smaller group agrees on preliminary drivers for the larger group session, where the principle, personality, and associations and other drivers will become solidified.

Do not grow attached to your preliminary brand drivers. They will most likely change during the brand team sessions, and the critical work of facilitating a session will not be effective if you or the facilitator is unwilling to listen to countervailing viewpoints or are otherwise biased and try to manipulate the process in any way.

STEP SIX: HOW TO FACILITATE BRAND MEETINGS
SUCCESSFULLY

The rubber is about to meet the road in your quest to bring your brand or brands to consciousness. To determine your brand and/or organization drivers, you will need to conduct a series of brand development meetings with your brand team, where you present the preliminary work you've done and develop final drivers.

You should plan for a series of meetings, although some brands can be developed in only one or two. It's better to schedule five to six meetings and cancel unneeded ones than have to scramble to schedule a dozen busy people for one or two extra sessions.

Before starting, send all participants a memo outlining the goals of the session, as well as any preparation you need them to make.

To: Brand Team
FROM: CEO
RE: Becoming brand-driven

I am delighted to report that we are ready to hold our brand development meetings. We will meet from three to six times for the purpose of determining how to become a brand-driven organization and then periodically after that to fine tune the development of our brand.

During the first meeting, you will be briefed about our brand environment, how we look from an internal, customer, and competitive point of view. We will then work on brand tools that allow us to differentiate and build loyalty with every customer interaction.

The process will be facilitated by a professional and unbiased third party, and we will walk through and inspect our brand from all possible angles. Our purpose is to create a high-quality, integrated brand that will permeate company actions.

Please plan to come to all of the meetings. Because of the cumulative nature of the process, if you miss one, we will ask you to excuse yourself from the remainder and wait for the results.

Regards,

The First Meeting

At the first meeting, you need to present the brand environment report. This gets everyone on the same page, highlights areas of concern and strength, and sets the foundation for the work of revealing the brand.

Next, you will begin to develop the brand drivers, starting with the brand principle. The facilitator, ideally, will be an objective third party from outside the company. The brand development process will fail if it is subject to the whims of politics, or if a specific hidden agenda drives the decisions. A trained facilitator can also ensure that no single person dominates, and that all viewpoints are heard and will know what to do when the group reaches an impasse or hits a slow spot.

The way to start the brand principle brainstorming session is by first putting on a white board the various concepts the smaller group unearthed as potential principle material. This demonstrates the lines of thought of the smaller group and gives the facilitator a place to go if the preliminary principle does not work for the group. The facilitator should ask for other principle directions from the group, both to ensure that no possibilities were missed and to get the group engaged in the process.

The facilitator should next reiterate what a principle is and how it is used and give specific examples of use. He or she should also explain what it is not—such as a slogan, tag line, or an other external message. Then the facilitator should write the preliminary principle on the board, articulating the fact that it is a first-step attempt, kind of a best guess, but it is not expected to become the final principle. This tells the group that their input is necessary and that they don't have to worry about hurting anyone's feelings.

The facilitator should articulate how and why the smaller group came up with the preliminary principle, generally making a case for its selection. Then, the facilitator should open it up to the group, asking them what they think, whether they have other suggestions, or whether part or all of the principle works as is. At the same time, it's helpful if team members have on the table in front of them a worksheet with the definition and criteria for an effective principle on it.

It's also necessary to tell the group what to expect during the process. Many people get frustrated if their expectations and subsequent reality don't align. They need to be told that the revealing process is like walking along a meandering path. You won't find the most direct way through immediately, but you will learn invaluable information and gain a perspective on the brand along the way. The process is not neat and orderly—rather it appears messy and requires patience of participants to create a high level of quality. Additionally, without wandering down these other paths, the group will not feel it has explored all possibilities and may miss key pieces of the principle. This may directly impact the strength of its final consensus and, most important, the quality of the final principle.

At the first brand meeting, ask participants not to share specific meeting results prematurely with other company employees. Without providing the proper context, people will often misinterpret results on the basis of their past preconceptions of brand—such as confusing the principle with a tag line or a positioning statement. This can create resistance to brand integration later on.

Once the preliminary principle is placed on the white board, team members will add, move, or subtract words or suggest entirely new principles—all of which need to be written on the board as a visual expression of the group's thought process. A good facilitator will honor the thoughts of all participants while keeping the process moving toward its goal.

During the ensuing discussion, it's the facilitator's job to keep the group on task, to encourage quiet people to speak up, to ensure the customer's viewpoint is considered, to point out whether a suggestion meets the criteria for the driver, and to suggest alternatives when the group argues or is stuck. What the facilitator must not do is try to influence the direction or force his or her ideas on the group.

When the group is close to determining the brand principle, you can feel a collective sense of excitement growing in the room. When it is put up, several people will voice their approval. The job now is twofold: make sure the principle *is* the right one, not just nearly the right one, and make sure everyone in the room agrees on it.

Alternatively, if there is no consensus, and the group seems to be going around in circles, the facilitator must know when to call a halt to the proceedings. Often, clarity arises by adjourning and sleeping on it—send the group home with the current concept, and ask them to consider it over the next few days. Starting again fresh, after cogitating on the principle, can often free up new ideas or directions.

If the group does reach a strong consensus on the principle, also ask them to take a few days to consider it. If it is not really the best final principle, team members will return to the next meeting with suggested improvements.

Personality Development

Final personality development is often an easier task. The best place to start is to offer up the preliminary personality, and ask whether it is true and inclusive. In the interest of brevity, encourage team members to group several personality traits together under one trait. Typically, a personality will boil down to just a few traits that are critical to company strengths and what customers value.

At the end of the process, offer the group the opportunity to choose one, two, or three traits that best capture the essence of the personality. Some groups choose to do this, whereas others feel that this is over-simplifying their personality. They may also wish to choose a famous person closest to the company's personality to communicate to others a greater understanding of the brand personality.

Association Development

One way to approach the complex task of association development is to have each participant pick his or her five top associative concepts from a much larger list. This will quickly show which concepts are most closely wedded to the company. Alternatively, you can present the smaller group's recommendation and try to get buy-off on that. Remind participants that the association is for meaning only; any graphical representation will be developed by a designer at a later date.

There's always the chance that people will try to short circuit the process, either because they don't believe in it or because they want to throw their weight around. There are several ways to deal with problem participants. One is to use the rest of the group to apply subtle pressure. For example, if the troublemaker is putting the kibosh on an otherwise great idea, look for the rest of the group to champion the idea.

Alternatively, go back to the criteria list and point out that the driver meets every requirement. Or ask for a better idea to replace the group's choice, then ask the group whether they like the new one better. Always be aware that what may look like a troublemaker to you may actually be the person with the best solution.

STEP SEVEN: HOW TO TEST FINAL BRAND TOOLS FOR EFFECTIVENESS

If all goes well, by the end of the second, third, or fourth meeting, you will emerge with consensus on the brand principle, the brand personality, and the brand association. Before deciding they are final, there are a few steps that you can take to prevent mistakes.

First of all, run each by the criteria list. Of the highest importance is that you can base actions on the brand principle. Second, hold off on finalizing the principle for a few days. A good principle, like a good design, gets better with exposure. Third, if you are tentative about your results, test them with others in the company or with customers. This testing process can be as simple as talking to customers about what the principle implies and what kinds of action result from the personality, or conducting focus groups with tag lines and advertising based on all organization and brand driver results.

Remember that you are not trying to act in lockstep with a process. What you are trying to do is create the very best drivers possible. If that means going off-process, or adding a step to ensure quality, then do it.

Once you have finalized all drivers, the next step is to educate employees in a series of workshops that begin the process of integrating brand into the work force. The objective of integrated branding workshops is to get employees to use organization and brand drivers as the basis for customer interactions and dialogues and as a way to differentiate the brand, product, and service offerings from the competition.

NOTES

1. *Millennium 1998–1999 Journal/Calendar* (Data Dimensions, 1998), June 29–July 5.

2. David Aaker, *Managing Brand Equity* (New York: Free Press, 1991), pp. 104–152.

8 Developing a Practical Brand Structure

> Brands do not exist in isolation but, rather, relate to other brands within the system.[1]
>
> —David A. Aaker, *Building Strong Brands*

There is a lot of brand theory in the brand business. The challenge for brand marketers is to go beyond theory to what works, without oversimplifying or overcomplicating the process and thereby losing its value. Oversimplifying is using brand as simply a marketing function—missing entirely how it drives actions throughout the company. Overcomplicating is using a brand model that you can't easily apply. One branding specialist defines brand as *strategic ambiguity*—saying that some aspects of brand defy easy characterization. The result of brand work is a powerful and sophisticated system for relating with customers—but getting to that system does not have to be a complex or ambiguous process. This is especially true when determining the brand structure of your company and products. Most companies use either one or a combination of the strategies discussed in this chapter.

Consider viewing your brands as a series of sovereign states. What you need to understand are the strengths of each state, their driving force, their unique aspects, and their boundaries. You also need to know how the states work together. Are they part of a confederacy, a union, or a monarchy? Or does your company practice anarchy as its model?

If your company has not defined its brand structure, and you have all product lines under one brand name, you may be confusing your customers and limiting your products' growth potential. In this scenario, customers may not have a clear understanding of what your company stands for or why they should purchase any of your products. They may also accept some product offerings but find others suspect because of your apparent lack of focus.

For example, Company X is a maker of software development tools called Outland. One day, one of its engineers has an idea for a nifty new development language. Without a clear idea of what its brand strategy is, Company X names the product Outland ++. Customers expect the product to be compatible with Outland. When they find out it isn't, many will walk away from your brand in disgust. They question Company X's commitment to its original Outland product line as well as to this new development language. They may anticipate that the company will pay less attention to either line than it did to the original.

Confused brand and naming strategies become even more of an issue when companies merge or one company acquires another. The result is often competing products in the same marketplace. In an effort to retain both sets of customers, management may be unwilling to give up either product brand. This creates great confusion inside the company in terms of which product continues to receive investment.

A brand-driven company has a rational brand structure that corresponds to company mission and product line strategy. This gives brand-driven companies a road map for finding their way through new product, new product line, and overlapping product challenges resulting from mergers, acquisitions, and actions by R&D departments.

There are three strategic models that we use for understanding and building brand structure. They are the *umbrella* (also known as *parent*), *shared-status*, and *product brand* structure. Each method can be effective, but each differs greatly from the others in execution and cost.

THE UMBRELLA BRAND STRUCTURE

The umbrella hierarchy is the most cost-effective of the three models. However, it is also the least market-focused and the one that leaves companies most vulnerable to attack from competitors. In this model the *company* is the brand and all of the products underneath have no or little brand equity and share the same organization and brand drivers. All products use the company name and then typically add a literal description of the product or a number. An example of an umbrella structure is that of Xerox, where historically every product was called "Xerox," with a model number after it, such as the Xerox 1090 copier. This helped make the Xerox name (which is derived from the Greek for "dry writing") so synonymous with copying that the company wisely took bold steps—such as running an aggressive trademark education advertising campaign—to ensure that Xerox was never in danger of becoming a generic term.

This is also representative of the other problem that faces umbrella brands—becoming too well known for one line of products. When you ask most people what they associate with the word *Xerox*, they will say "copiers." Although this type of unaided awareness of a positive association would have some brand managers drooling, when the association places narrow boundaries on your business or puts the company's trademark at risk, it is not helpful. That is why product naming at Xerox today is different, with some product families identified with additional category trademarks—such as the Xerox DocuPrint N20—followed by the generic descriptor, networked laser printer. Yet it isn't always possible to change either external perceptions or internal inertia around a brand's boundaries.

Microsoft also uses the umbrella strategy, but because the company has such a commanding market position in the software industry, it can do so without as many drawbacks. In situations in which the company is the brand, the company name will be used as the bridge to new product areas and hold brand meaning. Microsoft is expert at this, branding every product from word processors and operating systems to development languages and Internet content with the Microsoft moniker.

In every market Microsoft has moved into, the Microsoft brand name and distribution system have been responsible for a large part of each product's success.

For companies that are contemplating launching new products, a well-known corporate brand is a great launch pad. Because brand is a promise, customers will expect that same promise in all future products. That's why low-end products from high-end brands often fail—people expect the same quality from the low-end product and are disappointed. If this happens, the company hurts both the chances for its new product and those of its existing products, because the brand promise has been broken and the trust in the relationship has been impaired.

It's like any relationship: if someone breaks a promise, the relationship can be irreparably damaged. If a company cheats on its customers, that is, breaks the brand promise, the relationship is damaged also. It takes great customer commitment to give a promise breaker a second or third chance.

If you are going with the umbrella approach, it's very important to spend the time to create high-quality organization and brand drivers (see

Chapters 4 through 7). By focusing on both the present and the future, company drivers such as the mission and brand principle can make you more effective in the short term and protect you from huge and costly brand reworks in the long term.

Redefining the Umbrella Brand

In the 1990s, Xerox has been conducting a global experiment in umbrella brand redefinition. The company correctly foresaw the potential of the new digital markets that would allow its existing business to act as a springboard to an even larger marketplace. In 1994, Xerox put together a new strategic direction and new brand image centered around the idea of *The Document Company*—being a leader in the digital document marketplace. *Digital document* is a much larger category than *copier*. It appears that the company has been successful in this process. Here's what chairman Paul A. Allaire told shareholders at the annual meeting in Chicago in 1998:

> By anticipating major changes in the marketplace, Xerox Corporation has successfully transformed itself from a copier company into a leader in digital document technology.
>
> For most of the past decade, we have been boldly reinventing Xerox—from a predominantly black-and-white light lens copier company to a digital, color and document solutions company. This is a real success story for Xerox. We have accomplished what few companies ever manage—foreseen, adapted to and led a major transformation in our marketplace.[2]

The ability to achieve this says a lot about the strategic acumen of Xerox management, and the discipline and skill of its work force. Although your brand is not a crystal ball for seeing into the future, a brand that understands its brand strengths will allow an easier transition when the market shifts.

Another way to transform a strong umbrella brand is by using its existing brand equity to create a new brand and market direction—one that was recently tried by Lucent Technologies. Lucent is the AT&T spin-off formerly known as Bell Labs. Bell Labs had its own brand, which was thought of as inventive and technically superior, but also slightly old-fashioned. With a series of text-heavy ads in major newspapers, Lucent launched itself as a new brand by highlighting its technology roots, but removing itself from the stodgy, slightly out-of-touch brand image held by Bell Labs. The result is a tour de force of branding—creating a

Figure 8.1
The WRQ Logo

WRQ®

Reflection and Express Software

The WRQ logo demonstrates the relationship of the company brand to its two product line brands.

Source: Reprinted with the permission of WRQ.

new brand that uses only the positive parts of a previous identity yet benefiting from its long and successful history.

THE SHARED-STATUS STRUCTURE

A company can protect itself by diversifying beyond the company brand. In a shared-status structure, a company will focus on building both product line brand equity and corporate equity through its strategies, communications, and actions. WRQ, discussed earlier, is an example of a shared-status brand. The WRQ brand can be viewed as a federal government and its Reflection and Express brands are its states (see figure 8.1). The federal government provides overall direction and union while the states provide products.

One of the major benefits of this structure is that the corporate brand can function with a more abstract principle (such as WRQ's *consultative partner*) and still be highly effective. This limits the danger that the marketplace will associate the company with an old, outdated technology or practice and that the company will be tempted to define its brand too narrowly. Meanwhile each product line brand will have its own set of distinct brand drivers (such as Reflection's brand principle of *software designed from an IT point of view*).

The shared-status brand can also be effectively used by the company as a way to transfer equity from the stronger to the weaker or from old to new. In technology markets, products often garner more equity than the company producing them. Effective branding (such as placing company and product logos closely together in ads) can transfer equity to the company from the product. Once the company brand has stronger equity, it can be used to help ensure the success of new product line

Figure 8.2
Organization Drivers Stay Consistent in Product Brands

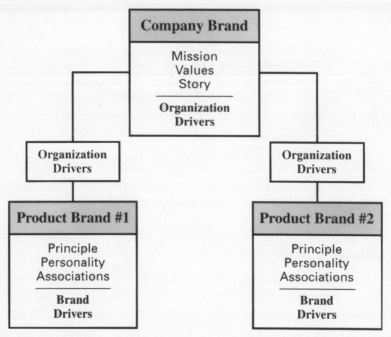

All product brands share the same organization drivers, which allow organizationwide brand consistency.

brand launches. Products that begin their life with a familiar name from a company with strong distinctiveness have a much better chance of succeeding than those that don't.

There's also the possibility of performing an equity transfer between two existing brands. This is done by linking the old and new brands, then slowly weaning the new brand from the old. For example, WRQ did this by telling users of its new Express brand that Express products were now "From the makers of Reflection software," a strong brand with positive equity (see figure 8.2).

Shared status can work from new to old as well. A hot new technology product may be able to accrue a vast amount of awareness in a short period. By tying itself to the product, a less well-known company can boost its awareness by riding the hot product's coattails. An example of this is the search engine Alta Vista made by the former Digital Equipment Corp. Alta Vista helped to position Digital as a leader in the Internet and away from its image as a proprietary computer system maker.

When a company has a shared-status structure, it is easier to sell brands off. This can be an advantage for a company that finds itself no longer able or willing to support a certain brand. Also negative company news will not necessarily rub off on its product brands as happens under the umbrella structure.

There are two negatives to the shared-status structure. The first is that creating and supporting new brands and product lines is an expensive process. Each brand takes investment. When successful, individual brands are viewed as independent assets on the balance sheet by the financial community. In the domestic U.S. market alone, it takes millions of dollars to sell a new product into the Fortune 500.

Second, each additional brand adds complexity to the company's communication process. Companies are faced with such questions as "How do we communicate the corporate brand within marketing pieces for a product brand?" It also becomes more difficult to maintain a consistent look and voice throughout all brands. However, the positives of a shared-status structure outweigh the negatives for most companies.

THE PRODUCT BRAND STRUCTURE

In the product brand structure each product is its own brand and the company takes a back seat in the awareness process. Product brands are beneficial when a company wants the focus to be completely on the product and there is no obvious need for company support behind the product. A product-brand-only strategy may also make sense in categories (such as gaming) where the marketplace values *uniqueness* and *novelty*. Not being tied to a company that's considered outdated could actually be an advantage in these markets.

The product brand structure is not typically used in technology areas, except in games. *Myst* is a good example of a product brand structure. When the same company produced *Riven*, it had "*Riven*, the sequel to *Myst*" on the box, never mentioning the company name, Cyan.

Another version of the product brand is a wholly owned subsidiary. For all of the benefits already mentioned, a company may choose to distance a product from its core offerings. It may also want to try out new ideas that might not fly in its corporate culture. This is the case with the carmaker Saturn. Faced with a market that did not believe Americans could make a low-end car that could compete in terms of reliability with those made by the Japanese, GM created an entirely new brand to attack exactly that portion of the market. The brand promise? A world-class car made in America. The brand personality? Down home, friendly, personable, and trustworthy. But it's never emphasized that GM owns Saturn.

If GM had made a big deal about Saturn's being a GM brand, the Saturn promise would be less believable. If GM had made the same car but given it a Chevrolet-brand name, it would not be credible. But by the creation of a new stand-alone brand, Saturn became one of the nation's most popular small cars—sixth among all automakers in 1996, and garnering a market share of the small and sport segment of 10.31 percent.[3]

HOW CAN YOU DETERMINE WHICH MODEL TO ADOPT?

How do you pick which of these brand architectures will be most conducive to your current organizational structure and future growth strategies? For most small companies, it probably means staying with the umbrella or parent brand structure until your first product is well developed and has captured significant market share. Using an umbrella brand is much less expensive and can still afford you the freedom to move to a shared-status system over time. The danger to this approach is being typecast as a one-category company.

If you are sure that you will be moving into several product lines in the future, the safest bet is to create a shared-status brand structure, in which the company and initial product brand purposely use different brand drivers—even though there is only one set of products involved. This system can help prevent the company from being typecast, without expending huge marketing dollars. Your first product brand may take years to reach its full potential. During that period you will be able to create equity in the company brand to use it as a product launch platform for a second product brand down the road.

If you choose to use the shared-status approach, be aware that each new brand requires some additional financial and managerial investment. Having fewer brands is always easier. Therefore, only add new brands when you are strategically compelled to do so.

THE BRAND MATRIX: HOW TO DETERMINE WHETHER CURRENT PRODUCTS FIT UNDER CURRENT BRANDS

How can you determine your brand structure? Which products should be grouped together?

You can determine brand structure by using a simple brand matrix that matches like product features, image, assets, and margin (see table 8.1).

First, create a table that lists all products in columns and assets in rows. Product assets include all assets—both tangible and intangible—that make up the product. This includes drivers, distribution methods,

Table 8.1
The Brand Matrix: Determining Brand Hierarchy

Brand X Audience = Scope/Direction =	Enterprise software utilities; to become a *must-have* element of IT desktops		Information technology managers
Asset	*Product 1*	*Product 2*	*Product 3*
Market share U.S. & ROW*	80% 15%	15% 15%	25% 30%
Margin	40% 25%	<1% 15%	15% 40%
Brand X audience overlap	100%	30%	50%
A Brand X association is integral to product sales	Yes	No	No
In line with brand scope; strategic direction	Yes	No	Partially; can be construed to be a utility but more of an enterprise management tool
Alliances	Yes; with number 1 enterprise systems reseller	Yes; same as product 1	Yes; with number 1 enterprise systems vendor
Co-branding	No	No	Yes; with number 1 enterprise systems vendor
Rational naming strategy	No	Yes	Yes
Other assets, differentiators, licenses, OEM* agreements	Considered "the gold standard" by European and Asian customers		OEMed to European system integrator

The brand matrix is a simple method for gaining perspective on brand organizations.
*ROW = rest of the world; OEM = original equipment manufacturer.

market share, margin, customer loyalty, patents, licenses, and alliances.
There are a number of questions that you need to answer to complete the matrix. Start the brand inventory by listing all separate brand product lines, for instance, software development tools and software utilities, in separate columns. If you have empirical evidence about market aware-

ness levels, percentage of audience that is positively disposed toward the product line, and other assets such as patents or associations, put that into each column as well. The brand matrix allows you to put a rational spin on brand structure. Answer the following questions to complete the brand matrix:

How high are the market share and margin of each product?

What percentage of the market overlaps with other product lines?

Is there additional value associated with the company or products such as associations, patents, or differentiators?

Do certain products have awareness that is not related to the brand?

Do all of your products fit under the brand's business scope?

Which products fit in with your strategic direction?

Which products are rising stars, cash cows, or over the hill?

In this sample brand matrix we can see that Product 1 is a perfect fit for Brand X, and Product 2 and Product 3 should not be under the brand at all. Given Product 1's status in the rest of the world (ROW), the matrix suggests looking for a way to create the *gold standard* association in the United States as well, and seeing whether it is a viable association for the brand in general. If Product 1 is this strong using a naming strategy that customers don't understand, imagine what could happen if this situation were corrected. The company's ROW marketing staff should also seek to capitalize on its strengths through alliances and cobranding initiatives.

Given Product 2's low market penetration and margins relative to other products, management should consider three possibilities. The first is moving Product 2 under another brand name—it may be confusing customers in its current incarnation as a software utility. Worse still, Product 2 may be diluting the strength of Brand X by confusing the customer on both the scope and the commitment of Brand X to its core business area. Second, if that does not seem feasible, the company should consider selling or licensing Product 2 to another company.

With Product 3, management is at a fork in the road. They are facing the question of whether to market (and develop) Product 3 more in the direction of a enterprise utility than they have done in the past. Or will they find more fertile ground by developing a new brand around enterprise management tools? This is the riskier course in the short term because it requires an understanding of a new market, as well as technical and marketing expertise that the company may not have. Over the long term, however, it creates a new product line for the company that could lead to increased growth and profitability. A factor arguing for a new brand is that the product has only a 50 percent overlap with Brand X's audience.

RECOMMENDING A BRAND STRUCTURE FOR A ONE-PRODUCT COMPANY WITH A BIG VISION

The following example will demonstrate how to apply brand structure to a typical technology company.

A common branding scenario in the technology market will be for a small but rapidly growing company ($10 million–$250 million in revenues) with one business-to-business product line and a small number of products in it. Typically one product in the line will be very well known.

If the company is seeking to grow and perhaps go public, the brand structure that makes the most sense is shared status. Shared status allows the company to create broad boundaries for its mission and its brand principle, while not diluting the focus of its product line brand. The company will be in much better shape over the long term if it starts using an integrated brand early in its existence. As the company expands, its integrated brand will help it to focus on the most appropriate products and features, deepen customer relationships, and retain its corporate culture.

One medium-sized company in the mobile communications area has a technology software product that is practically a household word. However, it has not made a consistent effort to develop meaning around the corporate brand. The company also has tried over the years to launch a series of new products, all of which have failed because the company had expected the unique set of circumstances that made the first product a success to continue. But the first product was launched into an immature and therefore noncompetitive technology market, where it was relatively easy to get new customers and be carried on store shelves. Without transferring the equity from the well-known product to the company, there is no foundation for new brands.

DETERMINING A BRAND'S BUSINESS SCOPE AND APPROPRIATE BRAND EXTENSIONS

It's as important to determine the business scope or boundaries of a brand as it is to determine the mission statement of the company. By setting clear boundaries, companies can protect themselves from costly errors in strategic direction. They will also avoid huge investments trying to change course in the future. In a recent study of fourteen leading high-technology companies, researchers Behnam Tabrizi and Rick Walleigh determined that in every case in which new products ran into difficulties, it was in the product definition stage. In one instance, the new product team, manufacturing, and marketing all had different definitions of what the product was, right up to launch.[4]

There are two factors that will help you determine the business scope of the brand. Both are also very important to brand extension success. The first is, *What offerings will customers believe the brand can successfully deliver?* The second is, *What strengths does the brand bring to a specific product or service?* Brand strengths include those things the company does particularly well that are crystallized in the brand principle, personality, and brand association drivers. They can also include technical, distribution, and marketing strengths.

The way to determine scope is similar to the way you rationalize your existing brand structure. Take an internal inventory of brand strengths, hypothesize the boundaries of the brand, and then test boundary-pushing product concepts with customers. If you are in a situation in which the company is the brand, then the scope needs to be set as broadly as possible. For example, if you make a web browser, could the broadest reach be about *all things related to the Internet*? Or should broadest reach be limited to *Internet navigational and organizational tools*? By having at least a rough idea of brand scope up-front, you can begin to set up messages and product directions to support future development.

Current Brand versus Possible Brand

Depending on your objectives, you may extend the brand in several different ways. For instance, you may use brand extensions to fill holes in current product lines. Customers may need scaled-down or scaled-up versions of a current product. They may want one that bridges the gap between two categories as well. For instance, at a certain point, desktop laser printers overlap with laser copiers. If you place a product directly at the convergence of these two categories, you may find an entirely new market (brand extension) for your product.

You may also look for new ways to use an existing technology. Consider the case of a management software product for computer networks, which analyzes a network and helps it to recover from system errors. This same product could be sold as stand-alone logic analyzer software and compete against an entirely different set of products.

DEVELOPING A SECOND PRODUCT BRAND: WHEN IS IT A STRATEGIC WIN?

When should a one-product-line company consider creating a second product brand?

One answer is when you are about to max out the growth potential of your existing product line. Another is when you want to create a more diverse set of profit centers. A third is when the business or category focus of a new product or acquisition opportunity does not fall within your existing brand's boundaries.

Before you jump into a new brand you need to determine whether the brand has staying power and potential for future growth and expansion. What are the market prospects for this product category over the next two years? Five years? What could make this category obsolete? Are any competitive giants likely to enter the category and take it over? You can use the brand matrix tool to determine whether the proposed product is a good extension candidate for the company. If it is just a "one-off" (a product unrelated to the rest of the product line) product, you may still wish to bring it to market to prove its viability for the purpose of selling it or licensing it to the highest bidder. If you are going to put the work into turning the product into a brand, however, you need to ensure a long-term payoff.

How long should you expect a brand to be viable? Forever, would be the best answer. But this is not realistic in technology circles, except for broad-based technology brands such as IBM and Xerox, which have been able to create very broad brand boundaries. The appropriate answer depends in part on company investment versus potential sales. Can you get the return on investment you require versus initial costs? Beyond this, a brand unit should be able to provide many years of consistent revenues and profitability to the company and serve as a cash-generation mechanism allowing R&D to create new products within the brand.

When developing a new brand, you also need to ensure that you have logistical support for it as well. Do you have sufficient internal resources to develop and support the product line? Is management willing to invest in the line up-front? Have employees bought into the promise of the new brand? Newly branded products tend to do better if they are handled by product teams that are distinct from existing brands.

BRAND DILUTION: THE BRAND'S WORST ENEMY

What is brand dilution? It's another way of saying *loss of value*. Dilution pushes a brand in the direction of becoming a commodity by degrading the customer experience. When a brand takes on meanings that either exceed the belief systems of its customers or just confuse them, it is said to be diluted. Unfortunately, there are a large number of activities that can dilute a brand, activities that are practiced every day by most companies. The only insurance against dilution is a clear understanding of your brand.

Message Dilution

When brand experts talk about dilution, they are typically talking about a defocusing of a brand into too many product areas. This lack of focus weakens customer trust. A brand that lacks focus is like a person who embraces a different belief system every week. He or she looks insincere or uncommitted to others.

There is a second type of dilution, *message dilution*. Message dilution most often happens to brands that aren't consciously managed. However, it may also happen even when there is a strong brand management system in place. Just as product dilution is often the result of opportunistic actions, message dilution is often the result of marketing that becomes enamored of trendy messages in their product area.

How do you determine when new messages are helping the brand rather than confusing it?

This is a judgment call for the brand and marketing managers. The brand manager must keep an eye on market trends and related messages, and be a collection point for them. He or she should have good relations with people on the front lines, including sales people, product managers, and customer support and marketing people, and work with the marketing and product managers to selectively add new messages that keep the brand fresh. To determine whether a specific message should be added, ask yourself whether it is in line with the brand principle, a benefit of the product's functionality, or is a current category benefit or differentiator. If your company needs to add new messages to the brand, this is an indication that your product positioning is no longer relevant and should be reworked.

Unbelievable Product or Services: The Principal Cause of Dilution

As mentioned earlier, brand dilution usually refers to adding new products, services, or messages to a brand that don't fit within the brand's boundaries from a customer's point of view. This dilutes the promise of the brand—it muddies the water. An example of dilution is the practice among high-end clothes designers of putting their name on all kinds of unrelated products including perfume and underwear. A brand that has established itself as unique and one of a kind, such as Calvin Klein, can easily lose that cachet when its name is sold on three-to-a-pack underwear in a discount store.

When Brand Dilution Happens

There are several scenarios that create fertile ground for brand dilution. Most often brand dilution is the result of

- opportunism
- a desire to maximize short-term profits
- R&D
- a lack of brand knowledge
- a desire for product line extensions
- mergers or acquisitions

Opportunism is something that happens all of the time in technology companies, where engineers drive new product development on the basis of their degree of interest in a particular new technology or marketers smell a new untapped market. Many technology management teams may not have had formal marketing education or experience. If their first product is successful, the classic mistake is to assume subsequent products will also be. Dilution happens when these subsequent products bear little or no resemblance to the original product, yet are grouped under the same product name, or when the company has been so niched in customers' minds (typically as a result of the company's own communications strategy of focusing only on product features and benefits) that customers believe the new product is outside the company's area of expertise.

R&D is a vital function for the future prosperity of any company. However, companies need to take care that the resultant technologies or products fall within the charter of the company. After expanding into too many product lines in the 1980s, Tektronix has done a good job of reducing the number of products it offers, while putting the results of R&D to productive use. Instead of commercializing every new technology it develops, the company now has an aggressive licensing and sales program. Therefore, it isn't as likely to expend time and energy in too many directions at once.

It's only natural for companies to expand brand product lines to meet new customer needs and to increase revenues. However, companies must act with restraint when it comes to new product introductions. The first question that the brand manager must ask is, *Does this product fall within the boundaries of the existing brand?* Unfortunately the answer to this question isn't always obvious, because brand extension is as much art as science.

When WRQ developed a product that allowed web-to-host connectivity as opposed to PC-to-host connectivity, it was simple to answer the question of whether the new product was within the boundaries of the brand. Connectivity is the focus of the Reflection brand. Although web-to-host offers a whole new way to access mainframes and minicomputers, it is clearly a connectivity product, so this product became branded under the Reflection name. But when WRQ developed a product for TCP/IP, the de facto standard for data packet transport on computer networks, the answer was less obvious. Is a transport a connectivity product, or should it be put in a new category? The company determined that its TCP/IP product was a classic connectivity product by allowing data to move between different operating systems. Therefore, the company kept the product within the Reflection brand as Reflection for TCP.

Brand dilution can easily happen in mergers and acquisitions, as companies often consolidate radically different product lines under one brand name. In the case of a merger, the brand manager must review which products fall neatly within the boundaries of a particular product line, which are clearly outside and need to be branded differently or sold off, and which are marginally inside the current brand definition.

False Claims

False claims—as a company promotes product benefits that don't exist—are another threat to a brand. Again this is far more likely to happen with an unconscious brand where company actions and brand message don't necessarily match. Making claims that customers value, without backing them up with actions, creates negative customer interactions and reduces brand equity each time it happens. If the claim is large enough, the brand can get a permanent black eye or the company may even become the target of a class action suit.

Acting against Customer Best Interest

When it comes to choosing between customer best interest and increased short-term profitability, many companies choose the latter. Is this an effective way to maximize profits over the long term? Not usually. Imagine having a friendship with someone who *always* puts his or her needs ahead of yours and who is friends with you only when it is convenient for him or her. How far would you trust the person and how much emotional rapport would you have with him or her? The same concept will be applied to your brand by your customers. If you choose short-term profitability over customer satisfaction, you will end up with a weak brand.

In the software industry companies sometimes act against their customers' best interests through releasing unnecessary product upgrades. Often termed "bloatware," many upgrade versions seem to add features to mature products just for the sake of increasing revenues. Young technology companies often don't fully consider the problems their customers will face when forced to change standards or upgrade to newer versions of products. Most customers are reluctant to upgrade operating systems and applications because of the training and installation headaches involved.

Inconsistent support for past standards is another sure way to lose brand equity. Sometimes this is unavoidable. This was the case in the videotape standard wars when VHS won out over Betamax. Those who bet on Betamax had to make a subsequent investment in VHS. Product cul-de-sacs have also happened frequently in the technology industry, as users have been forced to change from custom systems to standard ones, proprietary to open, and DOS-based to Windows-based systems, for example.

Inconsistent Product

All strong brands are based on strong products. If a company guts its product, its brand can fall from grace quickly. In study after study of IT managers, they say that there are only two reasons they will switch brands in a mature market. One is that the product stops delivering. The other is that there is a major improvement in the technology being offered.

Five Tests to See Whether Dilution Is Taking Place

The following tests will help you identify and prevent brand dilution.

Test one: Have you defined the brand's business scope? Is the business scope stated in a brand plan or other strategic document? Has the executive team agreed to this scope, and is it defined so that everyone can understand it?

Test two: Is the brand's business scope still obvious from looking at the product line? Or do you have to explain it to people?

Test three: Are customers, employees, or analysts questioning your reason for offering a certain product? This is an area in which advanced product concept testing can really help determine whether a product should be part of an existing brand or not.

Test four: Check for one of the following dilution scenarios: Are you introducing a new product that is different from existing ones? Are you merging multiple product lines into one? Do your actions and messages match? Are you making decisions that will harm customers? Are you supporting your products as long as customers need you to? Are you continuing to produce a great product?

Test five: Do you have integrated brands? Do employees know and use organization and brand drivers?

Carefully answering these questions will prevent you from making brand dilution mistakes.

NOTES

1. David A. Aaker, *Building Strong Brands* (New York: Free Press, 1996).
2. Xerox web site: http://www.xerox.com/investor/irconf/1998/paa/index. htm.
3. Saturn news release, August 1, 1997.
4. Behnam Tabrizi and Rick Walleigh, "Defining Next Generation Products: An Inside Look," *Harvard Business Review* (November–December 1997), pp. 117–118.

9 Using Integrated Branding to Expand Market Share

Brands matter. People are looking for something to hold onto, not just generic products they can buy.

—Marian Salzman, Director,
Brand Futures Group, Young & Rubicam

The secret to the power of the brand is in how it enhances your company's relationship with its customers. A good relationship is worthwhile because it leads to long-term customer retention and market share leadership. A company's raison d'être is profit, and by dominating your market, you will be less vulnerable to competitors and will be able to maintain leadership with less additional investment.

Integrated branding helps companies expand market share through a variety of methods. In some cases, an integrated brand helps companies hit a market that has become a moving target; in others it ensures a continuity of focus; and in still others it helps them maintain rational product lines.

TYPICAL INTEGRATED BRANDING SCENARIOS

Here are some typical scenarios demonstrating how companies can leverage company strengths and expand market share using integrated branding.

You Are a Small Yet Rapidly Growing Company

Many successful companies are started by a founder who has a passion for a particular idea or has found a better way to do something. In the early years, that passion can be passed to new employees through close team interaction. But as the company gets larger, new people enter who are out of touch with top management. Many companies watch their organization fall to pieces just as they are reaching a dominant market position. Brand, as a central driver of corporate culture, provides clear direction to people at every level, for everything from new product development to customer service. It also acts as a guide for hiring and new employee orientation to maintain the best aspects of the existing culture.

Your Product Line Is Growing in Size and Description

As companies extend their product lines, they tend either to continue using the same name and logo as their successful initial product or to go to the other extreme and create new names for everything. Using the same name risks confusion and reduces the company's ability to expand market share. Naming everything differently means creating many brands—a strategy that requires a huge, ongoing investment of time and money. The brand process can create the most effective path between these two extremes by determining the realistic scope of an existing brand and the potential for new ones. If there is no current potential for launching new products from your existing brand, this process will help you determine how to create a platform for cost-effectively launching new brands.

You Are Acquiring Another Company and/or Its Products

Acquisitions bring up a number of thorny questions that, if answered in a disjointed way, can hurt a company. How does a company integrate an acquisition that has unique brand attributes, new or overlapping product lines, and a unique company culture into its existing organization? Does the company keep the new product line or service as a unique brand, does it use the acquired company name as a brand name, or does it relegate it to being a product name? If products are overlapping, does it choose to sell both? How is this explained in direct sales?

Integrated branding provides answers to these questions. And it does so in ways that create actions and decisions that lead to and sustain a cohesive organization and lower the chances of customer cannibalization or general customer confusion.

You Are in a Changing Market

Integrated branding can help companies stay on track—this is particularly true of technology companies, where a new innovation completely changes the face of the market. If a company focuses too narrowly on current product features, it can easily get sidelined by shifts in market direction.

For instance, faxes are gradually being replaced by electronic documents sent via email attachments. If a company defined its business as "making fax machines" it might be at a loss for what to do next and probably flounder for several years trying one blind alley and then another. Integrated branding keeps companies on course.

You Are a Company Adrift

This typically happens when a company has either attained or totally failed to attain its original mission. Once it has accomplished its goal, what direction should it take in the future? Or if market changes have made its goal impossible to reach, does it keep trying until it runs out of money? Many companies have died without making a clear decision when facing this scenario. Integrated branding provides a path that encourages a broader market view and movement to markets where brand strengths can be effectively used.

You Are a Start-Up Company

Start-ups have more to gain from branding than almost every other group. Most start-ups assume that focusing on brand is a luxury, to be done once you have already made it. Start-ups justifiably feel that they have their hands full just getting product out the door.

Many start-up companies also believe they don't have the financial resources to do integrated branding. However, integrated branding is both easier and less costly to implement when a company is at start-up stage, because there are fewer layers of management, greater focus, and a smaller customer base from which to sample.

By focusing company strengths from the start, the company is much more likely to gain market dominance over its unfocused competitors.

You Are an Unfocused Conglomerate

If a company gets big without a conscious brand direction, it is susceptible to several problems that can be prevented through a brand-driven focus. Many companies do well for long periods because their core product or core concept is so strong that normal competition is slow to overtake them. An example of this is retailer Sears Roebuck. For decades, Sears did well from both catalogue and store sales. One of the most basic reasons Sears ran into trouble was its move away from being the *buying expert for the American family* to something more like *low-end one-stop shopping services*. It added financial and real estate services while paying less attention to the quality of the shopping experience within its retail stores. The organization went through a multiyear slide and has made a comeback only after recommitting to its core brand strength of offering a high-quality shopping experience.

THE ROAD TO MARKET DOMINANCE

In each of the preceding scenarios, companies required the focus and discipline of integrated branding to achieve market success. So how does branding lead to market dominance? Besides the intrinsic benefits of integrating brand, the brand process will allow you to determine who your best customers are. Your best customers are those who have the most affinity with your company strengths that you exhibit through actions, messages, and personality. At the same time, this group is made up of those most prone to be repeat purchasers and word-of-mouth ambassadors for your company.

By identifying what these customers are like, you can design your interactions with them to meet their needs and reflect their values even more closely. This will also allow you to identify new customers who are like existing ones cost-effectively and to find those who are not quite so similar but still may be considered second-tier purchasers for your brand. Thus, your messages can encompass a wider and wider set of people, all linked by what they experience with your brand.

For example, Starbucks started out by being closely linked to Italian cafes—providing the intense coffee experience previously only available in Europe. These extreme coffee aficionados—Starbucks' best customers—prefer their coffee dark, rich, and strong. But there is a set of customers related to this group who view themselves as drinking a high-quality brew but who also like their coffee a little lighter, a little less intense. For this group, Starbucks expanded its brand to include lattes versus espresso, Frappuccinos, and a house blend that is lighter and less hardcore than many of its other coffee varietals. Starbucks could then both dominate the apex of its market as well as expand downward into the larger mass market. The company provided the trendsetters and early adopters with a unique experience, then created a less difficult way for a larger market to cross the chasm into fresh-roasted coffees.

In this example, Starbucks positioned itself for *early adopter customers* (those who are trendsetters), then expanded its messages to include the *early majority* (those who like to learn from other people's experiences before trying something, a group many times larger than the early adopters). Is there room for an ultra-high-quality coffee company to position itself above Starbucks? Not easily, because Starbucks has positioned itself through its customer experience as the highest-quality coffee experience possible.

Will the brand achieve its objective of becoming accepted by a large market? Look at the figures—sales of canned coffee (Yuban, MJB, and the like) have been dropping precipitously for the last ten years, while sales of whole beans have climbed, according to the Specialty Coffee Association of America.[1] Since 1989, canned commercial coffee has dropped 12 percent, while whole bean specialty coffee has increased by 62 percent during the same period.

As these figures show, what once was specialty coffee is now on its way to becoming mainstream. Starbucks rose to the top of its market through a clear and well-executed brand, by creating a brand that appealed to its best customers, and then expanding the appeal of the brand down market. And because Starbucks owns its stores rather than franchising them, it tightly controls all aspects of its brand. The company is positioned well against its current competition, which includes a number of coffee manufacturers such as Tully's and Seattle's Best Coffee with less defined customer experiences, as well as against wherever the market may go in the future.

For Starbucks, finding this "market sweet spot" was the result of

1. discovering its best customer (the sophisticate or sophisticate "wannabe" looking to duplicate the Italian cafe experience).
2. optimizing its company strength of producing a coffee experience with what customers value—having their sense of self worth reflected in an affordable luxury.
3. creating a brand wide enough to allow for brand extensions (jazz, Frappuccino, ice cream, cafes), yet narrow enough to guide actions (highest quality, some snob appeal, a rich experience rather than just the sale of a product).

As a result of its brand, customers know exactly what to expect from Starbucks, see their self-image reflected in its products, and become committed adherents and advocates for the company's products. Starbucks is able to increase its share of the market, and, through extensions, its share of each customer's income. It does this through extensions that give its best customers more reasons to spend money at Starbucks.

Potential Threats to Going Mass Market

Starbucks has also tried to increase its market by expanding into house-branded teas called Infusia and Café Starbucks, a full-service restaurant. Can Starbucks bring the same ambiance into these experiences? Tea drinking has not been a traditional part of Italian cafes and usually conjures up tea houses—a different experience and a different set of customers—and restaurants take Starbucks into uncharted territory. The restaurant business is very different from the serving of coffee and snacks.

But the real danger of moving into the mass market is the possibility of Starbucks' brand's losing its premium image. This is even more probable, for instance, when Starbucks licenses its coffees to other providers, such as airlines, who will not maintain the same care in brewing and serving as a tightly controlled Starbucks outlet. This potentially large taste difference can alter a customer's perception of the entire Starbucks experience, causing him or her to stop frequenting Starbucks' stores. At best, this negative experience would force them to create two Starbucks' brands in their minds—a good one and a bad one—casting a pall over the brand experience.

The danger of going mass market is either having customers perceive a change in the experience of the brand or producing confusion or skepticism about the motives of the brand. Continually spreading a brand to meet a broader market is one cause of dilution, discussed in Chapter 8. A brand becomes diluted when it has tried to be so many things that it is the master of nothing and, therefore, no longer appeals to its original core customers.

As the Starbucks example illustrates, brand can be a powerful tool for moving companies up to the top of their markets. It prevents competitors from encroaching on market share, as well as opens doors to growing its market share in the future.

Leveraging Brand Equity into Market Leadership

How do you gain greater market share by leveraging an existing brand's equity? The first and most obvious step is to put the name of the existing brand on the product, on the box, on the advertising, and in the name. But beyond this, the new product must encompass the characteristics of the existing brand, and messages to that effect must be used in marketing communications materials.

Hewlett-Packard, a company with a very strong brand for its LaserJet printers, has successfully transferred its equity to other products. At last check, the company owned more than 50 percent of the desktop laser printer market. This brand equity has translated into the company's PC business. According to the July 13, 1998, issue of *Business Week*, HP vaulted from the twenty-seventh-place PC manufacturer in 1992 to number 4 by 1998.[2] Good experiences with the brand means you will be a repeat buyer or look to the same company for similar but different products.

In another example, Maytag has a great brand in the arena of washing machines centered on *the dependability people*. That brand equity has been successfully transferred to all kinds of appliances.

USING BRAND TO BUILD AWARENESS

One of the benefits of branding is that it allows you to leverage your marketing communications investment. When all customer interactions have the same flavor and tone, people know products are all from the same company and carry the same brand promise. That's why HP ads always look like HP; that's why Kodak uses yellow and Healthy Choice uses green on their packaging and printed communications. If you know and love Healthy Choice low-fat ice cream, you'll look for the green in other brand extensions; similarly, if you know and love HP printers, you'll pay attention when HP is advertising other products.

This is especially true in mature or highly competitive markets. The clearer your brand, the easier it is for customers to differentiate among products. In a mature market such as soft drinks, brand speaks louder than taste, cost, or promotions. Coke drinkers identify with their brand to the point that they avoid Pepsi, even though in blind taste tests, more people liked Pepsi than Coke, including longtime Coke drinkers. In the book *Pepsi: 100 Years*, Bob Stoddard states, "Blind taste tests, in which samples are not identified, were pursued with subjects who had claimed not only to prefer the taste of Coke over Pepsi but also to be able to tell the two drinks apart by their taste. In fact, when unaware of which cola they were sampling, of the initial group of participants who claimed to prefer Coke, 50 percent said that Pepsi tasted better."[3]

Competitive markets can also benefit from the lessons of branding. In a competitive market such as long-distance carriers, many vendors have tried to sell on price. This leads to training customers to *buy* on price, competitive price wars, and downward pressure on margins, with no associated uptick in long-term customer loyalty. As a result, some of the more savvy providers use lock in programs (MCI's Friends and Family), and others use sound quality as the differentiator, as in Sprint's dropping pin association.

If a company has fallen into the addictive habit of selling through discounts or promotions, it must move to differentiators that help define the customer experience. Typically these are built on either emotional issues or unique service aspects.

Let's take PCs, a potential commodity, as an example. One Intel-based PC with the same specs is like another, right? Not if branding comes into play. *Safe buy*, an emotional hook, can be owned by IBM. Dell Computer Corporation can own *customization*, a service-oriented hook. Gateway can own *made by nice, trustworthy Midwesterners*, another emotional hook, reflected in its Holstein cow graphics. Compaq can own *innovation with quality*. This company has found ways to innovate that appeal to PC buyers, such as a "sleep button" on the PC, which, when pushed, puts the computer into sleep mode, saving energy for the home user.

In each of these cases, the brand strength is defensible if the company chooses a course of action that finds what customers value. If it consistently strengthens and owns meaningful differentiators over time, no one will be able to wrest customers away. Companies looking for customization at a good price will go to Dell; those looking for a computer they can trust will go to Gateway; safe buyers will turn to Compaq or IBM.

Each PC manufacturer in this example has identified its best customer and what he or she values, has compared that to the company's strengths over time, and has worked to build that brand strength into every aspect of the customer relationship.

But you don't need to have a big business to use brand as a way to escape commoditization. One of the authors of this book lives in a small neighborhood in Seattle called West Seattle. West Seattle has a strong sense of community and a neighborhood gas station, Barnecuts, that has been a neighborhood institution for over forty years. Even though competition has been growing over the past twenty years, Barnecuts has continued to be a preferred brand experience for local residents.

According to its customers, Barnecuts stands out for several reasons. One is that it provides a personal experience. At Barnecuts they pump your gas and the attendants are personable and pleasant to interact with. Their mechanics are known for being honest and for doing the work right the first time. Finally, customers go to the station because they have beautiful boxed flowers sitting on top of each gas pump.

NOTES

1. Ted Lingle, "Avenues for Growth: A 20-Year Review of the U.S. Specialty Coffee Market," *Specialty Coffee Association of America* (January 1993), pp. 1–7.

2. Peter Burrows, "Lew Platt's Fix-It Plan for Hewlett-Packard," *Business Week* (July 13, 1998), p. 128.

3. Bob Stoddard, *Pepsi: 100 Years* (Los Angeles, CA: General Publishing Group, 1997), p. 163.

10 The WRQ Story: The Steps to a Successful Integrated Brand

> Focusing on brand is one of the three most important activities we have done in the past four years.
>
> —Kevin Klustner, Vice President, WRQ

WRQ, the seventeenth largest U.S. PC software manufacturer, specializing in connecting, managing, and securing corporate networks, is a good example of a successful integrated brand. Besides being one of the largest privately held software companies in the United States, WRQ has significant overseas sales with offices and distributors in Europe, Asia, and Latin America.

WRQ started on the road to integrated branding in 1994. At that time, it had one product line, Reflection, which was connectivity software that allowed people on personal computers to access the information their companies stored on mainframes directly. As computer local area networks gained in popularity in the 1980s and 1990s, companies had to find a way to integrate the information from mainframes into the network. WRQ, through its Reflection software, was one of the companies doing this work.

The company began by integrating HP minicomputer data with PC data and quickly became the market leader. From there, WRQ moved into Digital, UNIX systems, X Window, and IBM connectivity. The customers for WRQ's products were information technology (IT) professionals. IT people are the ones in companies who are responsible for all computer systems, from operating systems to PCs to the Internet.

In 1994, WRQ wanted to increase market share and company awareness. It sensed it was on the edge of becoming much larger and wanted to make sure this growth was controlled and focused. The company also had some brand issues it wanted to solve.

As in many technology companies, at WRQ, Reflection had much greater name recognition than did the company. The company wanted to know whether it would make sense to change its name from WRQ to Reflection. Second, WRQ's marketing communications, including advertisements, did not have a consistent look over time. WRQ hoped that the integrated branding process would create this consistent image. It also wanted to make sure that the WRQ corporate culture, which excelled in customer service and personal initiative, stayed strong.

WHAT WRQ DISCOVERED

WRQ has gone through two phases in its branding process—revealing and determining its brand structure in 1994 and revisiting and fine-tuning its brand in 1997. In 1994, WRQ interviewed a broad cross section of employees, including the remaining business founders, upper management, and representatives from each department. Externally, the company questioned current and past customers and suppliers. The results of the research were very positive and indicated that WRQ had strengths around *quality/does job/best of breed, long-term customer commitment, customer service, smart, friendly,* and *a great place to work.* This would be the raw material for the company's brand drivers.

ONE BRAND OR TWO?

The brand team also discovered that employees and customers strongly identified with the Reflection brand name but not with WRQ's. This indicated that WRQ had not been differentiated to the point where it was recognized as its own brand. The brand team asked, "Is Reflection (host connectivity/transport diagnostics/networking) the total WRQ brand?" and, if not, "What does the WRQ brand stand for?"

WRQ's brand team, which included top executives and influencers from every department, met to hammer out the answers to these questions. During the course of this work, they discovered that the WRQ brand included elements that did not need to apply solely to Reflection but could work for a number of brands or product lines. The WRQ brand could focus on *solving the problems of the information technology department.*

Specific WRQ brand elements included *providing a solution to difficult existing problems, outstanding service and support, strong, stable, high quality*, and *a long-term relationship with customers to understand their future needs*.

These elements allowed the brand team to consider creating a separate WRQ brand. This was a critical strategic decision, because WRQ contemplated moving beyond connectivity with additional product lines sometime in the future. Research on product introductions indicates that products that are related to an existing strong brand stand a much better chance of succeeding than those that aren't. By creating a strong WRQ corporate brand, the company could create a platform for new product line introductions not tied to the connectivity business scope of the Reflection brand.

The following table shows how the brand team viewed the differences between the two brands (see table 10.1).

This left the company with a *shared-status brand structure* that included a company and a product line brand, with the door open to additional product brands in the future.

DETERMINING BRAND DRIVERS

Principle

After defining the brand structure, the brand team began creating brand drivers, beginning with the principle. Through a series of facilitated meetings, the team decided on a WRQ principle of *consultative partner*. Acting as a consultative partner was a unique industry approach to solving IT problems. This appealed to IT professionals because they generally need as much outside support as possible to do the difficult job of managing computer networks successfully. WRQ elaborated on the principle, using the following supporting statements:

- WRQ is dedicated to solving customer problems.
- WRQ provides superior service and support.
- Navigating change: WRQ has a proven system for steering customers in the direction that best fits their needs for enterprise solutions while avoiding technology cul-de-sacs.

Personality

WRQ's personality came through clearly in the research, which indicated that its current IT customers really enjoyed their relationship with WRQ. They felt that WRQ employees genuinely cared about them—that

Table 10.1
WRQ/Reflection Brand Comparisons

WRQ	Reflection
Outstanding service and support	Connectivity software
Strong	Industrial strength
High quality	High quality
High performance products that answer established (early majority/ late majority) Fortune 1000 customer IT needs in information access category	Meets Fortune 1000 customers' needs for high performance in connectivity
Complete solutions	Designed to changing customer needs
Consultative partner/products where customers want a high degree of interaction with company	Strong support; customizable
Easy to do business with	Easy to use

Source: Reprinted with the permission of WRQ.

this was a company they could trust with their critical information systems, which typically ran everything from the company's inventory to accounting. The WRQ personality also reflected a company that was careful about what changes it made to its products, listened carefully to customers about future needs, and generally treated employees, customers, and vendors alike with respect.

Many young companies have flat, one-dimensional personalities, but given the strong and varied personality of WRQ founders, a lot of personality traits had been injected into this company. The brand team agreed on a personality of *a listener, thinks carefully before speaking, friendly, empathetic, humorous, open,* and *intelligent.* They also agreed upon using the trait of *respect* as a way of summarizing the rest of the other traits.

WRQ exhibits respect for customers, employees, community, earth, vendors, and prospects in everything it does. Respect shapes the attitude the company takes in any action. Not surprisingly, respect as a personality trait derives from one of the company's three core values. See the discussion of values in Chapter 4 for details.

As mentioned previously, another way of understanding the personality of a brand is to imagine the person behind the personality. This person can be either completely fictional, borrowed from an existing person everyone in the company is familiar with, such as a company founder, artist, or actor. The following is WRQ's interpretation of its personality, which is used to give employees an idea of how to create the WRQ voice in action as well as in written and spoken communications.

If WRQ were a person. Walter R. Quinn is a fictitious employee who exemplifies WRQ's personality. In his late thirties, Walter is an expert in enterprise software. He's assured, intelligent, and articulate, and he is driven to always do his best. A thinker, he is not only good at solving problems, he truly enjoys it. He respects his customers, listening to them intently before recommending a solution or purchase. Many of Walter's peers consider him a "visionary," and he is frequently invited to sit on discussion panels to talk about industry trends. He is an accomplished speaker who exudes confidence. He often anticipates customer problems before they become an issue, and always has a solution to suggest. Although he is quick to respond to a customer's question, Walter doesn't hesitate to say, "I don't know," and offers to research the problem until he finds the answer.

Walter is passionate about his job. He approaches it with great enthusiasm, always happy to explain the advantages of his products. While he may offer comparisons with a competitor's product, his approach is positive. He is respected by his customers because he doesn't resort to name calling, and he is always a thorough professional. When assisting a customer or prospect, he takes the long-term view, placing the highest priority on what is best for the customer—even when it doesn't mean an immediate profit for him. Because of these qualities, people trust him. They know he will never let them down.

Associations

Finally, the brand team agreed upon three associations to build over time.

The first association is nature. WRQ is closely linked with nature. It supports several conservation efforts. In technology terms, nature can be interpreted as evolution and migration to new systems.

The second is navigating change. WRQ has a proven system for steering customers in the direction that best fits their needs. WRQ solves customer problems. Navigation can suggest organizing data, not just moving it from place to place, the original definition of connectivity.

WRQ's third association is respect. Respect is central to WRQ's business style. This is an emotional association that is in keeping with WRQ's personality and values while being a differentiator to customers.

THE REFLECTION PRODUCT LINE BRAND

Principle

The Reflection product line brand principle was focused on the idea that Reflection helped information technology professionals do their job. The principle reads, *Reflection designs its products from an IT point of view.*

Competitors' messages included *one interface, the most features,* and *the easiest to use.* *Designed from an IT point of view* stood out from these by focusing on IT, rather than the end user of the product. Further, this was what the company had been already doing with its Reflection product on an unconscious level. People frequently think of the integrated branding process as *revealing* a brand, rather than creating something altogether new. Reflection product developers had made a product that was industrial strength and could be relied on by their IT customers. By adding the consultative aspect of the WRQ brand to this Reflection approach, the company had brought to consciousness a very powerful one–two punch (*consultative* and *IT point of view*) that has served it very well with Fortune 1000 and medium-sized companies, WRQ's primary targets.

Reflection uses three supporting messages:

- The Reflection feature set is designed to provide IT with the perfect tools for their enterprise connectivity needs; it helps IT manage the enterprise and users.
- Reflection is reliable; it is industrial strength and it works.
- Reflection is supported by WRQ's outstanding support services.

Personality

Because the brands grew up in tandem, WRQ and Reflection share WRQ's personality traits.

Associations

The first association is nature, primarily in the form of a nature scene visual within a triangle. The second association is the TCP/IP icon. The purpose of the TCP/IP icon (see figure 10.1) was to build awareness for a new component of the Reflection product line—its TCP/IP transport and related products. TCP/IP is the data transport used to carry information on the Internet, and it's the de facto standard for computer net-

Figure 10.1
TCP/IP Icon

The visual TCP/IP icon helped raise Refection awareness in the TCP/IP marketplace.

Source: Reprinted with the permission of WRQ.

works, as well. Reflection had a strong TCP/IP product. The icon, which was used on all advertisements, direct mail and collateral, brought immediate brand recognition to this product and positioned WRQ as a company that was committed to continuing to develop and improve its TCP/IP offering.

THE RESULTS OF THIS FIRST ROUND OF BRANDING IN 1994

The first round of branding helped move WRQ into a new understanding of what core drivers guided its brand. The company successfully reached consensus on a shared-status brand structure, including the number and relationships of existing brands and their brand drivers. Finally, through employee seminars and presentations, the company was able to integrate its brands into various departments and witness the resulting focus.

For example, in the direct sales department, sales people used the *consultative partner* principle of the WRQ brand as a way to strengthen their sales efforts. This did not represent a departure from what they had done previously, but gave WRQ a consistent way to talk about why it was unique.

One of the steps the direct sales force took was to include a software engineer on every large sales call. These experts could speak to prospective customers in technical terms about how to implement the Reflection product line in a way that would be most productive for their enterprise. The consultative approach strategy has been responsible for several Fortune 500 sales, even in situations in which competitors already had larger installed bases than WRQ.

By crystallizing its personality, WRQ also attracted customers with similar or complementary business styles. These customers purchased Reflection software because they felt comfortable with WRQ. In addition WRQ customers within each company tended to be loyal champions of the company, adding essential word-of-mouth momentum for additional sales.

The company highlighted the Reflection software *designed from an IT point of view* principle in its first major multiad campaign. This included two-page advertisements that demonstrated how IT people would handle a typical situation, such as rush hour traffic or Mondays, and then compared that to WRQ's connectivity solution. This campaign was the first step in the process of raising external awareness of what the brand stood for and reinforced the brand principle internally as well (see figure 10.2).

The *designing software from an IT point of view* message also worked well with technology industry analysts. WRQ spokespeople explained how specific features and entire products had been designed from an IT point of view. This gave analysts reasons why Reflection should be positioned as a premium product in the connectivity software category. Favorable reports from analysts also helped the product line with magazine article mentions and product reviews.

The company saw evidence of the developing brand in almost every department, from human resources (which was sharing brand information with new hires and using brand messages in its recruitment ads) to new product development. In the most recent round of Reflection product updates, the brand introduced a new feature, *hands-free administration*. Hands-free administration allows IT professionals to reduce both troubleshooting and maintenance on Reflection products greatly—solving a problem at the top of every IT professional's wish list. This is the logical outcome of brand thinking: creating products and features that reinforce the brand principle.

WRQ'S PHASE TWO BRANDING IN 1997

In 1997, WRQ conducted the second phase of its branding work, designed to find out what was and wasn't working and make appropriate changes. For the first step, WRQ conducted a benchmarking study on how well the brand had performed from both an internal and a customer perspective. The study included two hundred quantitative interviews of IT professionals in all sizes and types of companies throughout the United States.

The study revealed that WRQ brand awareness had increased to a much higher level and the brand attributes such as *consultative, listening,* and *respect* had begun to be played back by customers. WRQ scored very

Figure 10.2
Reflection Brand Advertisement

ENTERPRISE-WIDE CONNECTIVITY,
AS DESIGNED BY NETWORK PROFESSIONALS.

MONDAYS,
AS DESIGNED BY NETWORK PROFESSIONALS.

If it were up to you, your hard work would finally pay off. Mainframes, PCs, minicomputers and servers would all fit together seamlessly, and Monday would be just another day at the beach.

Impossible? Not with Reflection® from WRQ. Reflection offers complete, integrated PC connectivity software for your entire enterprise—including transport protocols, PC X server software, and terminal emulation. All with the management features, open standards, and service and support you need.

To try connectivity designed from your point of view, call today for a free evaluation copy. We'll make sure that from here on out, your Mondays go swimming.

REFLECTION® SOLUTIONS

REFLECTION PC-TO-HOST CONNECTIVITY SOFTWARE
▲ UNIX, X, HP, DIGITAL, AS/400, 3270 AND TCP/IP CONNECTIVITY
▲ WINDOWS, DOS, AND MACINTOSH PLATFORMS
▲ INTUITIVE OPERATIONS, FAST FILE TRANSFER, ADVANCED TEXT AND GRAPHICS EMULATION, AND POWERFUL PROGRAMMING TOOLS

REFLECTION NETWORKING SOFTWARE
▲ COMMUNICATIONS: TCP/IP, UDP, LAT, NOVELL IPX/SPX, SLIP, CSLIP, PPP
▲ ARCHITECTURE: VXD/DLL DESIGN, 100% WINDOWS SOCKETS COMPLIANT
▲ FULL-FEATURED APPLICATIONS (FTP, LPR/LPD, INTERNET ACCESS
▲ EASY CONFIGURATION AND MANAGEMENT
▲ OPTIMIZED FOR MOBILE/WIRELESS COMPUTING
▲ AVAILABLE AS SUITES AND INDIVIDUAL PRODUCTS, TAILORED FOR ANY ENTERPRISE CONFIGURATION.

For a FREE evaluation copy of any Reflection product, call
800.926.3896

CALL 800.926.3896. IN EUROPE, CALL +31.70.375.11.00.
OUTSIDE EUROPE, CALL 206.217.7100.
INTERNET: sales@wrq.com. WEB: http://www.wrq.com/

Reflection
WRQ CONNECTIVITY FOR A CHANGING WORLD

The first Reflection ad campaign after WRQ's integrated branding process highlighted Reflection's brand principle of software designed from an IT point of view.

Source: Reprinted with the permission of WRQ.

high in customer loyalty. This research was later verified by a separate, independent study by Prognostics, in which WRQ's loyalty ratings beat out other major industry players.[1] To continue the company's transformation into a more outspoken industry leader, the WRQ brand team decided to add the traits of *visionary* and *practical* to its personality. And to raise awareness for the WRQ brand further, the company changed its corporate signature from the then-current small WRQ/Reflection logo combination to a logo that simply used the WRQ name.

The *Reflection TCP/IP* icon appeared to help awareness of the TCP product; however, the WRQ and Reflection *nature triangle* visual association did not break through into customer awareness. This forced the brand team to review its association strategy. Ultimately, they dropped this association and developed another visual association around networking. The brand team concluded that the nature association was too much of a mental reach for customers, even though it had shown up in earlier research as an association of WRQ and Reflection.

The earlier research represented a narrow market that the company had grown beyond. As WRQ expanded into larger markets where it was not as well known, the nature association could not make the transition. It remains an organic association of WRQ, because of the company's commitment to the environment, but it is no longer being promoted to customers.

After the purchase and integration of the Express product line, explained later, WRQ realized that it had a unique impact on any product line that came under its umbrella. WRQ engineers make sure that any product offered by WRQ is *rock solid*—it works the way it is supposed to and is highly reliable. Therefore, the brand team decided to use *rock solid*, which shows up in background graphical textures, as a new association for WRQ. It also decided to use *networking* for Reflection (see figure 10.3), which is a three-component illustration that shows a globe, a computer, and a monitor connected by electronics.

In a subsequent benchmarking study in late 1998, WRQ's Reflection brand had vaulted to the top of the competitive list (after not even placing in the top three a year and a half earlier) in terms of top of mind and unaided awareness—primary methods for tracking product leadership. WRQ also led competitors in a majority of customer satisfaction categories and scored highly on being *visionary* and *practical* with customers. When asked what they associated with Reflection, customers picked the WRQ brand as their top choice—demonstrating a successful sharing of Reflection equity with the WRQ brand.

Figure 10.3
Reflection's Networking Association

Source: Reprinted with the permission of WRQ.

THE EXPRESS BRAND

In 1996, the company purchased the Express Software line of products. Express Meter, the first product in the line, is a software tool that allows companies to track software licensing and use by their employees. In 1996, telephone research among more than three hundred Express customers suggested that Express was known for *detailed and helpful reporting* and for *helping companies keep accurate track of what software they were running*. The Express team was differentiating the product by developing a software category of *software management*, rather than more narrowly defining the category as a utility for metering software use or for tracking licensing, as its competitors have done. Express also sells a Year 2000 product for the desktop, Express 2000 Suite—a textbook brand extension into this critical area of software management.

Express fit into the existing WRQ brand structure as a product line brand under WRQ on the same level as Reflection. Express used to sell primarily to small and medium-sized companies. It now uses the WRQ brand platform to create legitimacy for its offering among large companies. Being a WRQ product implies that Express will "solve the problems of IT in the enterprise" and be an *industrial strength, rock solid* product line.

The Express Brand Principle

The Express product line did not come into WRQ with an articulated integrated brand. On the basis of the Express research, the brand team agreed on the following brand drivers. The Express brand principle is *software management for informed business decisions*; this means that Express

Figure 10.4
Express's Archer Association

On-target for expert IT decisions

Source: Reprinted with the permission of WRQ.

delivers the information that IT managers need to make strategic business decisions for software purchases, upgrades, training, and providing
help desk support.

This is a markedly different approach from that of competitors, who
view software management as a set of utilities, rather than a strategic
tool. If the Express development team viewed this software as strictly a
utility, they would have drastically changed the way they developed the
product. For instance, they wouldn't have put as much time into the
analytical and reporting features of the product.

Personality

The personality of Express is slightly different from that of WRQ and
Reflection. Because Express had an existing installed base of users, the
brand team determined that Express should retain its personality. The
Express personality included the traits *innovative, leader, quick, responsive,
focused, confident, efficient, competitive, expert, reliable, intelligent,* and *consultative*.

One benefit of being conscious of brand is WRQ's ability to learn from
Express. WRQ could add Express personality traits, such as *innovative*,
to make itself stronger. In the future, the brand team expects the two
personalities to move closer together and perhaps become one.

Associations

The Express brand association is an archer (see figure 10.4). This is a
bold way of saying *on target*—which is something that happens from

making informed business decisions. This association implies that the Express product allows customers to become software management experts within their companies.

ORGANIZATION DRIVERS

WRQ had existing organization drivers that it refined subsequent to the integrated branding process.

WRQ Mission

WRQ's mission was recreated in 1998, on the basis of the experience of introducing more than twenty successful high-technology products under its Reflection and Express brands. The brand team sifted through many aspects of what the company had done, including past brand research, to determine its new business focus. Throughout that process, certain concepts kept reappearing, including *rock-solid quality, long-term partnering, technology systems expertise,* and *following its customers' pain to solutions.* Whereas some of its competitors may shy away from the hard knots, WRQ has a tradition of providing elegant solutions to problems that may seem less than glamorous, but clearly frustrate its customers on a regular basis.

WRQ's brand handbook states that the company's mission is:

Driven by customer needs, we do whatever it takes to anticipate and solve complex problems of information systems.

Driven by customer needs means we partner with customers with a long-term perspective.

We do whatever it takes means we provide rock-solid quality, we do it right.

To anticipate and solve complex problems means we follow our customers' pain—both current and future.

Of information systems means our business category includes all types of information systems and related audiences.

The brevity, clarity, and distinctiveness of this mission provide an understandable direction for the company. It gets immediately down to business, raises the bar for both products and services, and has an aspirational aspect as well.

WRQ Values

WRQ has three values that encompass many others: *personal responsibility*, *respect*, and *business success*. These values work in concert to drive quality in everything the company does.

Personal responsibility means

- taking the initiative to find a solution.
- bringing new ideas to fruition.
- being self-motivated and hardworking.
- doing a job right *and* taking risks.
- being responsible for themselves, coworkers, company, customers, community; being team players.
- living a balanced life.

Personal responsibility fits well with WRQ's flat organization model. The company has relatively few layers of management for its eight-hundred-plus employees, yet the system works well. This value requires hiring people who are personally responsible. Responsibility is difficult to determine in the short period typically set aside for the interview process. WRQ has solved this problem by putting all of those interviewed through a lengthy process, involving up to ten or so interviewers and dubbed by some as *the gauntlet*. This technique ensures a good fit between the prospective employee and the WRQ team.

Respect means

- listening and honoring others' opinions; respecting diversity.
- trusting.
- being honest.
- communicating differences of opinion.
- making decisions that are best for the company—not avoiding confrontation.

Having respect as a central value has been a mixed blessing for WRQ. Although it perfectly summarizes how the company values human interaction and complements its principle of "consultative partner," some employees have misconstrued it to mean not confronting people or not disagreeing with people when necessary.

Business success means

- growing market share.
- growing revenue.
- increasing earnings/profitability.
- evaluating success by measuring both short- and long-term results.

Although business success has always been a value at WRQ, it has only recently been called out for special emphasis. WRQ has done such a good job of creating a high-quality work and entrepreneurial environment that the company now wants to make sure that employees continue to focus on business success.

WRQ Story

The WRQ story helps the company maintain and strengthen its culture through periods of rapid growth. Note that the story is used as a way of bringing context to company values and product quality.

At WRQ individuals are valued. We are made up of hundreds of individuals who are responsible for driving the company forward. Employees do what is right for the company and the customer. Employees work hard and efficiently through focusing on our values of personal responsibility, respect and business success—with the overriding principle always being "doing what is right for the customer, company and individual." The result of our values is that we do things right everywhere—quality products, services, relationships and communications.

WRQ Elevator Statement

The elevator statement takes WRQ's story to its external audiences:

WRQ makes software that connects, manages and secures networked information systems. We take the IT manager's perspective to:

- reduce network complexity
- manage and control costs
- exceed expectations of quality

This elevator statement is succinct yet gets quickly to what the company does without using jargon. It also focuses directly on brand messages.

THE WRQ BRAND TOOLBOX

Many companies have style or identity guides for both their marketing communications departments and outside vendors. These guides demonstrate usage rules for logos and fonts. Typically, they scratch the surface of an integrated brand and don't do anything to help employees and agencies to think from the brand perspective. Also, the other elements of brand, such as visual motifs and associations, templates, and brand messages, are often more or less left to chance. The WRQ Brand Toolbox addresses these needs.

The toolbox helps users conceptualize their marketing pieces. "We keep the brand in mind at the outset, and carry the brand momentum forward through the various stages of product development," explains Darcie Wolfe, director of marketing communications. "If you try to apply the elements of the brand only as an afterthought in later stages of the project, the brand's message will be weakened."

The Brand Toolbox, spearheaded by Wolfe, the creative director, Carmen Carbone, and the senior writer, Rachel Imper, was created to keep everyone on the same page. It has a hard-copy and a CD-ROM version. The CD has a browser interface that allows people to download the files they need and to hook up to WRQ's internal intranet site for more current information.

The Brand Toolbox educates graphic artists, writers, creative directors, and others who create marketing materials or communications of any kind about the way WRQ sets itself apart from its competitors. The toolbox helps people capture the essence of WRQ in their projects and create a consistent look, feel, and tone in all communications. It includes a graphic tools section on logos, colors, fonts, images, and templates and general information on copyrights, WRQ trademarks, address blocks, and telephone numbers. Writers' tools are also part of the toolbox, including writing to communicate the WRQ brands, index of terms, numbers and symbols, general rules, and additional standards.

Branding through Graphic Design

Perhaps the method for developing the greatest awareness around a brand is the use of visual elements. All three WRQ brands can be depicted gr ph ~lly, both in terms of general graphical treatments and through ; pecitic visual associations.

All companies and product lines wrestle with the problem of creating a recognizable identity among their many communications and product lines. The trick is often one of balancing *creativity* and *memorability* on one side of the scale and *consistency* on the other. Depending on a company's culture, brand structure, and product line, solutions to the problems vary greatly. WRQ has achieved a balance that it believes will provide maximum creativity, allow product brand differentiation, and "say WRQ" in everything the company does.

The company created a series of graphical templates (see figure 10.5) that reflect the personality and consultative partner aspects of WRQ. They feature a bold use of concave lines that can accommodate a multitude of formats and different graphical treatments. The toolbox also includes tools for developing custom templates.

The graphical style of WRQ is related to its consultative partner brand principle. What does a consultative partner look like in terms of graphics? According to the toolbox it is "strong, without being heavy-handed, just as the ideal consultative partner is strong, but not heavy-handed."

The company also wishes to express its personality traits *visionary, confident, practical*, and *respectful* through its photographic style. It features photographs that make dramatic use of light and monochromatic use of color and have a limited focus (one or two objects only). One of WRQ's associations, *rock solid*, is represented through graphical rock textures to be used as page or screen backgrounds and on the Reflection product box (see figure 10.6). When possible, the company also uses its other association, *the triangle*, as the shape for bullet points. The triangle is also the shape of the WRQ logo itself and is suggestive of the Reflection *networking* association.

As mentioned earlier, Reflection's networking association grew out of its principle *designed from an IT point of view*. The toolbox explains, "The PC and the host in the main image represent different devices in a network, while the globe represents the wide scope of the brand. These three elements are linked by different types of electronic connections." Reflection illustrations support the brand principle by showing an overhead perspective, which suggests the perspective of IT managers as they oversee the enterprise. The use of organic texture behind objects in an illustration ties Reflection into WRQ brand textures, creating a common look and feel between the brands. Reflection also has an additional set of textures (see figure 10.7) that reinforce the association by suggesting networking.

Figure 10.5
The WRQ Brand Template

WRQ **Express Meter**

WINDOWS NT®
WINDOWS® 95
WINDOWS 3.1x
DOS

WRQ

Improve your IT control and make more informed business decisions with advanced software metering

Express Meter is a complete license management solution. It puts you in control of desktop software across your enterprise. Express Meter works on the most popular desktops and network platforms and delivers:

- **Complete desktop software metering and control**
- **Comprehensive reporting**
- **Automatic application discovery**

Today's enterprise plays host to an ever-expanding influx of desktop software. From approved applications to Internet downloads, gaining control over the sprawl—and assuring that you are in compliance with license agreements—can be a huge challenge. Express Meter makes it easy by managing your software and giving you the information you need to make IT decisions that benefit your entire operation.

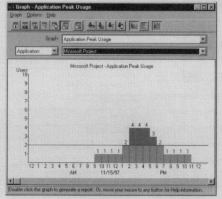

Sixty customizable reports show you clear ways to improve software deployment, training, and help desk support.

---

5 ways Express Meter puts you in control and lowers your cost of ownership:

1 Exclusive technologies keep you legal and save you money.

- **Auto Discovery** automatically detects application launches, so you can have 100% confidence in your license compliance status.
- **Auto Add** lets you sit back while Express Meter automatically adds new applications to the recognized library and presents them for you to set up monitoring parameters.
- **The WRQ Express Application Database** and sophisticated matching algorithms provide advanced application recognition.

2 Clear reports help you make better business decisions.

- **A comprehensive report library** offers more than just data; you'll see a clear path for action.
- **Precise software usage information** helps you cut waste and make improvements in software and hardware purchases and upgrades, training, and help-desk support.

3 Innovative management tools put you in control of software across your enterprise.

With Express Meter, you can:

- Determine which users can access which applications.
- Create groups of users with common access parameters.
- Respond to requests for unlicensed usage by locking out users, warning them, or simply monitoring their use.
- Set up waiting lists for applications.
- Warn users when they have been running a program for a certain time, or when the program has been open and idle for too long.
- Close idle applications.

4 IT-friendly features make Express Meter a worry-free addition to your networks.

- **Network platform independence** assures compatibility with all PC networks.

- **Integration with network management platforms** lets you build a complete management solution.
- **Fast installation and easy-to-use interface** means you'll start seeing benefits immediately.
- **Background operation** makes Express Meter transparent to the user, so productivity remains high.

5 WRQ's award-winning technical support team backs you up—every step of the way.

- **Telephone and online support** gives you easy access to expert advice.
- **Specialized support and training options** address your IT-level needs.

Ensuring Desktop Year 2000 Compliance
Express Meter is also part of the WRQ Express 2000 Suite—your complete solution for Year 2000 compliance on enterprise desktops.

WRQ Express software management tools ensure intelligent IT decisions with clear information about software across the enterprise. Express tools help IT drive the financial and strategic success of the company, by ensuring license compliance, reducing costs, and increasing control over software and related IT resources.

Visit WRQ's Web page at www.wrq.com for more on WRQ Express software management tools.

This graphical template using bold concave lines helps create consistency among all WRQ brands.

Source: Reprinted with the permission of WRQ.

Figure 10.6
The Reflection Software Product Box

The Reflection networking association and WRQ rock-solid textures play a prominent role on the product box.

Source: Reprinted with the permission of WRQ.

The central image of the Express brand was based on its brand principle of *software management for informed business decisions*. The archer association is designed to be a visual cue suggesting the idea of expertise—and further suggesting that Express can help an IT manager become a software management expert. One of the benefits of being "on target" is creating a complete picture of enterprise software usage and efficient and effective decision making.

Express photography is similar to the WRQ style with more aggressive graphic elements such as a special high-contrast look and a blurred-edge "glow," which support the Express personality traits *innovative, leader, focused, confident*, and *efficient*. Express also features additional on-target textures (see figure 10.8).

Writing for the WRQ Brands

WRQ has created a set of writing examples to demonstrate "how to write WRQ." It also shows specific examples for its Reflection and Express brands. According to the toolbox: "The tone changes slightly depending on the medium, and a white paper or data sheet will be a bit more formal than a direct-mail piece, but writers will want to avoid 'stuffiness,' preaching, or talking condescendingly. Keep in mind that as a consultative partner, WRQ wants to help customers solve their enterprise computing problems, and we are simply letting them know why

Figure 10.7
Reflection Textures

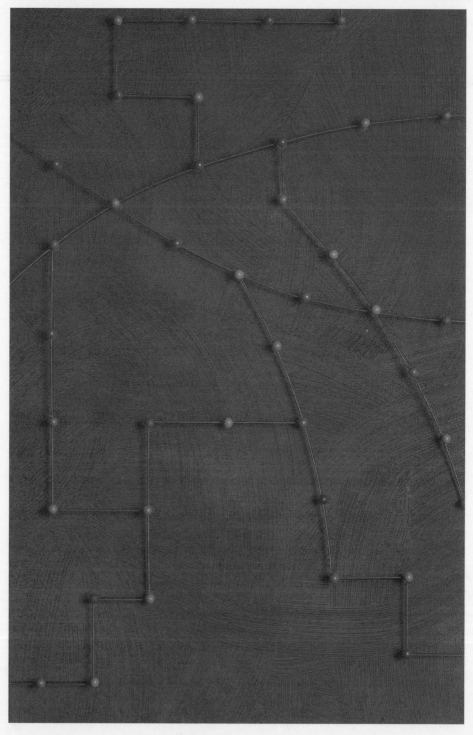

Textures reinforce Reflection's networking association.

Source: Reprinted with the permission of WRQ.

Figure 10.8
Express Textures

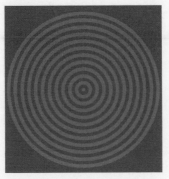

Textures reinforce Express's association of being on-target.

Source: Reprinted with the permission of WRQ.

we are the best choice."

The toolbox then goes on to give specific writing examples. Here is one to demonstrate the idea:

Straightforward, like this: WRQ beat Company Y in 19 out of 20 tests. WRQ outperforms Company X, again and again. Your users demand a lot from you, which can be frustrating. But WRQ's award-winning products can make your job a lot easier.

Not disrespectful, like this: Company Y made a poor showing—which is just what you would expect from an inferior product. Sorry, Company X.

The difference between these two examples is not the facts but the way in which they are presented. WRQ writers put themselves in their reader's place and think about how they would like to be addressed. Although WRQ is proud of its achievements and willing to promote them confidently, the tone is never arrogant. It is always respectful. The company often relies on statements from customers or analysts, or facts and awards, to do the promoting for it. As WRQ says in the toolbox, "Respect also means giving customers the information they want—solid facts and evidence, versus unrealistic or exaggerated claims."

Other tone differences between the two examples include using active rather than passive voice. In addition, using "you" messages rather than "we," as in "your business is important to us" rather than "we think your business is important," is important.

WRQ makes sure that its writers understand the context of specific personality traits. For instance, *practical* has always been a part of the WRQ way of doing things, but *visionary* is relatively new. WRQ defines *visionary* as meaning "they are always anticipating the problems their customers will face in the near future, and how they can quickly step in to provide solutions for them." The goal is to help customers make a smooth transition to the future. *Visionary* for WRQ means preventing customers from making wrong turns and going down blind alleys. It is about short-term vision, which most technology experts will agree is the only type of vision that has a chance of being accurate in the swiftly changing technology marketplace. This constitutes the company's trait of *practical within visionary*.

An example of this kind of visionary thinking is WRQ's acquisition of Express. Recognizing the growing importance of software management, WRQ acquired the expertise it needed to offer this service. It moved to provide a practical answer to an emerging problem that its competitors simply have not addressed.

Writing about the Reflection Brand

Reflection writing uses the same voice as WRQ. What distinguishes the brand is the principle of *products designed from an IT point of view*. WRQ understands how IT managers use Reflection—to access business-critical information. This means product development is based on what capabilities IT needs and creation of a product that works every time. When writing about Reflection, the toolbox says:

> You may—or may not—mention that Reflection is 'designed from an IT point of view,' but it is useful to elaborate on how a particular product feature benefits IT staff. To reinforce the 'designed from an IT point of view' message when you are writing about Reflection, clarify how a particular product or feature benefits IT managers. Whether your audience is the IT manager or a channel partner (your product distributor or dealer), those benefits need to be in the copy.

The toolbox goes on to elaborate on specific messages that put into words the concept of the principle. Examples of how to indicate "designed from an IT point of view":

Use specifics, like this: Reflection Profiler lets the system administrator control user access to settings and features—eliminating accidental configuration changes and reducing demands on the Help Desk.

Or this: Reflection's intuitive features make it easy even for non-technical users to master—which means lower training and support costs.

Not just stating it: Reflection Profiler is an example of how Reflection products are designed from an IT point of view.

Writing about the Express Brand

Because the Express product line is relatively new to WRQ, the company has had less experience in writing about it. A brand voice becomes stronger and more distinct over time as people get used to using it and as it evolves to meet new circumstances. The toolbox says:

> The Express voice varies slightly from that of WRQ and Reflection. It has the consultative nature of WRQ, but it also has a youthful directness to it and a "splash of attitude," challenging the status quo with tasteful irreverence.

Examples for writing about the Express brand:

Direct, like this: How much software do you really need? Find out with Express Meter.

With a clever attitude, like this: 30 days to a better figure.. . .Order your Express Meter Audit Kit today.

Not impudent, like this: Do you like wasting money? Then why aren't you using Express Meter?

Not staid, like this: Try the Express Meter Audit Kit and watch your software costs go down in 30 days.

WRQ's Brand Toolbox demonstrates how closely integrated a brand can be in terms of messaging and marketing communications. Close-to-the-brand messages tied with brand-driven actions create a powerful combination. Even as its original business has matured, WRQ has continued to post strong gains and commanded price premiums for its products.

NOTE

1. *Prognostics* (October 1997), research commissioned by WRQ.

11 How to Get and Keep on the Same Path

We have a virtual brand team of 60 who represent all of the major product lines—we keep in touch through a series of yearly meetings, and constant emails to work through issues and share answers.
— Brian Burch, Worldwide Consumer Brand Manager,
Hewlett-Packard

Trying to keep a company on the brand path is like taking a group of toddlers to the zoo—someone is always wandering off. And, as when taking two-year-olds on an outing, planning, eternal vigilance—and some clever techniques—can stave off disaster. For some companies, this just requires bringing existing brand practices to a conscious level, for most it is about building a new discipline within the organization.

Implementing conscious brand management takes change. And change is where most companies fall short of the mark. In a *Harvard Business Review* article, "Why Transformation Efforts Fail,"[1] Professor John Kotter of Harvard Business School states, "In the final analysis, change sticks when it becomes 'the way we do things around here,' when it seeps into the bloodstream of the corporate body."

MOVING BRAND INTO THE WORK FORCE

Planning is a cornerstone of successful brand integration. There are many ways to plan for brand integration. Is brand development part of people's job descriptions? Do you have a global brand manager, either by title or by function? Are your brand team members educating their respective departments on the content and usage of organization and brand drivers? Does the brand manager cite his or her brand activities as examples to other employees? Are employees rewarded for using brand messages in their actions and communications?

You may recall planning also comes into play when you are selecting your original brand team. This group, if it is made up of people from many departments, can be called upon to become ambassadors for the brand to their peers. They understand the relevance of branding to their specific discipline, and they are the best at translating and communicating that message to people of a similar professional bent.

Because organization and brand drivers are most meaningful to those who helped create them, the brand team members are the best people to explain how the drivers pertain to strategic decisions. You should build incentives into brand team participation, because of the many extra hours it takes to complete the process. These incentives work best if they include both monetary and recognition-based rewards.

The Role of Brand Seminars

For both the brand team and the rest of a company's employees, the use of brand seminars can help people apply brand to their day-to-day decisions. In brand seminars that promote hands-on training employees are introduced to

- the value of branding.
- top-line results from the research.
- the actual brand drivers.
- how they can implement brand to enhance their interactions with customers.

To develop an integrated brand, training is necessary for every employee. In some cases, the "train the trainer" model is used: a company designates a group of brand trainers, who then share the brand training with a larger group. Other companies videotape one seminar and show it to everyone else. Still others create an intranet site for ongoing education on brand.

It is critical for top officers, beginning with the CEO, to begin using the brand and pointing out effective brand activities to others in the organization. It's a good idea to create a video in which the president or

CEO of the company speaks to the benefits of the brand and expresses wholehearted support for it. Without the support of a continuing champion in senior management, the process of becoming a brand-driven company most likely will flounder.

Whatever communication model you choose, the careful design of the seminar is paramount. It must provide enough theory to put branding in its proper context, but not so much that people get overloaded with abstract information. It must be lively to keep people interested and packed with content so that no one thinks it is a waste of time. It must be an advocate for integrated branding without turning people off. And finally, it must balance lectures with interactive exercises for most effective results.

One way to structure a brand seminar is to schedule a three-hour block of time. The first half hour is to communicate *what is a brand?* and *why brand?* This part is typically half multimedia and half questions and answers from the participants. Without this context, the necessity for branding will not be obvious, and employees will not understand how to use brand drivers.

It's always a good idea to have a reward system to inject some fun into the education process. You may want to have lots of brand name products to toss to people who ask or answer questions; Oreos, Cracker Jack, and Hershey's Kisses are crowd pleasers.

The second half hour is structured around highlights from the research and the resulting brand drivers. This time will be dedicated to explaining the brand principle, personality, associations, and other drivers as necessary. You will walk people through the process used by the brand team to reveal the brand elements. Unusual gifts that demonstrate brand concepts, including toys and novelties, are useful to hand out as rewards for getting up in front of the group, having a great idea, or demonstrating branding knowledge.

This second half hour is important because many people have to have the research results before they will buy off on the brand team's conclusions. They also will need to have the company or product brand drivers explained in detail, so they understand what they are and how to use them.

The second and third hours are when the employees learn by doing. Have people brainstorm ways they can implement the brand in their departments, through both words and deeds, and then present these ideas to the larger group. The variety and depth of brand thinking that come out of these smaller groups can be remarkable and useful for the company as a whole.

ANALYZING THE CUSTOMER EXPERIENCE: BRAND IS IN THE DETAILS

The second and third hours are spent getting people to begin *living the brand*. You're trying to stimulate brand thinking and decision making as automatic responses. The best way to do this is to take all employees to the places where they will need to use the brand—to define the customer experiences and conversations that they control.

First, do this brainstorming exercise with the brand team so that they can lead others in their divisions and departments through it. Next, split up employees into departmental groups. Have people from the brand team be part of each group to answer questions employees may have and help guide the process.

Where do employees interact with customers? If you are in sales, it's in your sales relationships and presentations. If you are in product development, it is through watching customer interactions with the product in focus groups or direct observation. If you are in accounting, it is your customer interactions about billing practices and invoices. The list of questions asked in the exercise will vary, depending on the area; for example, in sales, questions will focus on the sales process. (See the Appendix for suggested questions by area.)

Product strategy experts Ian C. MacMillan and Rita Gunther McGrath have created a process for mapping the customer experience that can also help your employees to begin living the brand. They ask five questions to determine customer experience at each link of the value chain. If the list of questions in the Appendix isn't appropriate for your department, consider using these as a starting point in the process:

- *What?* What are customers doing when they interact with you? What would they like to be doing?
- *Where?* Where are your customers when they experience your interaction?
- *Who?* Who else is with the customers? Do these other people have influence?
- *When?* At what time of the day or week are they interacting with you? Does the timing cause any problems? When would they like to be with you?[2]

Once the group has made an exhaustive list of the different ways they interact with customers, the next step is to have them brainstorm additional ways to improve their role in the customer experience—based on organization and brand drivers. Do not let employees assume that because they are not on the front lines of customer interaction their part in the process is less important. Any customer interaction has the potential for enhancing loyalty or destroying brand equity. For instance, one company's accounts receivable staff was so unfriendly to late payers that the company lost several customers. Most interactions, regardless of how mundane, provide openings to differentiate the customer experience positively. By building on experience after experience at this nitty gritty level, employees can create a very high level of customer affinity.

Thinking about your customers' experiences and conversations is also a great way to create new possibilities for the brand. Whether you implement the results of such brainstorming will depend on the costs associated with each idea, how much a new process will change the company, and how much value the company derives from the change.

Another method for improving the customer experience is getting customers to understand and use your product or service in new, beneficial ways. Ask the following questions as you brand each customer experience: Is the brand highlighting all product and service features that might offer customers benefit? How easy is it for customers to understand a new feature and use it? Is the new use consistent with your brand drivers? By implementing new brand uses, you can increase your market share and deepen customer relationships.

Branding the Customer Experience at a Service Firm

The following example demonstrates branding the customer experience using a small service.

Company DEF has a brand principle of *authentic relationships*. This means we help our customers develop authentic relationships and we develop authentic relationships with our customers, other publics and among DEF employees. The company's brand personality includes traits of *passion, integrity, empathetic, collaborative*, and *creative*.

Company DEF is small enough that the whole company can go through the brand process as if it were one department. The company began by looking at customer interactions:

Where we interact with customers (we determined that the following were our primary avenues and places for customer interaction):

- Telephone
- Email
- Fax

- In meetings
- U.S. mail
- FedEx or courier
- Press/analyst tours
- Trade shows
- Lunches/dinners
- Social occasions

After listing these interactions we asked the questions, *Are there any activities that we should be doing more of? Are there any new activities we should add to encourage authentic relationships?* Our group felt that we needed to do more socially with customers such as having lunch, and hold more meetings and workshops at the DEF offices, because our space does such a good job of visually representing who we are.

How we make these interactions more about building authentic relationships. The team felt that although we do a good job of living our brand there were areas where we could improve.

Telephone

- Make sure that the person answering the phone personalizes the experience for our customers—specifically by calling them by name
- If the requested person is unavailable ask *how can I help?*
- Treat whoever is on the phone as if he or she were the most important person in the world
- Don't do a second activity while on the phone
- Reiterate action items at the end of the conversation
- Thank people for their time—end the call with a positive interaction

Voice mail

- When leaving a message, have your name and number be the first and last thing you say
- Use your own voice on your prerecorded message

Email

- Use the auto signature function to include your name, company, address, URL, fax, phone number, and a quote derived from your personal experience

- Always put a salutation and your name in the body of the email—this makes it more personal and reduces confusion on forwarded messages
- CC to other appropriate team members

Fax

- Create an electronic template for faxes to improve the look
- Add something personal to the message
- Include appropriate directions when necessary
- Always follow up the fax with a phone call telling the recipient that it is coming
- Internally, deliver received faxes as soon as they arrive

FedEx or courier

- Create a letter on Company DEF letterhead to accompany the package
- Attach a business card to the letterhead
- Alert the recipient with an email or phone call
- Use judiciously—only when time is of the essence

Meetings—at Company DEF

- Put a clock in the conference room
- Offer refreshments
- Put team biographies in the reception area
- Validate parking at the garage down the street instead of forcing customers to use street parking
- Make sure everyone on the Company DEF team is participating in each meeting
- Use the park area of Company DEF for customers who like a more casual atmosphere
- Create exercises and workshops that use all three brainstorming areas within the office
- Name the brainstorming areas
- Let other team members know who is coming for each meeting via email, so that everyone can properly welcome visitors
- Pull in team members during meetings who aren't on the account to help with general brainstorming, to share experience, or to facilitate the meeting

- Track and reward both great company and great customer achievements
- Ask ourselves each time the customer leaves the building, *was the meeting an authentic, creative, and reality-based experience? Did we bring knowledge, passion, and empathy to the table?*

Meetings—customer office

- Be punctual
- Be prepared with any back-up materials that you could possibly need
- Dress appropriately for the customer's culture
- Mix up the seating among Company DEF and customer team members
- Make sure everyone in the meeting is engaged
- Treat everyone at the customer's office with the same high level of respect
- After the meeting, offer to bus cups and plates
- After the meeting, type up and confirm all action items

Branding the Customer Conversation

In addition to changes in action, you can ask employees also to brand their customer dialogue by recreating how they talk with customers.

Ask employees, in a typical experience, how they start the conversation. What types of phrasing do they use? How does the customer respond? If there is a problem, what words or messages does the employee use to resolve it? This process works best as a role play in which one employee plays a specific customer or type of customer and another employee takes his or her normal role in the customer interaction. Other employees in the group observe the process and everyone, including the two in the role play, analyzes it afterward.

Role playing to draw this information out of employees makes the experience much more immediate than trying to imagine past customer conversations. To bring brand down to the individual level, role play each of the interactions (when customer interactions take place) that the group listed in the customer experience example.

Questions each group should ask during the role play include the following:

Is the dialogue on-brand now?

Does it reflect the principle and demonstrate the personality?

What other actions and messages might say the same thing but reflect the brand more exactly?

Company DEF Role-Playing Example

Employee: Hi Janice, how are you doing?

Customer (employee as customer): Fine. How's married life treating you?

Employee: It's great. Not too much has changed really. How about with you?

Customer: Oh, it's going good! You know my son's in soccer so I get to cart him around everywhere; that's a lot of fun.

Employee: Right. Now, with Bob on board at work, you have a lot more help, haven't you?

Customer: Yeah, I have a bit more help but you know, uh, with the strategic stuff, I really need to be more involved, you know what I mean?

Employee: Yeah, absolutely. So what have we got on the agenda today?

Customer: Well, I thought we would get back on the white papers and also talk about general public relations.

Employee: Right.

Customer: So, are we giving you enough information to do everything you need to do?

Employee: So far, yeah. I've had a really positive backup from Bob on things. We've had a great summer press tour and we have some great coverage coming out from that.

Customer: So how do you think the editors responded to us?

Employee: They responded well. I mean they are really pleased that you take the time to go out there and meet with them at the shows. And they are really pleased with our interactions as well. We've supplied them with story angles that they are using.

Customer: How did the time-to-market message go?

Employee: That went well. We have about five articles coming out of the press tour. We have another one coming out in September, which we're looking forward to.

Customer: What other angles did they tune into?

Employee: The fact that people could activate your web-based services by themselves. And what we are trying to do is get a bit more mileage out of that and provide some trends, story pieces to editors as to what does the future of handheld PC users look like. What are these people going to be able to do in the future using the web?

Customer: Maybe we should put a white paper together around the web and the future of the PC handheld?

Employee: I think that would be a very good idea!

Customer: Do you think you have enough information? Do you think editors and analysts would be interested in that?

Employee: I think so, definitely. I think it would create some good pitches not just to handheld editors, but also the business press.

Customer: That's great.

Employee: Now in terms of rough information, do you want us to write it or do you have internal people to write it?

Customer: Well I don't really trust in-house writing talent, so I would prefer to have you guys write it.

Employee: Okay.

Customer: So, the thing is, we could really use that for our show on the 25th—do you think that is possible?

Employee: Yeah, we have outside writers that we could give that to.

Customer: So when do you think you could show me the first draft?

Employee: Well, I should think in about a week or so. As long as we get some input from you guys early on.

Customer: Okay, well, I'll get Norm to give you a call.

Employee: Yeah, great!

Customer: Have you met Norm before?

Employee: Yeah, I have, and I heard that he did great on the press tour. I look forward to speaking with him.

Customer: So what else should we be doing?

Employee: I think we should explore more web pages. Not only are these educational, but we can also put directional info into our press kits and turn the content into articles. This would be more on the contributed article side, which we haven't done too much of so far.

Customer: Aren't those magazines we don't really want?

Employee: No, some magazines will take those and some don't. Certainly *Handheld Review* does because we have such a good relationship with them. They would be more than happy to look at a few pieces.

Customer: Is there any way we could get a contributed article that talks about all three of our products?

Employee: I think so! It could be about the future of the handheld user and the big picture on customers and web communication.

Customer: There was something else we were going to talk about. I can't remember what it was. Do you have anything to add?

Employee: Let me see, uh, we have the show coming up, the story angles; um, another story angle we wanted to brainstorm was how the company's products are going to help handheld manufacturers segment their markets. I think that would be a great story angle to pitch to the business press, such as *Wall Street Journal* and *Business Week*.

Customer: You know, I could really see that with Product U especially.

Employee: Yeah, I think that would really help with the story. By the way, are we going to do any strategic consulting for you?

Customer: Yeah, you know we've tried but Elma keeps dragging her feet on it.

Employee: Right, is it just a matter of time and resources or is it a matter of budget?

Customer: I don't know; I am pushing as hard as I can. Yesterday in the meeting with Elma, I got her to agree to a category, which we need to brainstorm on. You should push Elma on that.

Employee: Okay, I'll make a note of that.

Customer: And, uh, I think that's it for now, as long as you think things are going well.

Employee: Yeah, I think things are going really well. Like I said, I think we should keep an emphasis on those vendor-contributed articles. We could write those for you.

Customer: Oh, which reminds me. One more question: is there anything we can do to get more visibility for the public relations we are doing inside the company?

Employee: Um, well, you could have a web site pressroom, maybe. Do you circulate the articles that come out about the company?

Customer: Well, that hasn't happened lately, as I have been out of that loop.

Employee: Right. Well, when the articles come out you could circulate them about the office, or have them framed or mounted, or put them into a particular room so that people can see what kind of coverage you get. Or, you could—do you have an intranet?

Customer: We have an Internet, not an intranet.

Employee: You could post them on a virtual pressroom.

Customer: That would be great. Could you guys help us with that?

Employee: Yeah, sure!

Customer: If we provide you with copy, could you help with the programming?

Employee: No, not the programming, but we know people who can— they can help you out. We can make recommendations for you.

Customer: Can we bill the whole thing through you?

Employee: Yeah, sure.

DEF Employee Commentary on the Role-Play

S: I just have two comments. You talked about giving extra work to other people. I think we could talk about the outside people as outside resources *or* an extension of the team. The way we talk about them could be really important as to how we position them to clients. Because I think if we talk about them as outside resources or outside writers like that, I think clients are going to feel that they are not getting the best of what we have to offer. I would call them simply resources or writers.

J: I thought you kind of dropped the ball a little on outside vendors, but you came back real fast on the programming side. I would say, if someone says can you do that? you say, Well, part of our philosophy is that we focus on what we do best and that we have made really strong alliances with partners who do those other things. So, I would start there and say that we have already made these alliances and used them more than once.

E: One comment I have is to ask the customer what needs she has. The interaction was so positive, but you needed to ask, Well, are we meeting your expectations? What do you need?

M: I only had one nit; that's when the customer asked what the editor's response was. I think the customer wanted a direct response as to what the editor said.

J: Is part of *authentic relationships* (the brand principle) being specific or precise? We should look at being as specific as possible in all conversations right down to quoting facts, figures, and what people said.

S: Another thing I really liked was the balance of emotional and task conversation. You also did a little probing when you saw the opportunity and it was totally appropriate. Like, How's the branding coming along? I thought that was really good, and when you talked about establishing a category, you talked about it hierarchically and it made perfect sense.

S: However, I thought the customer would want a little more assurance, a little more proactive something. I felt like she needed something or that it was a needy relationship from the standpoint that she wanted you to provide her with something more.

M: Maybe suggest article topics to her.

S: Just something like, I would recommend this; does this apply?

J: That's really good.

S: And then that would be specific because it seemed like she wanted that.

J: So would you call that reassurance? Or assurance?

S: I would call it leadership.

S: I thought that, but on the other hand, if you look at the customer's personality, she's pretty robust and likes to lead the show.

J: She wants reassurance but then she comes out with something else, because she's looking for arguments to support something else she's thinking in the back of her head. And then she'll throw that idea out and say, Well, what I was really looking for was an answer to this and seeing where you would go—kind of a minitest.

E: I was going to say it looked like there were some problems with the conversation but overall it was such a lovefest.

M: This customer is like that; you're in such a lovefest that you have to make yourself consciously stop, step back out of the lovefest, and say, "Am I actually doing what I need to be doing for the customer in the middle of this?"

E: Right. And it's tricky balancing getting things done efficiently with the emotional element. Because you're mixing business with pleasure so much.

M: I kind of get lost in that, sometimes, and wonder if I'm really servicing her enough.

J: So, I think one of the things you could have done more was affirmative statements, assurance statements such as, Yes this is going well, and You should feel really good about this. That kind of stuff as long as you believed what you were saying.

E: It almost turns situations into where, in a partnership, you could be patting her on the back. Making her understand that her part of the relationship is really going well. That she's adding value.

S: I did that with another customer yesterday when he provided a lead for the demo; I thought it was a really good demo, and that it would work out well.

J: So, I would end this dialogue with a question. I'm trying to put structure to this thing. What else could the employee have done in this relationship to be more authentic, areas we didn't go over at all? Does anything come to mind? Or, what else could she have done to further the relationship?

Empl.: Set a date for the lunch.

S: Yeah, set the next step of any sort, whether it's lunch or talking about the white paper.

Empl.: I think we need to do that more with our clients—take the time to take people out to lunch. Not even for business. Have more time to do relationship building.

S: I agree.

J: Okay. That's a goal. You're encouraged to do that. Anything else about either *relationship* or *authentic* that you could have done more of?

Once you have explored dialogues for customer interactions, you can publish instructional excerpts so that everyone in the department can review them. Dialogues are used by employees as a starting place for customer discussions. As the preceding dialogue demonstrates, they also allow employees to generate other ideas about applying the brand.

OTHER SEMINAR WORK

In addition to defining customer experience and dialogue, your marketing department may want to take the step of reviewing all communications material for brand message consistency, tone, and associations.

For the initial seminar consider specific situations such as, *How could you demonstrate brand at a trade show?* What would you do? How would you engage customers in conversation? What would you say?

Review and critique company ads, brochures, or direct mail for how well they demonstrate brand principle, personality, and associations.

Once each group has come up with plans for injecting brand into the customer experience and conversation, bring everyone back together to share what they have learned. This generates additional enthusiasm and gives employees and management a much broader picture of how an integrated brand works throughout the company.

ETERNAL VIGILANCE

The dirty little secret of branding—and the reason so few companies do it well—is that it's hard work. For most organizations, it requires an entirely new way of thinking by every employee. This amount of change is difficult to initiate and, once started, difficult to keep on track. Like the proverbial tanker making a hard turn, the typical organization absorbs and adjusts to change slowly. The inclination is to revert to old patterns, to the known. That's why the eternal vigilance of the brand team is so necessary.

As with any communications program, getting employees to make decisions using the brand is something that needs to go on for a very long time to be really ingrained in the company. This does not mean that it needs to cost an extraordinary amount of money.

Besides companies deciding they are done thinking about their brand once they have all of the drivers in place, the second major stumbling block is deciding that they have a complete brand once they have communicated it to employees and integrated it into communications. Professor Kotter adds: "In the recent past, I have watched a dozen change efforts.. ..In all but two cases, victory was declared and the expensive consultants were paid and thanked when the first major project was completed.. ..Within two more years, the useful changes that had been introduced slowly disappeared."[3]

Getting employees to start thinking from a brand perspective is comparatively easy. What's hard is to keep them on the straight and narrow. The temptation can be great to move to new messages without examining their effect on the whole brand.

Like businesses that run everything by the legal department before it goes out the door, some companies run everything by the brand manager. The brand manager ensures that no piece detracts from the brand and, in best cases, that each strengthens brand messages and tone.

But looking at materials and practices after they have been designed is buying the security system after they steal your TV: a nice idea, but a little late. The best method for ensuring brand compliance is to build deep brand awareness into every fiber of the organization. The seminars start this process of deep imprinting. But there are other ongoing techniques to prevent veering off-course.

An important one is to distribute a desktop published brand handbook or an electronic version over an intranet (see figure 11.1). This reference acts as a resource for reviewing what the organization and brand drivers are and how employees can use them. Another technique is a CD-ROM brand toolbox that walks employees through the brand process and even gives them question templates for making brand decisions.

The Emergence of the Global Brand Manager

There's a new senior management position within many larger corporations. That is the position of global brand manager. This person or team has the responsibility for the well-being of the brand in all divisions and departments of the company, from product development to advertising. In medium-sized and smaller companies, this is often part of the job of a VP of marketing or even the president.

To be effective in this position, the global brand manager must have the support of senior management and preferably should report directly to the CEO or president. Officers and managers must understand that this person is speaking on behalf of upper management and that he or she will be supported by upper management on most decisions. According to David Reyes-Guerra, manager of corporate identity at Xerox Corporation, "You need a champion who understands branding and our CEO, Paul Allaire, has been great at communicating brand to the ranks. His successor, Rick Thoman, our current president and COO, brings a pro-brand background with him to the job. He was Lou Gerstner's right hand at IBM and was instrumental in bringing a brand focus and mindset to that business."

Figure 11.1
Brand Handbook Excerpt

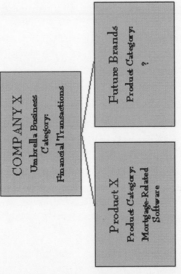

We have two brands at Company X, one is the company brand, the other is the Product X product line brand. Our company brand, Company X, is used for company-related partner and product-related service messages and as a platform for introducing new brands to the marketplace. The business scope of the Company X brand is financial transactions. This means that in the future Company X could use its existing equity in mortgage transactions to launch new product brands in other areas of financial transactions. By not tying Company X too closely to our Product X product category, we can successfully introduce products in a broad range of areas within our company's business scope of financial transactions. This equity lowers the cost of introducing new brand products and increases their chances for success.

COMPANY X
Umbrella Business Category:
Financial Transactions

Product X
Product Category:
Mortgage-Related Software

Future Brands
Product Category:
?

The Business Scope of Our Brands

Our product brand, Product X and all that it means, is the brand for all of our mortgage-related products. When thinking about Product X, think in terms of the entire product line.

A simple brand handbook helps keep employees on track.

Job Description

To be effective, the global brand manager must be able to give input into all aspects of a company's operations related to each brand. This means helping coordinate upper management strategy with R&D, product development, and marketing. In essence, he or she needs to be responsible for every aspect of the brand. "I don't have the title of brand manager," explains Joe Kennedy, vice president of sales, service, and marketing for Saturn Corporation.

> But the biggest difference is our point of view—people tend to think of someone who manages advertising and promotion when they think of brand. We think of the brand as *the brand is the company*. The retail experience of buying car services is every bit as much a part of the brand as buying the car. Managing the whole service delivery process and the service profit cycle is key to a strong brand. You can't deliver consistently great service unless you have enthusiastic employees. My job is to make sure it all comes together.

Skills of a Successful Manager

To be successful in this position requires several important skill sets.

The first is the ability to work well with people and teams. The global brand manager is most effective as a persuader or leader rather than an enforcer of policy. This person needs to be able to share the vision of the brand and get people excited about it. At the same time he or she must like and feel at ease with a very wide range of people and personalities. A strong sense of humor is also an important prerequisite for this person. Bringing brand to a conscious level is asking people to think differently. In the first few years, there will be all kinds of challenges to conducting effective brand activities, and these challenges must be met with grace, goodwill, and a nondefensive attitude.

"You need someone who can look strategically to see where to take the brand and also who will be a nuts and bolts implementer," explains Reyes-Guerra.

> My job is to educate as well as ask the question, "What is a particular action going to do to the Xerox brand?" We use an internal web site that's been a wonderful tool for strengthening the corporate brand. We have developed a common brand language within the company; given people opinion pieces written by experts; provided standards and handbooks and cultivated a brand mind-set

even for financial decisions. For example, the value of our brand is increasingly important to the corporation, our affiliates around the world, and potential licensees. How well we support, grow, and expand the brand globally will have a measurable effect on its value and, thus, the royalties others are willing to pay for its use.

The global brand manager must understand the company *globally*. This person should have had either direct work experience or exposure to most company activities. He or she should understand both strategic and financial objectives of the company and its brands. If the brand manager doesn't understand how the accounting department functions, or how the engine division does business, he or she won't be effective in helping to integrate the brand into those areas.

Globally also means an understanding of brand, culture, and customs on a region-by-region and a country-by-country basis. For example, one computer hardware company discovered that it was the awareness and preference leader in several product areas in China while being number two or three in those areas in all other countries. The company had to ask itself, *How does this affect brand actions and messages in China?* That question opened up significant new revenues by introducing a new product into the Chinese market at a higher price than was planned.

CLEVER TECHNIQUES

At the beginning of this chapter, three methods were stated to keep an unruly brand in line: planning, eternal vigilance, and clever techniques. Under the category of clever techniques are several tactics, including bribery, peer pressure, and use of rewards and fear to motivate branding behavior. Seriously, though, as in any organization, what gets repeated is what gets rewarded. Small rewards offered on a consistent basis are more useful than a big brand push at the beginning, then nothing. That's a sure recipe for failure.

It's important to show examples of brand results as quickly as possible. Successful practices have a way of feeding on themselves. When brand wins take place, it's important for the company to communicate its role in the win. Don't assume that people will make the connection. They usually won't. One sales force successfully used its corporate brand principle to make large sales—yet no one in the sales force realized that their actions and messages were based on the brand principle. Although brand works whether you understand specific brand terms or not, it is important for employees to understand the role it plays in a success so they will repeat the brand-based action in the future.

Several ideas, including using a company's web site or intranet to reinforce branding messages, demonstrating good brand compliance via a brand bulletin board in a commonly visited location such as the cafeteria, and using promotions to build employee acceptance, will have a positive impact on the consistency of your brand.

A company can also use the power of peer recognition as a motivational device for keeping employees on-brand. For example, a bulletin board, kept in a central area such as the company lunch room, can be designated for great examples of how different people are conveying brand, including letters, ads, and memos. The latest news releases, direct mail, and other brand conveyors can also be displayed here.

Because marketing to employees is increasingly moving online, this is a good method for brand communications. Consider starting a brand chat room, where employees struggling to live the brand can find support. Brand success stories, a brand Frequently Asked Questions (FAQ), a brand handbook, publicity that reinforces brand, and messages from upper management about the importance of brand can all be uploaded to a company's intranet. Anytime you find an example of how an employee has successfully used brand, hold it up for the company to see.

Other techniques are also effective in reinforcing brand-driven behavior, including:

- Offering online learning programs and giving those who successfully complete them a giveaway such as a screen saver or mouse pad that reflects brand messages.

- Giving a monthly award to the department that best exemplifies brand in action. This award could be either extra perks (free movie tickets, latte certificates) or a physical trophy that moves from group to group. Use whatever motivational techniques work for your corporate culture.

- Use advertising and public relations to build employee enthusiasm around the brand. Consider employees and prospective employees as a target audience for advertisements and articles. Companies also insert regular brand columns in their newsletters. Newsletters are a great way to get brand messages out to employees at a very low cost.

- Almost all medium-sized companies have quarterly meetings in which company officers explain company direction and next steps. These are excellent places for senior people to talk about and demonstrate the brand.

- Another technique used by Saturn employees keeps the brand front and center. They use their organization drivers of mission, values, and corporate philosophy every day. As a visual reminder of these drivers, many wear them directly below their ID badges (see figure 11.2). Joe Kennedy, the acting brand manager for Saturn, says of his company's

Figure 11.2
The Saturn ID Badge

Saturn employees keep brand close to their hearts.

Source: Reprinted with the permission of Saturn Corporation.

mission and values, "There is nothing totally extraordinary from what other companies write down. The difference is that ours are used and we can get quite weepy-eyed waxing on about them."

Company promotional events are one exciting way to keep employees on-brand. For example, company anniversaries or annual meetings can be a venue for highlighting the success of brand actions and communications during the past year. Alternatively, an outside event, such as a fund-raising corporate run, can have a brand-centric theme.

Microsoft uses an annual meeting with division managers as a way to agree on brand positioning and messages. This allows it to maintain brand consistency while refreshing the brand as needed.

Brand Event Checklist

The following ensures that brand will be central to any internal company event. Does the event provide opportunities for the following:

Messages supporting the principle

Messages supporting positioning

Employees seeing or experiencing brand associations

Employees thinking from a brand perspective

Reinforcing company values and personality

Employees receiving a brand promotional item

Employees being encouraged to take an additional brand action after the event

By continually reinforcing brand messages with employees, rewarding and acknowledging on-brand behavior, and being vigilant about compliance activities, your company and product brands will become stronger and employees will be excited about living the brand.

NOTES

1. John P. Kotter, "Leading Change: Why Transformation Efforts Trail," *Harvard Business Review* (March–April 1995), p. 59.

2. Ian C. MacMillan and Rita Gunther McGrath, "Discovering New Points of Differentiation," *Harvard Business Review* (July–August 1997), pp. 133–145.

3. Ibid., p. 66.

12 How to Conduct Brand Planning and Benchmarking

> As new companies become more familiar, the Bells' brand edge will be diluted unless it's continually built. If they just live off the fat of the brand without building, they will eventually lose to newer companies with innovative services and new exciting brands.[1]
> —Jeffrey Kagan, *Winning Communications Strategies*

Creating brand structure and revealing your brands are only the first steps on the brand management road. Becoming a brand-driven company requires an ongoing commitment. As with any other company activity, brand activity needs to pay for its keep. The most effective way to determine and communicate the value of your brands to others is to create a brand plan that includes objectives, strategies, tactics, and measurements. Planning keeps you on track; benchmarking tells you how you are doing.

HOW TO CREATE A BRAND PLAN

How do you keep your brand or brands focused? Companies use many tactics to create brand effectiveness. IBM uses an intranet page for training. PhotoDisc conducts a brand seminar with all new employees. Both of these activities have one thing in common—they are supported by a strategic brand plan.

The following plan will give you an example of how to conduct the brand planning and implementation process. Although this plan is exhaustive and assumes a good size staff and budget, most tactics can easily be adapted for small to medium-sized companies.

XYZ Company Brand Plan

Situation Analysis

In this Section, Describe the Current State of Brand Development. The XYZ company has successfully defined its brand structure, brand drivers, and the customer experience and conversation that our brand offers our customers. We have not yet communicated this brand to the outside world, nor has it been internalized by any company group other than corporate and the brand team. The objective of this year's work will be to take the next step in this process.

The challenge is to integrate brand into every employee action and to win over longtime company employees who are saying, This is not the way we've always done things around here. We believe this will take a concentrated effort of all senior management, particularly of our CEO, in order to exhort people to use our brand wherever possible, and show positive results from brand actions as quickly as possible.

Objectives of the Plan

Explain What You Want to Accomplish for the Year. This plan has three objectives.

- To integrate brand into all departments, including sales, marketing communications, product development, human resources, and customer support
- To enhance employees' understanding of the experiences and their dialogue with the customer
- To introduce our brand to the marketplace

We will measure the results of this work by benchmarking both employees and customers at the end of the year.

Please reference the brand toolbox for our most current brand structure and an explanation of brand drivers and other brand characteristics.

Strategy

General Approaches to Meet Our Objectives. We will create an internal campaign designed to reach every employee and each of our agencies to educate them about the brand, with additional tactics aimed at the core departments in question. We will use our CEO as the spokesperson for the XYZ brand way. We will use seminars, sales, and marketing communications tools to define the customer experience further and develop a customer dialogue. We will create cobranding opportunities with other products and services that are a good fit with our brand experience. We will use marketing communications activities to focus on our new brand messages.

Messages

What We Want Customers to Believe about the Brand. We will focus this year's efforts on making customers aware of messages based on our principle and our visual association.

Tactics

Specific Activities within Each Strategy. The following tactics will create a more integrated XYZ brand that projects a strong customer experience and dialogue.

The CEO = Brand Spokesperson. The CEO will perform a number of brand-related activities as part of her or his duties. These will include

- Giving quarterly state of the brand addresses.
- Creating an eight-minute brand video for distribution on CD-ROM to all employees and agencies.
- Creating an opinion article series on the XYZ brand to be published in prominent industry media during the year and posted on the company's intranet.

Brand Seminars. Brand trainers (initially members of the brand team) will conduct seminars created by the brand manager to learn how to apply the XYZ brand in direct decision making. Part of this seminar will be a software presentation for use in combination with the CEO video. We will create a special brand seminar for human resources, to be used as part of new employee orientation.

Brand Success Education. We will reinforce the brand through communicating brand successes. A brand intranet page will

- talk about how the brand is being applied by various people and departments and what the result has been.

- have a frequently asked questions section in which each question asked by employees will be published and answered.
- contain an electronic brand suggestion box.
- feature a brand expert chat room with brand speakers on various subjects directed at creating a stronger, integrated brand.
- be linked with the existing brand toolbox, allowing employees and agencies easy access to updated information on the brand.

A regular brand column in the company newsletter will

- explain brand from the perspective of each department. For example, one column will talk about brand's impact to margins; another about its stabilizing influence on corporate culture.

Brand Promotional Items. We will create promotional items that reinforce the brand to be handed out at seminars and awarded to employees for brand suggestions and questions. These will communicate either our values, our principle, or our visual association.

Teaching Marketing Communications Personnel How to Use Brand. The global brand manager and his or her staff will be members of the review committee for all marcom tools in the first year, in order to teach marketing communications personnel how to develop and execute programs using the brand. In the second year, this job will shift to the manager of marketing communications with indirect oversight by the brand staff.

Refining the Customer Brand Experience and Dialogue. Starting from the XYZ brand experience template, we will refine current customer brand experiences and level of dialogue through a series of intensive, one-on-one interviews with customers. We will be looking for what works in terms of messages, product features, and company interaction from all departments. We will determine how well this is supporting the brand drivers and differentiating us from competitors. The results of these one-on-one interviews will be fed immediately into the system for continuous improvement. Large changes will be held for consideration in next year's brand planning cycle.

Building Customer Awareness and Value Around the Principle and Associations. To kick off the XYZ brand publicly, we will use an advertising and direct mail campaign that raises awareness of our visual association and brand principle. We will support this education process on the website, where we'll have a special section telling our story and explaining our visual association.

Co-Branding. We will explore cobranding opportunities with our alliance partners to take advantage of our mutual customer base. These will include product bundling, special offers, and joint advertising campaigns.

Benchmarking

Semi-Annual Brand Team Meetings. The brand team will review the state of the brand and evaluate brand actions and communications, address brand logistical issues, and plan additional strategies for strengthening the brand. The every six-month meeting will allow us to make course corrections and help to communicate brand momentum to all areas of the company through each brand team member and via our brand trainers.

Annual Benchmarking. We will conduct an annual benchmarking study at the end of the year. This benchmarking will include a quantitative brand survey supported by research conducted on each marketing communications activity as well as anecdotal information from sales, customer support, and human resources. This will provide feedback on what areas of XYZ brand actions and messages need strengthening in the coming years. It will also indicate where we have made gains over the year.

We will measure success on the basis of increases in aided and unaided awareness of the brand name and of specific brand elements including personality traits and the visual association.

The preceding brand plan focuses on the aspects of brand building and management that create strong brands or make successful brands even stronger. They include creating a consistent customer experience, building customer loyalty and dialogue, educating and implementing brand by department, and continuing to develop brand over time.

When you first implement your brand, crawl before you walk. Start with the big picture and focus on training strategic internal departments. Then move gradually into other areas.

BENCHMARKING YOUR BRANDS

One of the most important activities that you can do for the success of your brand is to measure progress. Benchmarking allows you to see the impact brand is having on the company in real terms, so you can demonstrate return on investment and protect the brand from being gutted through counterproductive, short-term actions.

Benchmarking is the process of measuring activities from year to year against a set of objectives. Tools companies use for brand benchmarking typically include anecdotal stories, online research, one-on-one phone interviews, customer visits, focus groups, and quantitative surveys. Research can be used to give companies a general idea of what customers are thinking (qualitative) or be statistically significant (quantitative). Although quantitative information is more accurate, it is also much more costly. But unless you have a tight budget, quantitative and qualitative research combined with customer anecdotes is the best way to go.

Because the brand is at the intersection of what customers value and company strengths, you should interview both internal and external audiences when benchmarking. For the *what customers value* portion, look for unaided and aided awareness of a company's general brand and measure the strength of its reputation, personality, and associations. Also determine what specific activities customers value and how greatly and how the company and its competitors score on each activity. By using a numerical rating scale, you can assign customer scores to the importance of each activity and rate each company's performance in comparison. A *gap analysis* measures the gap between those two scores. This shows how close the brand is to hitting the mark. You should also ask questions that help determine the customer's experience of the brand, loyalty, and level of dialogue.

Developing a Comprehensive Benchmarking Program

People tend to conduct the type of research that they are most familiar with, even if it isn't the most appropriate for the job at hand. One Fortune 500 company almost exclusively uses focus groups, a qualitative measurement, for market research, even though its customers number in the millions. Here is a recommended mix—one designed to give you the best return and strategic knowledge for each dollar spent.

Internal

When getting a sampling of internal audiences, interview all corporate officers and selected representatives from each division or department. Interview top officers in person to delve into issues and follow threads of information to their conclusion. If you have a highly consistent pattern of answers, you can have a high degree of confidence in your results even if you have interviewed only a small number of people. For small companies, you often end up interviewing from 25 to 50 percent of employees. With medium-sized companies, this drops to 5 to 10 percent, and for large companies, from 0.5 to 1 percent.

Quantitative

When you are in the initial process of revealing your brand, plan to conduct quantitative interviews of all customer groups, including both domestic and international audiences. Consider your first questionnaire carefully. As it will be the benchmark for future research, it should be as comprehensive as possible. Avoid asking questions that relate only to a current event, unless you understand that those questions are not part of the annual benchmark and you really need the answers for current work. Set up a template to specify how you will report information collected. This will help you to see whether you are asking the right questions.

The current medium for in-depth research is the telephone. However, web interviews are going to replace the telephone in the not too distant future because they are easier, faster, and less expensive.

You can reduce costs by limiting the number of open-ended questions you ask; these are questions that require more than a yes/no or check box answer. However, in brand work, these are some of the most important questions that you need to ask, because they give you more insight into how your customers are thinking. If you present customers with a list of traits, such as *friendly* and *respectful,* and ask to what degree the brand manifests them, you will get an entirely different picture than if you ask what the business style of the company is.

In-depth

In-depth interviews are the most important piece of the brand research puzzle. They allow you to unearth and reveal brand strengths through deeply understanding both employee and customer points of view. When facilitating brand drivers, in-depth interviews provide important context for discussion. In-depth interviews are typically conducted either over the telephone or face to face.

Focus Groups

Focus groups are a very important part of the brand process because they give an up-close-and-personal view of customers and let you approximate real world brand communications, dialogue, and experience.

Since organization and brand drivers result in both rational and emotional reasons for brand preference and loyalty, seeing people in a room rather than as written responses on a piece of paper allows you to make observations about emotional states and motivations that you couldn't obtain any other way.

However, group dynamics can alter people's answers. Often a group will have one or more participants who have a strong personality and influence everyone else. People also tend to be more negative in focus groups because they are being asked for their opinions, rather than experiencing a brand in a less judgmental, natural setting.

Face-to-Face Interviews

Face-to-face interviews are a useful tool for measuring the customer experience and hearing customer dialogue. Interviewees must be people who have a lot of experience with a brand, such as recent heavy users of the product who have experience with the sales force, collateral material, advertising, public relations, or customer support. These interviews are used for fine tuning the brand experience and customer conversation.

Anecdotal Information

Because of its immediacy, anecdotal information can have a powerful impact on management, sometimes too powerful. Often managers will make a policy change based on hearing something from just one or two customers. If this information comes through the filter of a second person, such as a sales or support person, what was said by the first person may bear little resemblance to what you hear.

When using anecdotal stories, try to obtain the same information that you use in your benchmarking. When used to support salient points from a comprehensive research program, customer anecdotes are an effective tool.

Web Research

Web research programs are able to provide almost real-time feedback on brands. This is because they automate fielding a questionnaire and compiling the results. What's most exciting about this is that web research does not have significant setup costs. Imagine having the ability to test a new concept, message, or name through a small customer panel for less than one hundred dollars a question. From a brand perspective, this could mean tracking effectiveness of brand drivers and conveyors at shorter intervals to make immediate corrections.

Developing a Brand Panel

The process of determining what customers value should extend beyond traditional research into customer panels. Creating a standing customer panel enables a company to have direct dialogue with a group of customers and influencers. These customers usually have a lot of history with the product and are considered product champions. The brand panel allows you to integrate customers and influencers more fully into the brand building process.

RESEARCH RESULTS: SEEING THE BIG PICTURE

One of the challenges of conducting any kind of research is how you get employees to read and act on the results. Corporate library shelves are stacked high with research reports that have valuable information yet are not used. That's because it is a struggle to put data into a context that is useful for employees. Also, the quantities of information are difficult to wade through—a typical medium-sized company or division may have ongoing research conducted by three or four different firms for as many departments.

The more comprehensive your view of brand research, the better. An optimal research process would pull from all existing company research for tracking category trends, aided and unaided awareness, loyalty, and repeat purchase likelihood. In this ideal reporting system, you would be able to see two years of quarterly benchmarking figures at a glance and easily identify areas ripe for action. For instance, if the first quarter 2002 report showed a huge lift in aided awareness and yet sales fell, this would indicate an area to investigate further.

KEEPING BRAND ACTIONS AND MESSAGES ON THE RIGHT TRACK

Your brand benchmarking efforts will show you how on-track your branding efforts are and what, if anything, needs changing. With the possible exception of the mission, the organization and brand drivers will need to change little over time. You may end up adding to the values, story, personality, and associations, but the brand principle should never need to change. Brand positioning needs to be changed whenever your product, service, or competitive offerings change; when new competitors enter the field; or when new technology has changed the market itself. Although this could occur after three months or three years, a typical position lasts for one to two years.

Each year, plan to conduct a quantitative program for the purpose of fine-tuning your brand. This comprehensive research will show brand weaknesses or brand approaches that are not working and help you track changes in the marketplace. The questions that you want to answer with benchmarking include, *What isn't working in the customer relationship? Are brand drivers resulting in more depth and differentiation in the relationship or not? Has the market changed to such a degree that aspects of what the customer experiences in the relationship need to change with it?*

When you find something that isn't working, determine what aspect of the driver or conveyor isn't doing its job. Is it a visual brand association or some marketing communications campaign? If research shows after the first two years of use that the association or associations you are developing do not even show up in unaided research, then you need to consider looking for and testing new ones. The caveat is that your marketing communications program must have given the associations a fair shot at exposure.

Customer and employee feedback may reveal that you have overlooked certain messages that are complementary to the brand but not currently stated as supporting points to the principle. Brand supporting points are an elaboration on your brand, giving employees various perspectives on what the brand principle means and various ways to represent the principle in communications. Part of the job of the brand manager is to assess additions to the brand continually.

How to Keep Your Brand Fresh

Just because you need to be consistent with a brand doesn't mean there isn't room for additions or updates. In fact, if you don't update your brand occasionally, it will be perceived as an out-of-date brand focused exclusively on low prices. Just as Oldsmobile had to update its brand image

Coca-Cola has been adding to and updating its brand over its long life cycle. In the early decades, the Coca-Cola logo, the bottle shape, and the color red were primary associations. Over time, new associations, such as the nickname Coke and polar bears, were added to provide depth and update the brand. New Coke was a failed attempt to update the brand— it didn't work because the brand promise of always the same taste had been broken for its best customers.

McDonald's has also been expert at adding associations and deepening its brand. To the golden arches were added Ronald McDonald, Happy Meals, play areas, Big Mac, and more. Many of its associations were designed to reinforce a key brand message of *kid friendly* food.

Montgomery Ward did not update its brand in a significant way for many years. Since filing for bankruptcy in 1997, the brand has been undergoing a transformation. Instead of competing on a commodity level, where price and only price matter, it has identified its best customers and its brand environment and has charted a new strategy. As a result, the company cut back its specialty stores and is repositioning itself around *affordable fashion*, targeting its best customers as women thirty to fifty-five with a household income of twenty-five thousand to fifty thousand dollars a year. This repositioning has been conveyed through image-oriented television spots introducing the theme line "Shop Smart, Live Well. Wards," and the idea that Wards offers fashionable merchandise that people want at affordable prices. Says Roger Goddu, chairman and CEO of Montgomery Ward, "By approaching our broadcast advertising as an ongoing image-building campaign, rather than developing a new standalone spot for every sales promotion, we can begin to enhance the value of the Wards brand and build brand equity with our core customer."[2]

Hewlett-Packard is adding innovation and a stronger consumer focus to its brand assets through a corporate brand statement of "expanding possibilities," providing new methods of delivering products. These include selling HP InkJet supplies through a vending machine distribution network, changing its approach to retail by focusing on category management over the sale of individual products, and renewing its emphasis on consumer product development with new industrial designs. HP will also concentrate on building long-term relationships with consumers through such vehicles as HP Business Centers in American Airlines' Admirals Clubs and the HP "At Home" newsletter.[3]

What are the rules for adding new value to a brand?

The first rule is not to break any promises. When adding new associations, ideas, and messages, make sure they fall in line with your existing brand drivers. In addition, look at your brand to see whether any associations or ideas need eliminating. Often brand associations are too subtle or linked to out-of-date ideas and need to be replaced with other ones more closely linked to key brand ideas.

One must be careful in the quest for freshness not to throw the baby out with the bath water. When, to update its image, Jack in the Box eliminated the brand association of the order-taking clown, the company lost a large part of its personality with which customers had a relation-ship. Jack in the Box ultimately reinstated the clown image, although in an updated, fresh way.

Applied Microsystems Corporation, a maker of embedded systems de-bugging tools, had an association of *expert at debugging*, articulated in a vi-sual form as a frog. Customers loved the frog motif, but the ad agency recommended removing the frog association as it was getting, in its opin-ion, stale.

However, just because internal people are tired of an association, or an ad agency in its quest for creativity believes associations do not have to carry over from one campaign to another, doesn't mean your custom-ers will agree. Typically, customers are much more attached to these brand reminders than you might realize.

That said, you can still update your brand. RCA added a new dog to the "Its Master's Voice" association. The company did this by including the customer in the naming decision and making sure the new dog didn't take away from the messages implied by the old dog. Volvo is adding performance and personality messages to its safety messages in its new cars but is not shying away from safety even in its sporty models.

The rules for adding new messages to the brand are to include your customers in the decision or implementation, not to eliminate or negate existing brand messages, and, if possible, to build, rather than change your brand's story.

Sometimes, a new VP of marketing or a change in the marketplace will spur revisiting the brand. A new person may have a different take on the customer, or the market may have made a wide swing. In either case, you still need to remain true to the brand. New messages can be put in marketing materials, but they should remain subordinate to the brand messages.

Similarly, just because you are committed to your brand it doesn't follow that you have to shy away from other messages. For example, when personal privacy became a big issue in the electronic commerce arena, some Internet companies added privacy messages to their com-munications. Does this mean the brand moved to a privacy focus? No, the brand principle remained the same, and the personality and associ-ations remained the same; what changed was the communication of new ideas in addition to the brand.

There are many reasons for advertising, and building brand is only one of them. If a competitive threat is looming and the company wants to respond to the threat via advertising, the messages may be issue based, and the brand reinforcement may be a minor part of the entire message. In this case, the *message du jour* is the reason for the ad, not brand building. The message will predominate, the brand be subordinate. In all cases, however, the new ads, whatever the message, should reinforce the existing brand.

Your positioning statements for individual products can and should change with the market. This is because positioning is related to competition, which changes over time. Your brand principle, on the other hand, is intended to be more or less permanent, changing only if a company becomes nearly irrelevant to the marketplace, à la Western Union and telegrams.

When is it time to integrate new concepts into the brand?

- When market forces change and you need to address them
- When you want to expand beyond your best customers to a related set
- When research with your customers reveals you have a flat brand
- When a competitive brand is stealing customers
- When you acquire or merge with a new company

If you decide to freshen up your brand with new actions and messages, how do you decide which ones will work the best? There are three tests for action/message appropriateness.

1. Do your core customers care about the new direction?
2. Will it have a long life, or is it a transitory response to a short-term issue?
3. Does it expand your brand's relevance to an increasing set of customers?

In most companies, decisions about updating the brand will be made at the upper management level. Alternatively, the brand manager and marketing manager recommend changes. The brand team should be brought together to review any recommended changes, as they have a long-term perspective on the development of the brand.

It takes patience to change a strong brand. Xerox Corporation built its first copier in 1959 and invented copying xerography. They were known as "the copier company" for over thirty years but have made changes in both product direction and messaging to support their claim of being "The Document Company" since the early 1990s. "Even today, the large wire services still describe us as the copier giant. Some people still don't get it," explains David Reyes-Guerra, manager of corporate identity, "which is why you can never stop communicating, marketing and investing in your brand."

How to Keep Company and Product Graphics Current

Once you make the decision to update the brand, you also need to decide whether a new look or visual association is necessary.

The truth about images is that they follow fashion and, as such, can become out-of-date. Companies are often updating the looks of their logos and packaging, because people's taste in these matters changes. But extreme care must be taken not to update just for fashion's sake, but because the brand's relevance depends on it.

A brand look can be as simple as a template and set of colors and fonts, or as complex as an entire new visual association.

FedEx updated its brand for a number of reasons, the most important of which was that the company had become global, and in many markets, the word *federal* had negative connotations, in terms of both slow-moving bureaucracies and the term *federales*. What was unusual was that FedEx chose to make this update from a position of strength, when the company was the leader in the field.

The update of the branding was the result of two years of research and design. As the Corporate Design Foundation[4] said in its case study on FedEx's brand image change, "Why would a company with a name so recognizable that it has become the generic equivalent of overnight delivery service choose to revamp its identity? For Federal Express, global success demanded a change. The challenge came in preserving its brand equity, while ensuring that its identity stood out from a growing field of global competitors."

The company's brand personality centered around "big and bold, but friendly and accessible." The brand principle—the key messages—were "global scope, accessibility, speed, reliability." In any event, the company did not want to lose existing brand equity strengths, including speed, reliability, innovation, customer service, and corporate colors—purple and orange—that communicated urgency and leadership.

The resulting update, which shortened the name to FedEx, replaced the 1970s typeface, removed the restrictive purple field around the logotype, and added the tag line *The World on Time*, capturing visually the company's strongest attributes.

Said the Corporate Design Foundation: "Federal Express management understood the delays caused by committee approvals and removed the usual bureaucratic barriers by designating one company decision maker. . . .Company vehicles have become moving billboards, airplanes can be read across an entire airfield."

Lindon Leader, senior design director at Landor, the graphics art firm that created the logo, explains, "People tend to look at a new identity and dismiss it as a logo change. FedEx understood that it's really a by-product of the overall repositioning of the company."

Since the name of the company and its corporate logo are two of the most important assets a company has, it would make sense to track what the company name means to customers and whether the look of the company logo works for them. Using the same reasoning, this is also true for product brand names and logos.

How can you tell whether your logo's graphic image is working hard enough for you? As a part of your research benchmarking, you should test logo relevancy with your customers. The most effective way to do this is through focus groups, in which a moderator can help customers explore their reactions to the logo and determine what those reactions mean. Because design styles change, every graphic element of every brand is in danger of becoming outdated. Companies can mitigate part of this problem when they create their company logo, by not getting swept up in current design fads. But even with an effort to create a classic design, logos will still show their age over time. And when companies go through an integrated branding process, they often find they desire to change logo graphics to correspond to the new brand direction. To keep a logo fresh, it's a good idea to test its relevancy every two years. To keep the cost of this research in check, you can conduct it in conjunction with other regularly scheduled research.

NOTES

1. Jeffrey Kagan, *Winning Communications Strategies* (Newport, RI: Aegis Publishing Group, 1997).

2. Montgomery Ward web site: http://www.mward.com/html/restruct.html.

3. Hewlett-Packard press release, November 11, 1997.

4. Corporate Design web page: http://www.cdf.org/issue/fedex.html.

13 How to Create Brand-Driven Marketing

Great companies pay attention to every point of interaction with the customer. That's how great companies become great brands.[1]
—Claude Singer, "Branding Worlds Collide"

When developing marketing strategies for the brand, brand managers are all faced with the same set of problems: how to build distinctiveness using the marketing tools of price, distribution, product, and communications?

All of an integrated brand's organization and brand drivers help guide marketing strategies. The *brand principle* moves marketing in a direction that creates strong distinctiveness. The *mission* sets the boundaries for all marketing strategy. The *principle* sets the approach to those boundaries. *Values* impact what a brand will and won't do. They build customer trust and are especially important in establishing long-term alliances with dealers, system integrators, and other system vendors. The *story* conveys meaning and perspective to all audiences. The *personality* adds a recognizable set of behaviors and voice to sales and marketing communications. It also helps build corporate culture. And finally, *associations* add distinctive concepts that help boost distribution and make marketing communications more effective.

Developing brand marketing strategies typically falls under the marketing VP's job description, in conjunction with the global brand manager. When a company has multiple product brands and a strong corporate brand, brand marketing becomes more of a challenge.

Brand marketing is probably even more important for small to medium-sized companies than it is for larger ones. Smaller companies can less afford to make a mistake in any area of marketing. Brand strategies can also open up opportunities for greatly increasing company/product awareness that would not normally be possible with smaller budgets.

The first questions the marketing professional has to ask are, *What are the range of marketing strategies and which will be best for our brand?* and *How can marketing help meet the short- and long-term objectives of our brand?* The following are some of the more common strategies that can help you determine the answers to these questions.

BRAND-BASED NAMING

Effective brand marketing starts with a strong naming strategy. That's the central premise of brand-based naming. Often, brand-based names reflect a literal promise of the brand: Peerless Coffee, Everready Batteries, Arrid deodorant, and Excite Inc. search engine. Other times, they merely evoke the brand promise; *Atta Cat* cat food, for example, evokes the energy your animal will obtain as a result of eating the product.

But naming is getting more difficult, especially naming based on meaning. Trademark registrations for computer hardware and software rose 112 percent between 1989 and 1994, and new product introductions are increasing at more than twenty-six thousand per year.[2] There were, at last count, 750,000 registered U.S. trademarks, a remarkable number when you consider the entire *Oxford English Dictionary* contains only 616,500 words.[3]

Although generating trademarkable names is getting more difficult, the process of using brand drivers to generate names makes the selection process easier. A company that knows itself may not find locating prospective names any easier but will have a good way to judge potential ones. Conversely, not knowing your brand makes naming a *very* random process. When a national maker of programmer hardware for programmable read-only memories needed new product line names, it came up with several dozen choices, each reflecting a different personality. Because the company hadn't articulated its personality, the choosing process was arbitrary, rather than helping to build the company's brand and relationship with its customers.

In brand-based naming, a company looks for names that convey a sense of the brand's attributes. Honda did this with its luxury line of autos. Working from the brand principle of *high engineering content*, its naming consultants broke down engineering into its component elements—science, metallurgy, precision—and matched them with a series of meaningful word units. The result—*Acura*—is based on *acu*, which means *precisely* or *with care* in many languages.

Alternatively, you can create names based on a company's personality. The search engine name Yahoo, for example, resonated with the founders' personalities: blunt, rude, and uncouth. Said David Filo, cofounder of Yahoo, "It fit us. We were well-regarded yahoos." Compared with Lycos, Infoseek, Alta Vista, and Excite, the name Yahoo is memorable and colorful, and it stands out, while being true to the brand's roots.

Although it's important to link names to brand attributes, be careful of linking a name too closely to a product's technical attributes. Says John Smart, managing director at Interbrand, a naming firm, "IT firms have a tendency to develop names that are too suggestive of product attributes. This can be very limiting as the industry is ever-changing."

Vixel, a maker of hubs and switches based on the Fibre Channel standard, wanted to let its users know how compatible its products were with the rest of the enterprise. The name chosen, *Rapport*, led customers to the right meanings. In this case, the product attribute selected will be one that Vixel can live with over the long term.

By naming based on brand, you ensure your customers see consistency and are not confused when you extend product lines or introduce new products. Thus, naming conventions should be consistent, easy for the customer to maneuver through, and, when possible, evocative of brand meanings. Metapath Software Inc. named its first product Ceos, an acronym of Communication Enterprise Operating System. Future products stayed with the *Ce-* word beginning for brand consistency, then added product-based meanings. So for a product that took network information from Ceos and packaged it for the marketing department to use to understand customers better, the name *Ceer* (evoking Seer, a future teller) was the right choice. When a provisioning service was added to the product line, the name *Cerve* (evoking service) made sense to leverage brand consistency.

Hewlett-Packard started a new trend for high-technology products when it named its laser printers LaserJets, rather than using the company name followed by a number. This gave the printers a personality, put meaning into the product, and made them easier for customers to remember. HP started to flounder when it introduced new models and product line extensions. Pretty soon, each HP LaserJet was followed by a string of numbers and letters, confusing both to the customer and to HP employees.

WRQ had a similar problem with its line of Reflection products. Initially, the company put numbers after the name, such as *Reflection 1* or *Reflection 7*. The numbers represented which platform Reflection worked with, but customers thought they were numbers of new versions.

After doing focus group research with customers, WRQ changed the Reflection naming conventions to center on the host platform to which Reflection connected. This was easier for customers to understand and was more in line with the company's brand principle of "consultative partner," that is, one who helps customers understand and choose software. The company changed to names such as *Reflection for IBM* or *Reflection for HP* and then took branding one step further and moved toward more evocative names. Today, you will find names such as *Reflection EnterView* (for a web-to-host access product that lets you Enter the web and View the host) and WRQ @guard (pronounced "At-guard") for a web ad filter/firewall product.

Often, a company needs to rename itself, either because a merger/acquisition occur or because the old name is no longer descriptive of the company's mission or charter. Deciding exactly how to do this differs from case to case, but a few rules of thumb are applicable.

1. Don't throw away existing equity whole hog. When Omega Environmental, a provider of underground storage tank removal services, bought a series of local companies, it attached its name to each, such as Omega Watkins or Omega Kelly. This way, existing equity with local customers was maintained, while Omega could move forward to build up a national brand for stockholders and other national customers.

2. Educate customers about a name change over time. CimWorks, a maker of factory floor automation hardware and software, used to be known as GageTalker before it merged with another firm. The earlier name, which was too limiting for the company's new markets, held a lot of meaning for GageTalker customers. To educate that segment of its customers, the company moved through a three-step naming process, from *GageTalker* to *GageTalker CimWorks*, to *CimWorks GageTalker*, then dropped the *GageTalker* name altogether and moved to *CimWorks*. By so doing, it could acclimatize CimWorks customers to the new name, during which time the company would be able to transfer its equity.

3. Use a name change as an opportunity to tell the world about your brand. When e-commerce retailer Software.net changed its name to Beyond.com, it did so with much fanfare to the press and its customers about why the name was changed, and how the new name reflected the company's underlying promise to customers. The news of the name change provided an opportunity for the company to discuss its brand attributes: *a better way to buy software* and *optimistic*.

COBRANDING: USING ALLIANCES TO BUILD BRAND AND LEVERAGE BUDGETS

One fundamental brand marketing strategy that you should consider is cobranding. In cobranding two or more brands team up to communicate to customers or provide a customer experience. Because of the fact that in high technology, most solutions are systems made up of linked components, cobranding is a very common activity among high-technology companies. These companies sell a complete product only as a result of integrating with each other. Cobranding activities can include two or more products represented in ads, at trade shows, at special events, or in public relations—such as a joint press conference, press release, or contributed article. Cobranding can also be used as a distribution strategy—bundling several products together, such as adding built-in software to new computer purchases, or adding Tabasco brand hot sauce to Heinz Ketchup.

There are other, less obvious activities that provide the benefits of cobranding. With high-technology products, cobranding includes the joint activities of system integrators, resellers, and dealers. Depending on the brand strength of the reseller, this can result in a good equity boost for a new brand software publisher or hardware manufacturer. Articles or even advertisements in newspaper, magazine, or broadcast media with strong brands, such as *The Wall Street Journal, Forbes,* or CNN, can add elements of credibility and innovation to a young brand. Finally, the Internet provides many cobranding opportunities as multiple brands are mentioned or displayed on web sites, online magazines, or portals.

Special events can be another particularly effective cobranding method if your customers fall into highly defined segments. There are associations, clubs, and sports out there for just about every interest these days.

In a cobranding situation, one or more of the partners is typically trying to gain either awareness or money from the arrangement. Companies with less equity stand to gain from those with more. More established brands gain from the innovative or exciting offerings of newer brands.

Many small and midsized companies make the error of not planning their cobranding opportunities because they don't know what they're looking for out of the experience. Often, the result is that smaller companies take a passive approach to cobranding, blindly accepting any opportunities that come their way. They also may measure cobranding experiences too narrowly, basing their ideas only on how much exposure their product received from the experience. The lack of a cobranding policy can result in mixed signals to your customer base and may even reduce your brand loyalty.

Cobranding can be very effective for the second- or third-place company in a market category. Cyberspace gateway Excite Inc. has used well-known partners to burst out from a pack of seven into the number-two spot behind market leader Yahoo. Cofounder and senior vice president Joe Kraus says, "We believe in leveraging partners' brands to make both companies successful." Yahoo has also used this strategy, negotiating partnerships with Intuit Inc., Netscape Communications Corp., and Ziff-Davis Inc.'s ZDNet.[4]

Prior to taking on a cobranding opportunity, you need to evaluate the brand you are partnering with. The old saying that you are judged by the company you keep is the operative principle when it comes to cobranding. Are the other brand's markets the same as yours? How is the other brand perceived by your customers? Are you only one of a multitude of cobranding partners? A cobranding opportunity may look perfect from an exposure point of view, but it can also do your brand great damage or may not be worth the effort.

Here are criteria that marketers should use to develop a cobranding policy.

Brand, product, or service strategy. What are the short- and long-term objectives of your brand? What do you want the market to believe about your brand? Are there additions to your brand drivers, such as personality traits, that leveraging another brand's image can gain for you? Service brands can be made more real and differentiated for customers by associating with a tangible product brand. For instance, several flavors of Visa and MasterCard differentiate themselves by offering purchase-based credit for hard goods such as Ford cars or British Petroleum gas.

Appropriateness. Is the cobrand one that will even help your brand equity? Or is it a bad fit?

Believability. Will your market find the cobranding activity to be believable? If your brand is known for being lukewarm on the environment or even participating in antienvironmental activities, will supporting an environmental conference gain you the goodwill you are looking for? As with all brand messages, cobranding needs to be backed up by company actions.

Strategic positioning. All participants in cobranding must ensure that it builds their brands in the directions they want to go and does not reduce existing areas of equity. Microsoft actively encourages cobranding with its third-party software suppliers and consultants through its Microsoft Partners program. This program allows these smaller companies to benefit from the Microsoft name in advertising programs, through using a

Microsoft visual association on company letterhead and through signage for their offices and trade show booths. Microsoft realizes the advantage of demonstrating critical mass.

Adding value to brand drivers. In a recent advertising campaign, U.S. Bank pictured an upside-down box of Cracker Jacks with a prize of an 8.25 percent loan falling out of it. The title read, "Now inside every U.S. Bank Home Equity Line—a low interest loan!" What is U.S. Bank trying to demonstrate by using the Cracker Jack brand in this way? It is leveraging the *prize inside* association of the Cracker Jack brand to reinforce the significance of the low interest rate of this loan. By tying its service to a product, U.S. Bank is attempting to make its Home Equity Line service more tangible to its customers.

Another result is that U.S. Bank borrows and benefits from Cracker Jack's well-established and popular brand personality traits of *fun, enjoyment,* and *an element of approachability* that banks sometimes lack. This transfer of brand equity in the form of personality traits could be very beneficial to the bank if it continued to do this and reinforced these traits with other actions over time. These traits make what is a very stressful decision for most people (mortgaging their homes) easier to think about and act upon.

Cobranding with Charities

Annie's Homegrown Inc. is a maker of Annie's Shells & Cheddar, Annie's Alfredo, and other dry pasta entrees that are sold in grocery stores on both the East and the West Coast, in well-known chains such as A&P, Safeway, Albertsons, and Whole Foods. This Hampton, Connecticut, company, run by Annie Withey, does no advertising, yet competes successfully against one of the largest food conglomerates in the world, Kraft/Philip Morris. Annie's gives a share of its sales to over one hundred small and large not-for-profit groups that benefit children, women, education, or the environment. The company is also developing a customer-based program for donating up to five free cases of its products to charitable events suggested by customers.

Why doesn't Annie's Homegrown need to advertise? Because it has created a very strong relationship with its customers through a powerful promise. It has promised that it will continue to provide great tasting products and support selected charities if customers hold up their end of the relationship, which is telling people about Annie's Homegrown and what it is doing. Annie's has developed a brand promise that requires participation of its customers to be fulfilled! This is the closest that brand/customer relationships get to the human model of friendship;

hence this also creates the most loyal customer base. In this way, Annie's Homegrown brand resembles Saturn's. Both brands appeal to people who are motivated by belonging to and doing work for a community.

Cobranding with charitable causes is an important part of brand development. It creates a reservoir of goodwill for the brand with the general public. As in any relationship, this goodwill is an asset that will help the company overcome adversities and misunderstandings when they arise.

IMPROVING THE PRODUCT AS MARKETING STRATEGY

Sometimes the best brand marketing strategy is to bring a product back to its former level of quality. Often companies will throw a poorly performing product with high brand equity onto the trash heap or change it beyond recognition, assuming the problem is the product itself. If brand loyalty is very strong, but the product no longer holds up its end of the brand promise, then improving its quality will typically result in an increase in sales and market share whereas changing the product might hasten the tailspin.

The over one-hundred-year-old Cracker Jack brand is a great example of this. Cracker Jack was developed by a German immigrant, F. W. Ruckheim, who began selling popcorn after the great Chicago fire of 1871, but really hit it big at the 1893 Chicago World's Fair. Originally marketed as a *great health confection*, the brand added the *surprise inside* association in the early 1900s. By the time it was purchased by Frito-Lay in 1997, Cracker Jack had watched an erosion of sales, with a 25 percent drop in its latest fiscal year. Some of the problems with the product were stale popcorn, very few peanuts, peanuts only on the bottom of the box, unappealing prizes, and the company's inability to provide a prize in every box.

A nonbrand approach might say, "Let's get rid of this poor performer." Instead, Frito-Lay approached improving the product as the answer to the brand's troubles. The company tested prizes among seven- to nine-year-old boys to create prizes that will hold a child's attention for about five minutes; made sure there are at least twenty peanuts to a four-ounce bag; and started shipping the bags upside down to ensure more even peanut distribution. Frito-Lay is also positioning the snack on store shelves next to candies as a healthy candy alternative (getting back to the brand roots), as opposed to putting it near popcorn, and has introduced a foil-lined bag to keep it fresher. The company has started using puffier popcorn and will use its extensive distribution system to make it more accessible to the American public. On the prize front, the company can now ensure that 99.7 percent of all packages have them.

Beth Strucknell, a vice president in charge of Cracker Jack, said that by 1999, "sales should be four times the current $45 million. Changing Cracker Jack would be the wrong thing to do."[5]

DISTRIBUTION AND BRANDING

Whatever distribution system you use will impact your customer relationships because of the delivery system's importance in shaping customer perceptions. The following outlines the brand challenges and opportunities of each distribution system.

Retailer, Dealer, Reseller, or System Integrator Channels

Most high-technology or electronic products and large-ticket consumer items sell through a third party such as a dealer, reseller, or system integrator. These third parties often vary greatly in the quality of service provided. What can you do to ensure that your brand stays whole in this environment?

Begin by creating a strategy for your reseller relationships. Although there are many hundreds to many thousands of dealers in the marketplace (depending on your product), don't assume that your only goal is to sign up as many as possible. The eighty/twenty rule tends to be true in this market—20 percent of your resellers will provide 80 percent of your sales. Your brand drivers can assist you in determining which 20 percent are going to work hardest for you.

When you are first developing the relationship with the dealer, explain your brand philosophy in some detail. Talk about the customer experience that you are trying to create and outline your expectations for the reseller's role. Look for understanding or even excitement from potential partners. See whether they understand your brand values and principle. Determine whether there is a common ground between your two firms. Where you don't see it, move on.

Ways to Brand the Third-Party Experience

Your direct sales force should be a support arm for your resellers and not in competition with them. When possible, have salespeople accompany resellers to their customers' offices and let resellers witness firsthand how you use your brand in the selling process. This will allow them to learn by doing and help them in future sales situations.

Create a very simple message platform for reseller use. If you ever played the game of telephone in elementary school, in which a single message is whispered down a chain to humorous result, you know how quickly messages can become garbled. One idea is to create a message cheat sheet that can sit in a salesperson's day planner or on the screen of his or her palm-size PC. Brand messages must be very direct, short, and memorable. If you were selling Xerox, for instance, you would explain how its products are superior because of its commitment to being "The Document Company."

Use incentives to imprint brand messages on your resellers' minds. If you use promotions such as vacations or cash as sales incentives, consider tying the theme for each contest directly to your brand principle. This type of repetition will reinforce your brand messages for high-achiever salespeople.

Annual Dealer Update

Create an annual let-your-hair-down session with your key resellers. Find out what they've been facing in the marketplace and let them know about new brand initiatives and new directions. Use this as a refresher course on organization and brand drivers and messages.

Online

Direct sales over the Internet are rapidly becoming an important part of almost all companies' distribution channels. In Internet sales, prospective customers will arrive at your home page, work their way through product information, choose what they are interested in, supply a credit card number, and then receive an order confirmation.

Where does brand fit into this experience? You should plan out a customer's Internet brand experience as carefully as you would any other customer/company interaction. This means a great deal more than putting your logo in appropriate places. The key is to create a differentiating experience to elevate the purchase transaction into a relationship. If it is just another transaction to your customer, or, worse, if it is confusing and time consuming, your brand experience is in trouble. Even if you don't sell on your web site, the same concept holds true—use your site to differentiate and deepen relationships.

Dell Computer Corp. is a good example of a brand-driven web site. The company has three goals for its online sales: making it easier for customers to do business with the company, reducing the cost of doing business for Dell and for customers, and enhancing the company's relationship with its customers.[6]

What are ways of differentiating? Differentiators should be things that customers want to know that only you provide. Or the buying experience itself can be a differentiator. For specific examples, see the sponsored content section in Chapter 15.

Catalog

Catalogs offer a great opportunity for branding, yet they are often underutilized as a brand conveyor. For every Banana Republic or J. Peterman, there are five companies that don't communicate their brand at all.

For instance, it's important to support through words what customers are shown in pictures. That's because most people won't take the time to understand a visual brand message unless it is very obvious. Unfortunately, most catalogs have few or no brand messages in them. One very strong retail brand, Nordstrom, is known for its unparalleled customer service, which includes a legendary no-questions-asked return policy, a personal shopper who becomes your eyes and ears inside the store, and incredibly friendly salespeople. Even though customers know about these services, reminding them when they are away from the store would be a positive, brand-building exercise. The company's catalog, however, doesn't explain or even mention any elements of its brand.

A catalog doesn't have to feature high production values to communicate brand. Morton, Washington–based Raintree Nursery puts out an extensive catalog every year highlighting its unusual and often hard-to-find fruits, nuts, and berries, such as the chop suey tree, the aromatnaya quince, and the medlar. The company's catalog is friendly and folksy with detailed how-to sections and highly educational descriptions of each plant, including icons that tell country of origin, disease resistance, and even whether the plant will attract birds. The entire catalog, with the exception of the first two four-color pages, is produced in black and white on a lower-quality paper, but the brand experience is still unique and compelling.

The Retail Brand Experience

What do you do when a salesperson on the floor of a computer superstore is trying to sell your product with very little knowledge? The answer is a point of purchase (POP) display or electronic demo that communicates brand. Even in the electronic age, POPs are still very effective at selling products, especially if you can attach them directly to the product, as in the case of a copier or desktop printer. They can, through tone, graphics, and promotions, create a brand experience on the retail floor.

An electronic demo can take the brand experience even further, through photos, sound, animation, and interactivity. But unless your product is part of the computer system itself, this will be more difficult to execute.

HOW BRANDING HELPS DIRECT SALES

The tension between marketing and sales sometimes rears its head in a company's branding efforts. The sales department may see no relevance of brand messages to their actions in closing a sale. Or even if they buy into the brand drivers, they may be at a loss as to how to demonstrate the brand in their customer and prospect relationships. Furthermore, salespeople have often been rewarded only for short-term sales. Sales also tend to attract people who enjoy the pleasure of the hunt and the relatively immediate, tangible reward that only making a sale can create.

But it is possible to get your sales team to use brand as the foundation for sales, if you listen carefully to their objections and their point of view, then demonstrate within their view of the universe how brand can help them sell. Typically you can begin this when you roll out the brand to the sales department. Helping salespeople apply brand to their customer interactions and customer conversation will allow you and them to discover specific activities that enhance the sales process and build the brand.

If your brand has a focus on *collaboration*, you may look at ways to approach the entire sales process as a collaborative effort. This could include conducting a customer audit prior to getting down to dollars and cents to determine current and future needs. It might also include recommending against a project or function, when it is not in the client's best interest, even though it will cause you to lose some short-term revenue.

But what if you have a sales force that is not open to brand? First, cultivate a brand champion within the sales department. This should be the person who is also a member of the brand team. If this salesperson actively took part in shaping and revealing the brand, he or she will typically stick up for it with other salespeople. Beyond that, the following are answers to five common sales department objections that may help you.

"I don't see how using brand messages will close the sale." Because a brand principle results from research into what customers care about and where the brand is competitively strongest, aligning with the principle can make sales happen. One network software company found this to be true when it decided to use its brand principle as a key selling message. It worked so well with one of the company's Fortune 500 prospects that the deal was struck even without competitive bids.

"The brand personality does not reflect my personal style." Using a company's brand personality doesn't mean salespeople have to change their personality. What it does mean is that their actions must reflect the company's personality. This subtle distinction is best illustrated by examples. Let's say a company's personality is summarized with the trait of *energetic*. In this case, all that a salesperson has to be careful of is that his or her customer interactions convey a high level of energy, whether or not the salesperson is energetic in his or her personal life.

"I have great customer relationships already." Integrated branding is concerned with taking what has made people successful and giving even more impact to their actions. Because a company's brand is revealed, not created from scratch, it typically reflects the same company strengths the salesperson used to build the relationship in the first place.

"That brand stuff is marketing fluff, selling is about what the customer wants." Even if branding is clearly manifested in product development, marketing, and customer support, customers want a *seamless* brand experience across the board. If the sales process is off-brand, the customers will wonder which is the real company—the one they experience with sales or the one that they experience elsewhere within the company. In addition, since brand messages are based on key customer values, using those messages will produce a good response from customers.

"My product line needs different messages." Ideally, all of a company's products should be closely linked to the brand principle. Sometimes different messages are really just elaborations on the brand principle or new product positioning. If they are truly different yet appropriate, then either the brand principle needs reworking, or the product line should be dropped, be spun off, or become a new, stand-alone brand.

NOTES

1. Claude Singer, "Branding Worlds Collide," *Wireless Review* (August 15, 1998), p. 72.

2. Gina Imperato, "Make a Name for Yourself," *FastCompany* (October–November 1996), p. 38.

3. Alex Frankel, "Name-o-Rama," *Wired 5.06* (June 1997), http://www.wired.com.

4. Jonathan Littman, "Driven to Succeed: The Yahoo Story," *Upside* (September 8, 1998), p. 115.

5. Constance L. Hays, *New York Times* (July 4, 1998), pp. B1–2.

6. Lisa Chadderdon, "How Dell Sells on the Web," *Fast Company* (September 1998), p. 60.

14 Using Marketing Communications to Drive Brand

It's difficult to get a lot of leverage off of marketing communications in its own right. It is the personal experience that people have with a brand that gives our marketing communication its credibility.
—Joe Kennedy, Vice President of Sales,
Service and Marketing, Saturn Corporation

Although the brand is a part of all company actions, marketing communications vehicles such as advertising, direct mail, public relations, trade shows, seminars, and collateral material play an important role in communicating brand. Thinking of these activities as *brand conveyors* is a useful way to understand their role. They allow you to communicate the *organization* and *brand drivers* that make up the heart of the brand.

Most marketing communication projects are kicked off with a creative brief or creative platform—a form that is filled out by product management and marketing communication management that describes the project's purpose, audience, content, message, and tone. Brand-savvy companies include a place on this form to fill in what brand messages will be woven or, at the very least, how the piece will strengthen the brand. This brings the role of brand up to consciousness, an important part of keeping branding efforts on track.

THE MARKETING COMMUNICATIONS PLAN

How do you integrate brand into marketing communications? Your first step is to design a marketing communications plan that incorporates brand meaning, visuals, and messages in a systematic way. If you are already familiar with this process, you can skip this section. For those of you who are in a start-up mode, or are just beginning to venture into marketing communications, we highly recommend this objectives, strategies, and tactics approach to marketing communications. Do not confuse this with the brand development plan described in Chapter 12. That plan helps you build the brand; this one integrates it into general communications. Depending on your company reporting structure, you may choose to combine both plans in one.

Your plan should look at marketing communications from the perspective of each driver and figure out the best way to weave in specific brand messages and actions. For example, advertising is one of the best ways to reinforce brand associations and personality, and public relations is tailor-made for educating customers on your brand principle.

Your marketing communications plan, of course, is attempting to achieve a variety of objectives. Implementing brand messages becomes one more objective in the plan, called out by individual brand drivers. Here's a sample plan to demonstrate how it works.

Company ABC Marketing Communications Plan

Situation Analysis

The software distribution market is going through a consolidation process. In the past, the market consisted of small regional companies founded by technically savvy entrepreneurs. Currently, the market comprises a handful of large companies such as Company ABC. Company ABC is made up of a group of geographically diverse companies combined through consolidation. It continues to acquire companies with a similar philosophy.

Company ABC is focusing on two primary goals: becoming the preeminent leader and becoming the employer of choice.

Company ABC practices a unique approach in acquiring regional partner companies. Its primary focus is to bring in new partners that have a similar corporate culture (companies built and maintained by entrepreneurs) and let them continue to grow as if they were still regional companies. It envisions maintaining the entrepreneurial spirit of each acquired company: not stifling but nurturing and empowering them, enabling the companies that join to function in a decentralized way while flourishing under the Company ABC brand.

This new entrepreneurial approach gives regional companies global strength through enhancing service offerings by adding partners with other services around the world. It allows the acquired companies to prosper by operating within their region as they see fit, while offering premier benefits packages to attract and retain the sharpest employees. The benefits of having one national infrastructure are streamlined operations and a larger employee pool.

The current market is encountering a shortage of qualified candidates and Company ABC views its employees as its greatest asset. Therefore, it takes care of them through flexible work programs, creation of a personal career challenge, a positive corporate culture, and an excellent benefits packages.

Because Company ABC is a new player, building awareness of the company is key to long-term success. Company ABC needs a plan for exposure in the marketplace that presents a unified front but clearly communicates the many services it offers, the uniqueness of its approach to acquisitions, and the positive nature of its work environment.

The following plan is designed to educate the marketplace about Company ABC, its focus on maintaining each regional entity's individual strengths, its diverse service offerings, and its positive corporate culture.

Primary Objective

• Successfully communicate the Company ABC brand to specific target audiences. This overriding objective will be infused into our strategic marketing communications approach. Company ABC brand components include:

Company ABC Brand Principle: Cooperation

Company ABC Brand Personality: Skilled, thoughtful

Company ABC Brand Association: Local and Global

Objectives

• Create widespread industry recognition of Company ABC as a market leader. We will measure success by conducting periodic audits to see how well key brand messages have been communicated to target audiences, that is, potential customers, potential acquisition targets, investors, potential investors, current employees, current customers, local management teams, and the press.

• Establish Company ABC as the preferred employer in the industry. We will measure success by conducting periodic audits to see how well brand messages have been communicated to target audiences: potential employees, potential acquisition targets, current employees, local management teams, and the press.

Overall Strategy

• Develop a solid message platform that clearly and consistently communicates Company ABC's features and benefits in a way that incorporates its brand principle, personality, and associations.

The overall strategy serves as a springboard to infuse our brand messages fully into additional strategies.

Strategies that *pull* messages to target audiences, by using third parties to help place Company ABC's messages in front of its target audiences, include

• Communicate Company ABC's messages via third parties to establish credibility with all target audiences. Third parties include analysts, media, award givers, happy customers, and online newsgroups/listserves.

Strategies to *push* messages to target audiences, by putting Company ABC information directly in front of its target audiences, include

• Use direct communications tools to seed brand to target audiences.

Tools include direct mail, advertising, collateral material, web site, and current employees.

Tactics

These tactics implement the goals and strategies explained. The result listed with each tactic maps back to the goal or strategy that tactic achieves.

The following tactics support the strategies to *push* messages to target audiences.

• Use direct communications tools to seed brand with target audiences.

Tools include direct mail, advertising, collateral material, web site, and current employees.

Direct Mail

We recommend two direct mail pieces to reach our target audiences. The following tactics support the strategies that *pull* messages to target audiences.

• Communicate Company ABC's messages via third parties to establish credibility with all target audiences. Third parties include analysts, media, award givers, happy customers, and newsgroups.

MEDIA/EDITORIAL ACTIVITIES

Press Materials Development

A recommended press kit will contain the following:

• Company backgrounder
• Press releases
• Contributed articles
• White papers
• Case studies

MEASURES OF SUCCESS

Clip Analysis and Periodic Audience Audits

An actual marketing communications plan will go into more depth in regard to timeline, measurement, and specific tactics, but this skeleton plan will set you thinking in the right direction.

EXECUTION

How do you take integrated branding out to customers?

If you're Microsoft, you create a set of Microsoft Brand Tools and the Microsoft Creative Resource Program to develop optimal agency relationships and efficient business practices worldwide. Microsoft wants to become one of the most famous brands in the world—symbolic of the benefits created by the information age. The tenets of its corporate marketing department are to bring the brand to life, create a unified voice for the Microsoft brand across all communication, improve the brand integrity and quality, and save time and money for Microsoft. Its goal is to own the founding proposition of *access to exciting possibilities through innovation* in the mind of all business customers and home consumers. At the same time, the goal is to prevent competitors from owning the *access* idea.

CREATING A BASIC TOOLBOX FOR MARKETING COMMUNICATIONS

For large companies, the first interactions with customers are based on visual information. Advertisements, web sites, direct mail, collateral material, logos, and photographs all play a big role in establishing a basis for relationship and defining the type of experience the customer will have with the brand. These guidelines will help you to create a visual toolbox for your brands that supports brand equity growth.

Define the Minimum Consistency Level for All Visual Communications

The problem with mandating visual consistency is that it can stifle creativity and eliminate distinctiveness among product brands. Therefore, consistency requirements must be as minimal as possible and also offer the ability to break some rules from time to time.

The most basic requirements are the placement, size, and color of a uniform corporate logo. One idea is to create two allowable logo coordinates for all pieces, with minimum sizes set as a proportion to the total viewed area. This will reinforce the corporate brand with every impression.

It's highly recommended to create a *visual element hierarchy* for other elements of the piece. This hierarchy is determined by where the reader's attention goes first, second, third, and so forth. Ranking first in the hierarchy should be the headline or image. Following it are other important brand elements, which might include the logo, product name, product brand template, background, and colors.

Brand Color Palette

Create a different palette of colors for each distinct brand. Color is a very easy way to set brands apart. The palette should include a dominant color and then a series of accent colors. Color is also an effective association for a brand because it is one of the easiest things for people to remember. Kodak and Symantec's use of yellow in their communications and packaging is a good example of creating distinctiveness and, in Symantec's case, of grouping products that don't necessarily have much in common.

Associations Revisited

This section covers visual branding as it relates to specific association usage. Associations range from the abstract, like the Nike swoosh, to actual people like Peter Norton, pictured on the box and on ads for Norton Utilities. The logo is a visual association, but integrated brands often have other associations as well.

The integrated branding process uses associations in two ways. One is as the center of an advertisement or other communication, to call attention to the benefit the association stands for, thereby creating a connection between the association and the brand value. This is the case with *Intel Inside*: each advertisement explains what having Intel Inside means to the computer buyer. Intel has tied this to a concept it calls *fantastic reality* to act as a graphic excitement generator for the beneficial power of technology in modern life.

The other way that an association is used is as supporting player in a print ad, commercial, or collateral piece, where the association is in the communication but is not the center of attention. In this case, the association triggers memories and benefits in the customer's mind, while taking up very little real estate, enabling the brand to communicate multiple messages successfully in a short period or in a limited space.

You may also choose to add new, long-term associations to bolster your marketing communications activities.

Brand Templates and Backgrounds

Visual templates are another way of creating distinctiveness. Hewlett-Packard has used a visual template for many years that controls the placement of photographs, type style, color, and logo to create a consistent effect across product lines and divisions. Although templates create strong consistency, they also can severely limit creativity. If you choose to create a template, keep it as simple and minimal as possible.

Backgrounds also can subtly reinforce a brand. For years, companies have put watermarks on their stationery. With electronic media, backgrounds have really come into their own. Many web sites use graphical watermarks behind other graphics and texts. Television networks put electronic watermarks in the corner of their programming. Electronic backgrounds can now be inexpensively purchased as clip art. Backgrounds add richness to the customer experience while allowing for more flexibility in the creative process.

Image Treatment

Consistent treatment of photographs and illustrations also adds memorability to the brand experience. Some brands choose to convey all visuals as illustrations; others use impressionistic photographs to soften a brand's visual image.

One word of caution about these visual brand conveyors. If you have several product brands that need to be integrated, use these tools sparingly. You can easily make the process too complex to manage or for your creative people to understand. Once you have a basic visual brand model put together, try it out on some test pieces. How easy is it to work with? If it isn't easy, pare your visual brand model down until you reach an effective balance of ease of use and distinctiveness.

The Visual Test

Once you have six months' worth of brand work completed, paste up each brand's marketing communications materials on a separate board and analyze brand and company distinctiveness among all pieces. If possible, include your outside agencies in the process. What succeeded? What didn't work? Were there any surprises? What should be changed or fine tuned for the next six months?

The Toolbox

Many companies create a printed or electronic toolbox for easy access to brand information. See Chapter 10 to learn about the specifics of the WRQ toolbox.

GETTING YOUR AGENCIES TO SING THE SAME TUNE

Besides integrating branding through the marketing communications plan, you'll want to get all your communications services vendors on board with the brand. Many advertising agencies do not have experience with integrated branding, have their own ideas about what your brand should be, or believe that a brand is an unnecessary straitjacket to their creative efforts. Alternatively, public relations firms may feel there is no place for brand messages in their written materials. Both of these attitudes must be identified and rooted out before they can sabotage your branding efforts.

Many who have no experience developing integrated brands will claim that they have, on the basis of creating graphic identities for their clients. Graphic or corporate identities usually include rules for *brand conveyors* such as fonts, logos, slogans, and specified placement on stationery, signs, vehicles, and uniforms. This is not the same as creating an integrated brand for a company that is consistent with, and flows from, its *brand drivers*.

Even when your agencies are familiar with brand-driven advertising, it is still a significant challenge to get agencies in several countries to stay on target. According to Brian Burch, HP's worldwide brand manager for its Home and Small Business division, "Keeping people in line has been a huge challenge. I have several team members who train agency partners. We need to be everywhere at once all over the world. This process requires lots of dialogue and thorny issues that we must work on together."

How can you determine whether you have the right third-party resources for the difficult job of branding? First, look at both their past branding work and their ability to work as part of a virtual international team. Does an agency really believe that it's okay if they don't invent the campaign themselves? Are they willing and excited to be team players? Second, explain your brand or brands in detail and ask them to feed back the brand in a way that demonstrates an understanding of it. If you feel they don't understand it, then move on to other firms.

Once your brand is in place, you need to train your other agencies on branding and how to use both the written and visual elements of the brand. It's a good idea to hold an agency conference for this purpose. This one- to two-day intensive exercise enables all agencies to hear about the brand, see it in use, and begin to use it themselves. Also, give the internal creative director, along with the global brand manager, authority over everything that is produced. This will eliminate the learning curve and help people get a feel for what the brand looks like in use.

Introducing brand drivers to customers and prospects requires a coordinated effort. Typically, using an ad campaign is the best way to kick off the process. Beyond.com did this when it moved from being Software.net to become an expanded brand that included feelings and aspirations beyond software. In large full-page ads in the *New York Times*, *Wall Street Journal*, and many other media outlets, the company announced its key brand principle loud and clear: *Beyond.com. A better way to buy software*.

At the beginning of a brand development project, you'll want your brand drivers to come through in your marketing communications materials in an obvious way. Typically, the first ad campaign after a brand process hits the brand messages extremely hard. Future campaigns can soft pedal the brand drivers, but they should always contain its key elements. For instance, the brand personality will dictate the tone of ads—the ad's message and tag line will be complementary to the brand principle. One way of looking at this is that no matter what product you are advertising, the message should deliver and strengthen the brand. On the other hand, even if brand is the focus of the ad campaign, it should also serve to strengthen your product lines.

USING PUBLIC RELATIONS TO CONVEY BRAND

Use public relations to add believability and depth to your brand messages. Public relations, because it dispenses its messages through independent third parties, is the most credible of all marketing communications tools; hence it can be ideal for getting across your brand principle. Public relations can help fine-tune a brand. It does this by gaining awareness and acceptance from customer influencers such as analysts and other companies and using them as your allies in customer interactions. There are myriad ways to get your brand messages across in public relations. Here are a few examples:

- When creating presentations for editor meetings, make sure the brand principle is one of the top three messages you're getting across.
- Write articles that demonstrate how the company is manifesting a specific brand principle.
- Write pitch letters to editors that contain your key brand messages.

DIRECT MAIL AND BRAND

Microsoft uses its brand personality as the basis for many of its direct mail messages. Unfortunately, Microsoft also has an unwanted brand association of *arrogance*. Because of this, the company tries to avoid arrogance-based messages. Instead, it uses a tone of *friendly, concise*, and *optimistic* in its communications and creates experiences in which customers feel they are talking to a trusted friend and adviser, in a two-way conversation. Through both tone and content, Microsoft demonstrates that it is deeply interested in its customers' concerns, enthusiastic about helping them meet their goals, and committed to steady innovation.

Here's an example of that tone, in an upgrade mailer to users of Microsoft Visual C++ 4.0 who had not upgraded to 5.0 despite two previous direct mail campaigns. The concept was to elicit useful information about why they didn't upgrade, while humorously pointing out the benefits of the new version.

Envelope banner side:
We want to know!
In 20 words or less, please tell us why you haven't upgraded to Microsoft Visual C++ 5.0 yet.

(Survey enclosed)

Envelope label side:
Don't smaller and faster applications make you feel better?
Does the Internet give you a rash?
Allergic to component-based development?
What?

Letterhead:
Upgrade now! Or at least tell us why you won't.

Letter copy:
Dear <name>:

Frankly, we're confused. With all the speed, productivity, COM and Internet enhancements we put into the Microsoft Visual C++ development system version 5.0, we expected you would have upgraded by now. But you haven't, and we're sure you have your reasons. Please clear up our confusion by filling out the survey on the back of this form.

Maybe it's simple forgetfulness.
Did you know the newest version of Visual C++ lets you produce the fastest, smallest 32-bit applications for the Windows 95 and Windows NT operating systems? With Visual C++ 5.0, both new and existing code will benefit from the improved optimizing compiler.

Visual C++, Professional Edition, features the best COM support available. New Internet features include wizards and controls that make it easy to develop dynamic Internet and intranet applications. Did you know that as a Visual C++ developer, you qualify for the special upgrade price of just $199.95?

And Visual C++, Enterprise Edition, gives you even more flexibility with integrated Visual Database Tools, remote SQL debugging, version control, Microsoft Transaction Server, Developer Edition, and Microsoft SQL Server, Developer Edition. Is it coming back to you now?

Read on for extra reasons to upgrade.

We're prepared to give you even more reasons to upgrade. How about six months of *Visual C++ Developers Journal*, filled with tips, articles, technical advice and more, for FREE? And so you can keep up to date on the latest technologies, we'll throw in a free Microsoft Visual C++ Technology Preview CD-ROM with new support for OLE DB, the new Internet Explorer 4.0, Common Controls, and Dynamic HTML.

Sound reasonable? Order today by calling xxx-xxx-xxxx, going online to www.developerstore.com or sending in the attached order form.

Sincerely,

Microsoft Product Manager

P.S. Get the most out of Visual C++ 5.0. Order *Mastering MFC Development Using Visual C++*, a CD-ROM training tool with more than 40 hours of multimedia instruction, along with your upgrade for the special price of just $99.95.

Survey head:
We want to know! Please fill out and return this survey.

Survey copy:

1. In 20 words or less, please tell us why you haven't upgraded to Microsoft Visual C++ 5.0 yet.

---

2. Why don't you want the latest and greatest technology?
   A. Smaller is not better
   B. Faster is not better
   C. There's no benefit to creating component-based applications
   D. The Internet is a passing fad
   E. Too expensive
   F. I'm in the middle of a project
   G. None of the above

3. If you were considering upgrading, what would push you over the edge?

    A. A free six-month subscription to the *Visual C++ Developers Journal*
    B. A free copy of the Microsoft Visual C++ Technology Preview
    C. Getting all five of the Microsoft Visual tools for about the price of two with Visual Studio 97
    D. All of the above
    E. Other _____

4. If you decided to upgrade, how would you order it?

    A. Via phone at xxx-xxx-xxxx
    B. Via mail through the enclosed order form (see back of survey)
    C. Online at www.developerstore.com
    D. Via fax at xxx-xxx-xxxx
    E. Through my favorite reseller,

    _____
                                  (fill in name)

Although many direct mail projects use flashy visuals and cute gimmicks such as the tongue-in-cheek survey illustrated here, the true power of Microsoft's direct mail is its using its brand to increase direct response. Internal statistics at Microsoft show equivalent responses with different messages: The reason people open and respond to the company's direct mail is the brand name itself.

EXHIBIT AND EVENT BRANDING

Until recently, exhibit programs were the poor cousin in the marketing communications department. Exhibit managers were not viewed as strategic members of the department and trade show messages were often different from everything else.

As trade shows have become larger, this has changed. But most companies still do not employ them for their best use: cementing relationships with existing customers.

Everything in your exhibit strategy should reflect brand messages and enhance the brand experience. Consider the following points: *How does the brand principle and personality affect the booth layout, look, and feel; staff-*

ing; theater presentations; training; and promotions? If you have multiple brands, how will they be represented in a way that prevents confusion?

Booth Design

The booth should represent both principle and personality. If your principle is access, does the booth allow easy access to people? Are they the right people? Does it show them how to use your products to access the information you need?

Metapath, a telecommunications software company, articulated its brand personality around the simplicity and functionality of Shaker crafts, the innovation and clean lines of modern Italian design, and the harmony inherent in things Japanese, such as rock gardens, shoji screens, and ikebana. This personality has driven the design of all collateral material, including the trade show booth, so that trade show attendees would experience Metapath's "Shatalianese" personality (see figure 14.1). Says Kathy Holm, manager of marketing communications at Metapath Software Corporation:

> Our tools are elegant, and simplify our customers' lives. We wanted the booth to reflect that in an elegant and simple design. And like Shaker-inspired objects, the booth's form is directly related to function, with easy to view introductory information guiding people deeper into the booth to the center, where a conference room is available for a personal explanation of our products. All of our marketing communication tools, including the booth, reflect the benefits of our products—they are intelligent, and make life easier, calmer and simpler.

Theater

What is the purpose of your theater? Is it to introduce new products or demonstrate how to use specific product features? Is it to tell the corporate story? The theater should tie into the larger strategic goals of each of your brands.

Highly Trained Staff

Because trade shows are where face-to-face interactions happen with the brand, it is important to conduct training with your exhibit team that focuses on the customer relationship. Many brands use only their exhibit

Figure 14.1
The Metapath Booth

The booth reflects an elegant and simple brand promise.

Source: Reprinted with the permission of Metapath.

specialists at trade shows or even hired performers for presentations. It's a good idea to take people from other departments to the show to expose them to customers and to demonstrate more of the brand to each customer.

If you do use a presenter, this person should look like the company. Develop a long-term relationship with a presenter who can then start to understand your products on a deeper level and appropriately represent the brand. An exception to this is the presenter who is a celebrity. In this case, the celebrity's personality and brand equity rub off on your brand but should also align with your brand drivers.

Promotions

The purpose of promotions is to build and retain awareness once the show is over. Many companies do not integrate promotions with the rest of their marketing communications messages. Why miss an opportunity? What could be more a part of the brand experience than the shirt on your customer's back?

USING ONLINE COMMUNICATIONS TO BUILD BRAND

At one brand seminar where the participants were discussing online branding, the presenter showed one web site that he said was doing a terrible job at branding because there were no logos in sight. But for the company in question, that was on-brand—they were about relationship, not advertising. It's not just the colors, logos, and images that relate to your brand on a site, but every experience needs to echo the brand principle and personality. Thus, if your company is *friendly*, your site needs to be easily navigable. If your company is *creative*, your site needs to be so, also. If *access* is your brand principle, then you need to provide links to related sites. If you are an *educator*, your site needs to be educational, and so on.

A DAY IN THE LIFE

How all these pieces of the marketing communications puzzle come together to convey brand differs from company to company. But there are similar activities that occur at all companies. Let's take a hypothetical example and visit a day in the life of a director of marketing communications who uses integrated branding.

Jane Dough is director of marketing communications at Com.com, a small-but-growing provider of Internet-related software. It's her job to ensure that the brand becomes part of all communications, differentiating the company from dozens of competitors, as well as building that all-important relationship with the customer.

In an ordinary day, she's reviewing customer registration information to determine her best customers, reviewing ad concepts from the agency, writing articles about how to choose an Internet software company, and planning the next trade show.

At each point, brand is uppermost in her mind. For example, when reviewing the customer registration database, she's looking for commonalties between customers who are upgrading, including industry, company size, and frequency of software usage. She's also looking at the lists for potential focus group participants for some brand benchmarking she's doing.

After this, she has a number of emails and letters to answer. When she's online, she puts on her Com.com personality hat, thinking in terms of the company's brand personality—*trusted counselor*. Thus, her email answers have that tone, and she's always offering people additional resources to address their questions.

By lunch, Jane has developed a focus group list, mined her database for some new insights into her customers, and answered twenty emails. The next meeting is with her advertising agency. She will see the results of their concepting session for a new series of display ads. Before she knew about branding, Jane reviewed ad concepts for memorability and unique selling proposition. To those criteria, she now adds whether they are on brand, that is, whether they reflect and strengthen the company's brand principle, and whether they follow the tone and manner of the company's brand personality. With that at the top of her mind, Jane selects a concept for the ad agency to run with.

Her next task is to review an article written by her public relations agency on how to choose an Internet software vendor. She looks at key messages, writing style, grammar, and how much it will serve the readers—as well as whether the company's brand drivers are clearly conveyed.

Jane's last task of the day is to plan a trade show. Her department, working with sales, wants to put on a breakfast for a selected group of customers and prospects. Because the company's brand principle is *educator*, she suggests hiring an Internet guru to speak on how people can get more out of their web site from a business perspective. She recommends finding someone with a name who is trusted in the community and able to draw participants.

In every action during Jane's day, she has looked at the company's brand and found ways to strengthen it through marketing communications vehicles. Or at the very least, she has kept strengthening the company's brand in her head as one of many criteria against which to measure success. She has made sure her actions and words reflected the brand. As a result, customers of Com.com will see a seamless, consistent personality and be assured that when they do business with the company, they know what they are getting—at least from a marketing communications point of view. Jane has also made sure others in the company will more likely keep brand uppermost in their mind as they make decisions, interact with customers and prospects, and otherwise communicate with outside audiences. She's a true brand advocate and an effective brand manager as a result.

15 The Digital Age: A Brand's Best Friend—or Worst Enemy?

WHAT YOU NEED TO KNOW ABOUT BRANDING WITH NEW TECHNOLOGIES

Have the changes in communications brought about by web technologies altered the relationship between brands and customers? Yes *and* no.

Web users are assailed by banners and "content ads" on almost every page they visit. Scores of cable channel and portal brands vie for mind share. Add to this electronic kiosks, in-air video infomercials, and the explosion of magazines and zines made possible by desktop publishing, and you have more than information overload: you have information paralysis. But because of an integrated brand's ability to create and maintain distinctiveness, companies and products that practice integrated branding stand out in a noisy electronic crowd.

Newmarket Networks' Tom Lix equates web site creation to other brand extensions. His firm holds the exclusive web license for National Public Radio shows including "Car Talk," "The Savvy Traveler," and "Whad'Ya Know." Lix says, "The key is to offer something that takes advantage of an existing name by giving customers something related, yet extra."[2] On the "Car Talk" site, web users can find information about the show and audio from previous broadcasts, plus trivia contests and a "virtual dope slap" (an animated postcard you can send to someone who did something stupid). Lix is using the web to differentiate brands in ways that reinforce basic product appeal and keep customers coming back for more. For example, the virtual dope slap reinforces the fun experience listeners get from their weekly Saturday morning "Car Talk" installment. The web can give audiences context for company and product brand relationships and a way to interact without being overloaded.

Web technologies represent at least three challenges for brand managers. One is the dispersion of viewer attention over so many different media. How can a small company with revenues of less than $100 million compete across so many media against multinationals?

A second problem with online technology is that it raises your customers' expectations for *real-time* interaction. In terms of new product introductions this can be an advantage or a company killer. The web makes it very easy to release a new product—especially if it is electronic in nature, such as software. You don't need boxes or trucks or shelf space, just the right e-commerce system. In fact, Amazon.com has expanded its product offerings from books to music with much less time and investment than a traditional retailer would have had to make.

E-commerce also softens the line between existing product versions and new versions. In software circles this is known as *dribbleware*. The problem with dribbleware and many electronic brand extensions is that inappropriate offerings have the ability to water down the brand's value in a customer's mind. The web reduces the length of time it takes between creating a product and getting it to market while reducing the costs of getting to market as well.

Integrated brands are able to resist some competitive onslaughts from reduced cycle time because of customer and reseller loyalty. Hewlett-Packard's LaserJet printer line has often been later to market with new features than competitors, yet it has held market share and its price premium through the strength of its quality, reliability, and durability brand promise.

The web is also a viable channel for the purchase of products and services. Customers who view the web as a way to buy will be frustrated with brands that don't offer either electronic commerce or a list of dealers who sell online.

On the other side, because the web makes it easier to be opportunistic, a brand may be tempted to sell whatever it can, without regard to its impact on brand equity. This is why many strong consumer brands have moved into web commerce very slowly and carefully, to ensure that customers receive the same brand experience from all sources.

This watering down effect often happens to companies who license their brand properties. These are brand elements that help boost the sale of an unrelated product. One popular licensable property is Mickey Mouse. In Kevin Lane Keller's excellent *Strategic Brand Management*, he describes how the Walt Disney Company discovered that its "characters were on so many products and marketed in so many ways that it was difficult to understand how or why many of the decisions had been made in the first place."[3] He goes on to say, "Consumers reported that they resented the large number of endorsements because they felt that they had a special, personal relationship with the characters and with Disney that should not be handled so carelessly."[4]

Another problem with real-time interaction afforded by the web is that it challenges the company to fulfill its role as a "real" personality. This means on the plus side that this is the best vehicle ever for conveying brand attributes. But, since interactions between the web site user and your web site happen within seconds, the user will expect faster response and a deepening relationship over time. The challenge for web masters and brand managers is how to convey brand when users expect to have an interactive dialogue. Amazon.com uses interactivity as a method for furthering the customer relationship and improving the quality of its offerings. Jeff Bezos, founder and CEO of Amazon.com, says: "If we've chosen poorly—if, say, there's a stupid jazz album on our list—we will get so much hate mail within such a short period of time that we'll [use the] feedback, and it will be perfect."[5]

A third is the potential to blur company focus through the lure of digital products. Although electronic media represent a break-through in communications and distribution, they will not take the place of other channels. In other words, a web site is not a new business, just a way to enhance existing business. It is easy for companies to get confused between the web as channel and web as product. Your web activities do not exist outside the scope of the brand. According to Nathan Shedroff, chief creative officer at Vivid Studios in San Francisco, "The key is to take brand attributes and build them into the experience of your site (the structure, the purpose, the messages, the content and the interactivity)."[6]

Finally, the web allows any brand, from a basement-based research service to a coin collecting store, to go global at the flick of the switch. Part of the challenge of global brand managers in the next decade will be determining how to extend the digital brand experience in a way that is relevant to potential customers throughout the world. This could be a great opportunity for small and medium-sized businesses to expand into national and international markets with very little overhead while challenging the existing leaders in the offline world. In 1997 when Barnes & Noble went online with its commerce site, many people predicted the end of Amazon.com. Instead Amazon actually grew faster in dollar and percentage terms than Barnes & Noble. Bezos explains, "I think the answer is that the consumer experience on the Internet matters. And the reason is the word of mouth is so powerful online that if you do a great job of servicing your customers and providing them with the best possible service, you'll turn these people into evangelists, and they will help you grow the business."[7]

SOME BRAND BUILDING WEB SITE EXAMPLES

Kodak encourages web visitors to create and send postcards based on digital images supplied by the company (see figure 15.1). This is a way to differentiate by creating an additional use for the company's main product, photographs.

Southern California Edison serves its residents with an online magazine called edison@home, which provides ideas and ways to save money on anything electrical related to a home. It includes "comprehensive home appliance and energy use information to tips on moving or conserving water with outdoor landscaping....In *Home Interiors*, you'll learn more about how you can better manage energy in every room of your home, and get valuable energy savings tips, and information on moving, setting up a home office and home safety."[8]

ELECTRONIC CONTENT AND BRANDING

In addition to e-commerce, the web may be best suited to information gathering and dissemination activities such as sponsored content, content aggregation, and surveys, as well as provide a new place for face-to-face interactions with customers.

Sponsored Content

Sponsored content hearkens back to the early days of live television when companies sponsored and produced weekly shows. This tradition is still carried on today by a few companies such as Hallmark. Sponsored content is the idea of giving your audience non-product-specific information that they need or want that bears some relationship to your brand. If done correctly, the process deepens an audience's emotional and rational appreciation of your brand.

An example of sponsored content is the festivals.com site managed by RSL Interactive. Festivals.com has listings and related information about

Figure 15.1
The Kodak Web Site

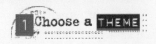
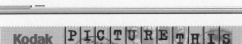

Kodak ⌜P⌝⌜I⌝⌜C⌝⌜T⌝⌜U⌝⌜R⌝⌜E⌝⌜T⌝⌜H⌝⌜I⌝⌜S⌝   TAKE PICTURES. FURTHER.™

Send Multimedia PostCARDS
in a FLASH

1 Choose a THEME

3rd: CREATE your Card

Miss You

. **Use your own picture!**
Register, or sign in if
you've done this before.

**Create postcards
using your own
pictures!**
Kodak.com membership
is required; Register
Now (it's FREE!). Or
Sign In if you've already
registered.

. **World Series**
. **Miniature Marvels**
. **NASA Mission Photos**
. **Lilith Fair**
. For Fathers
. Perfect Pairs
. Mother's Moments
. Beautiful Creatures
. Color in Bloom
. Digital Dreams
. Fresh Faces
. Great Cities
. Natural Wonders
. Night Lights
. Walls and Windows

Don't forget to read our tips on How to Prepare your
Pictures.

For more info about sending and receiving cards,
see Picture This Tips.

Once you've created a card or two, check out our
high-resolution Sample Digital Pictures .

OR . Multimedia Postcards
(requires Shockwave,
get it here)

Home | Find | Products | Support | Shop | Member Services |

🖅 Done

🅰 Start   🎜 CD Player   W Microsoft Word   📧 Inbox - Microsoft Outlook   🖅 KOD

Source: Reprinted with the permission of Eastman Kodak Company. Courtesy © Eastman Kodak
Company, 1994–1998.

more than twenty thousand festivals of all types in many parts of the world. Festival.com's sponsors provide information that their potential customers are looking for while creating goodwill and brand identity related to the information for themselves. According to Jim Shanklin, chief operating officer at RSL, "Sponsored content will be one of the predominant ways of using the Internet to build brand awareness. It allows companies to become leaders in their category by becoming a valuable information resource."

Another example of sponsored content is the Butterball Turkey site (www.butterball.com), which the Butterball Turkey Company uses to en hance its position as the number-one turkey brand. Butterball uses the site to educate its customers about the speed and ease of turkey preparation. It helps customers extend product usage throughout the year through recipes that feature new ways to use turkey in American cui sine —including recipes that tie the concept of "fast and easy" to turkey. These are two ideas that people don't associate with fresh turkey products but that could have a big impact on the company's bottom line.

Between 1995 and the beginning of 1998, Butterball provided assistance to more than 1 million cybercooks worldwide. "Last Thanksgiving season, the site received more than 5 million hits, nearly 2 million during Thanksgiving week alone," explains Jean Schneller, director of Butterball Turkey Talk-Line™.[9] Butterball also uses "push" technology, by providing an emailed turkey newsletter to interested readers. This second-step interaction creates an opportunity to extend the Butterball brand relationship into the home in a different way. This e-mail group currently has more than five thousand subscribers.

Hot Butterball Recipes for the Grill

Searching for new recipes to add sizzle to your barbecue menu? Look no further! Butterball offers a selection of mouth-watering grilling recipes ideal for any occasion, along with some light and delicious sandwich and salad recipes perfect for picnics. Summer may not last long, but the delicious ways to enjoy Butterball Turkey last all year round.

Butterball Grilling Recipes

- Grilled Teriyaki Turkey and Vegetables
- Grilled Jalapeño Turkey Burgers
- Grilled Citrus-Curry Turkey Cutlets with Cucumber Yogurt Sauce
- Grilled Tex-Mex Turkey Kabobs
- Skewered Turkey Satay on the Grill with Peanut Dipping Sauce

- Grilled Barbecue Turkey Burgers
- Sweet Red Pepper Sauce for Grilled Turkey Picnic Patties
- Caribbean Grilled Turkey
- Italian Garden Style Grilled Turkey Medallion Kabobs
- Barbecue Turkey Roast with Santa Fe Sauce
- Grilled Turkey with Cilantro Salsa
- Grilled Turkey Italian Sausage

Cool and Delicious
- Dillicious Turkey Sandwich
- Turkey Tea Sandwiches
- Turkey al Fresco on Mixed Greens

Super Easy Sandwiches and Salads
- Turkey Bacon Sandwich
- Turkey Super Sub Sandwich
- Zesty Turkey Breast Sandwich
- Cool and Easy Turkey Salad (Excerpted from the Butterball Turkey web site)

Content Aggregation

Content aggregation takes advantage of the ability of a web site to offer easy access to and use of other companies' services. The term, coined by Yahoo cofounder Jerry Yang, describes Yahoo's ability to provide "an independent, efficient and friendly medium to take advantage of other companies' content and services."[10] This something extra that the web provides in this case is a blending of multiple brands under the Yahoo experience. Can a brand do this in a way that doesn't dilute its focus? Yahoo COO Jeffrey Mallett says, "We're the executive producers. We're not obligated to produce or distribute anything we don't think is in the best interest of users."[11]

DATABASE MARKETING

The other important impact of the digital age on brand is the use of large, powerful databases as a way to manage the customer relationship. The creation of massive data warehouses is a significant step toward deepening relationships with each customer. The ability to access a central file on customer style, likes, and dislikes can allow relationships to develop as customers feel better served.

Some people claim that using this type of knowledge is not real relationship building, just another example of companies becoming too powerful and knowing too much. But it's actually like using notes and reminders on a calendar to flag a friend's birthday or other special occasion. Customer databases perform the same function—augmenting your knowledge so that you can better represent the brand.

To maintain your credibility with customers, don't collect customer data that you don't need or sell information to other interested parties without permission. The sanctity of the relationship between brand and customer should be guarded as carefully as you guard your personal relationships.

Databases can help build the brand in a number of ways. They can provide you with a map of the entire customer experience and conversation over time. This will allow you to determine what level of loyalty the customer feels toward the brand. What is the frequency of customer contact? Does the customer have a pattern of interaction that would allow you to serve him or her better? Have all experiences been good? Did the customer get to experience brand drivers in action? Did you do something above and beyond the call of duty for the customer? How many negative experiences occurred? How were they resolved?

Databases are already a powerful force in brand development. In Apple Computer's *Strategies for Building Digital Brands*, the authors cite the following statistic: "In 1994, Proctor & Gamble reported that it had over 250 unique 800 telephone numbers, each affixed to one of its brands. These numbers generated over 6.2 million telephone calls from consumers in that year. The teleservice representative handling the phone calls, aided by a powerful help desks system that contains answers to thousands of questions, captured not only the name and address of the caller but also four or five choice questions."[12]

One aspect of web surfing, the practice by web site publishers of putting cookies (web site additions that record information regarding your visit to a site) on a viewer's machine, has come under close scrutiny by the public. As part of the trust you build with customers, ask for permission prior to installing cookies and then explicitly state what the cookies will be used for. Southern California Edison puts a cookie use notice directly on its home page that says: "Our cookie isn't nosey. We're using a cookie to personalize graphics only. It does not record data. If you get a cookie warning, please ignore it, or use the preferences file on your browser to turn it off. Thank you."

VOICE MAIL AND EMAIL

Voice mail and email have the capacity to build up or tear down the brand.

Voice mail allows customers to leave more comprehensive messages, more quickly than ever before. It also allows customers to leave messages any time of day or night and doesn't require the employee to be physically present to pick up their messages.

However, improperly used voice mail has several negative implications for the brand. First, it is often used by both companies and individuals as a way not to talk to people directly. There is nothing that hurts the brand relationship more quickly than getting an electronic voice rather than a human one during business hours. It is worth a company's investment to have a living person on the other end of the customer's phone line.

The other potential negative of voice mail is that people use it to leave confidential or negative messages that they would never put down in writing. Voice mail captures the message for all of posterity.

Email also has the advantage of being very convenient for the employee. If it is too convenient, it too can detract from the customer relationship by never encouraging a face-to-face encounter. As with voice mail, people will write things in email that they would never put on company letterhead. Yet customers view email as coming from the brand or company, not just from the individual. This even applies to such things as typos and poor grammar—would you trust your business to a brand that is sloppy or can't spell? Create a voice mail and email policy, complete with email templates, that drives good brand communications.

One company, whose brand principle is *collaboration* and personality is *competent, energetic,* and *responsive,* uses the following as one of its email templates:

Dear   Name,

Thank you for the update on the progress of the Good Fix project. It sounds as if the first two steps are working toward the solution we developed together. I will work on steps three and four, as you suggested, and will keep you informed when I have new ideas for review. Please let me know if I can be of further assistance.

Looking to the future, the web and the technologies that follow will allow brands to become increasingly rewarding, one-on-one experiences for customers. Companies should watch for new technologies that will further enhance the relationship with customers. There is already webbased research that can be sent out to gather customer feedback, precisely and at a low cost. As video becomes commonplace in the office, we will see the customer and the brand take one more step closer to each other.

For the latest information on integrated branding on the web, go to www.parkerlepla.com.

NOTES

1. Bruce Haring, "Site Scramble To Be Your Gateway" (August 3, 1998), USA Today web site: http://usatoday.com/life/cyber/tech/.

2. Tom Lix, *Computerworld* (April 13, 1998), p. 41.

3. Reprinted with the permission of The Free Press, a Division of Simon & Schuster, Inc. from *Strategic Brand Management: New Approaches to Creating and Evaluating Brand Equity* by Jean-Noel Kapferer. Copyright © 1992 by Les Editions d'Organisation. Translated by Philip Gibbs. First published in the English language in 1992 by Kogan Page Ltd., p. 375.

4. Reprinted with the permission of The Free Press, a Division of Simon & Schuster, Inc. from *Strategic Brand Management: New Approaches to Creating and Evaluating Brand Equity* by Jean-Noel Kapferer. Copyright © 1992 by Les Editions d'Organisation. Translated by Philip Gibbs. First published in the English language in 1992 by Kogan Page Ltd., p. 376.

5. Kathleen Doler, "Interview: Jeff Bezos, Founder and CEO of Amazon.com Inc.," *Upside* (September 1998), p. 76.

6. Nathan Shedroff, *Online Branding*, NewMedia.com (July 1998), p. 28.

7. Kathleen Doler, "Interview: Jeff Bezos, Founder and CEO of Amazon.com Inc.," *Upside* (September 1998), p. 76.

8. Southern California Edison web site: http://www.edisonhome.com.

9. Butterball Turkey web site: http://www.butterball.com.

10. Jonathan Littman, Yahoo web site: http://www.yahoo.com.

11. Yahoo web site: http://www.yahoo.com.

12. Apple Computer, *Strategies for Building Digital Brands*, p. 72.

16 Using Brand to Clear the Path to an IPO and Beyond

Recipe for a sizzling initial public offering: Take one profitable company. Add a highly recognizable brand. . .and watch IPO boil.[1]
—David Kaufman, *Fortune*, March 18, 1996

If there is one area of a company's activity that can immediately benefit from integrated branding, it is investor relations. Most companies doing an initial public offering (IPO) are smaller and don't have as much name recognition as long-time public companies. Therefore, the pre-IPO company is most in need of brand's ability to bring focus to creating awareness and positive relationships. A strong brand can broaden a company's appeal with both the strategic and the calculating institutional investor and the individual who buys for emotional reasons—because it provides strong rational and emotional reasons for buying.

Brand experts David A. Aaker and Robert Jacobson discovered a positive correlation between brand equity and stock return in a study on thirty-four stocks between 1989 and 1992. Firms who experienced the largest gains in brand equity saw their stock return average 30 percent. Firms with the largest loss in brand equity saw stock returns average −10 percent.

What are the implications for investor relations programs and the global brand manager?

First, there is a strong financial incentive to create a high level of brand equity, especially for companies that are going to do an IPO in the near future. Strong brand equity properly conveyed to prospective investors will result in a higher initial offering price.

Second, companies with small capitalization (under $1 billion) are notorious for experiencing wide stock swings. These swings are caused by many factors, most of which relate to the investor's understanding of the company as well as the total number of investors interested in the brand. A strong brand will have both a positive effect on demand and serve to quell rumors caused by the typical investor's penchant to trade on insufficient or inaccurate information.

Brand makes a stock more attractive to investors buying for strategic or fundamental reasons as well. A brand-driven company is more clearly focused on its own strengths and is typically more consistent at communicating them. This process creates a simpler story for the financial marketplace, where brokers and analysts have less and less time to spend with each company. With the Internet's information gathering capabilities, a focused message can shine through to individual investors as well.

Because of the visionary and emotional qualities of effective brand principles, companies that have a well-crafted brand principle have placed a driver at the root of their actions that adds sexiness to their investment profile. The term *sexiness*, as used by financial types, means a company or product generates excitement, through either a new way of doing things or a unique approach to an existing market. These are both part of a brand principle's criteria.

For example, Lucent Technologies came out with a focused messaging campaign just prior to being spun off from AT&T. The campaign talked about the value and types of inventions that had come out of this Bell Labs division of AT&T over the decades. It established brand distinctiveness around "brain trust" and "inventiveness." In fact, the market got so excited that *USA Today* featured analysts recommending a "buy" on the stock even before it went public.

Brand personality and associations also help drive the emotional side of the brand. People will invest in a company such as Ben & Jerry's because they like the quirkiness of the company's product offerings or the way the company searched for a new CEO through an essay contest open to anyone who cared to enter. Coca-Cola has cultivated a friendly and familiar brand image that makes its stock a *comfortable* buy. People associate Berkshire Hathaway with the investment style and philosophy of Warren Buffett.

Companies that practice integrated branding also score more highly on the critical management team analyses performed by financial analysts. Most financial analysts say that their evaluation of a management team represents 50 percent of their valuation of an IPO. Yet management cohesiveness and management depth are typically two of the greatest weaknesses of smaller companies. Creating a brand focus around a brand principle or personality (or both) gives small companies a head start with the financial markets because it gives these companies a jump in creating management cohesiveness.

Brand drivers are simple enough that management can keep them in the top of their mind when speaking with analysts and, more importantly, when making decisions that will have potential impact on stock price. Companies that go through a brand process say that the most important up-front benefit was getting everyone in the company on the same page.

Regionality is often a positive brand attribute for investors. Investors buy what they know. In its "Rodeo Grandmas" commercials, Washington Mutual, a Northwest-based savings and loan, highlights its locally owned status by showing rodeo grandmas chasing the invaders (riding a stage coach to symbolize one of its Californian competitors) out of town with guns blazing.

One of the best sources of investors for small-cap stocks is the immediate region around company headquarters. Most companies receive more attention in their own region from the media or from word of mouth started by people who do business with them, including suppliers, service companies, and the government, than outside their region. Companies also tend to do more advertising or community support programs in their local area. The depth of prospective investor awareness about a company, its strengths, and its personality is also greater in its local area.

Regionality is not a substitute for a strong brand, however. What this means is that two companies that have relatively equal-quality products and distribution (say, two coffee companies in the Seattle region) that do a good job of courting local investors will have very different IPO and stock volatility experiences based on the difference in their brand strength. The one with the stronger brand will be able to go public at a higher price, experience less volatility, and register larger trading volumes.

"THE STREET" CAN BE A DANGEROUS PLACE FOR BRAND

Although strong brands command higher share prices and have less volatility than others, Wall Street does not understand how integrated brands are built and therefore can suggest actions or messages that may harm your brand. The problem with financial analysts, investment bankers, and large investors is that they often feel it is their place to give advice on how a company should conduct its business as well as how it should communicate. Even worse, companies often take their advice unquestioningly. This has historically led to actions that are at odds with driving brand value. Such actions as making leveraged buyouts, breaking conglomerates into smaller pieces, creating conglomerates from smaller pieces, and even repurchasing stock through cashiering assets may all look like the way to maximize profits for shareholders but actually have the power to cripple a brand.

A recent case in point is Sara Lee, which is selling many of its core assets including its hog slaughtering and textile businesses and possibly its bakeries and meat processing units. The reason? To increase profits and share price. According to Roger Lowenstein in his "Intrinsic Value" column of *The Wall Street Journal*, "Sara Lee will be a virtual company, putting its virtual name on things it doesn't make. Sara Lee will be the brand alone, the label without the shirt."[2]

Although the financial aspect of company operations cannot be ignored, it should not be put in the driver's seat in place of the brand. It is hard to just say no to your financial partners, but past history suggests that sometimes you should at least just say maybe.

INTEGRATING BRAND INTO IR

How can you integrate brand into your investor relations (IR) program? By using investor relations as one more brand conveyor. Here are some ways of incorporating brand throughout your investor relations program.

Reporting Structure

The surest way to integrate brand into IR is through your reporting structure. All company departments responsible for external messaging need to report indirectly to your global brand manager. By making your IR team an indirect report to your brand manager, you ensure continuity in message and action. For instance, if one of your brand values was "community" and your IR department began a program of forcing shareholders with less than one hundred shares either to buy more or to sell their shares, your actions as a company would not be supporting your brand. Your brand manager or the brand manager's staff should also be involved in general financial messaging (along with IR professionals and the CFO, of course) and have review input into presentations and the annual report.

Integration of IR Messages and Collateral Material with Marketing Communications

Many companies relegate IR messaging and strategy to the CFO or abandon it altogether to their securities lawyers and investment bankers. This is most often true prior to the first IPO, where the company is depending on the expertise of an investment banker to "do the deal." Most CEOs and management teams are unfamiliar with the IPO process, so they tend to abdicate their position—just when it is most critical to the process. This will almost guarantee that your IR messages will differ from other marketing messages, will not communicate your brand, and will confuse customers. This is not to dismiss the critical role that CFOs, investment bankers, and attorneys play in the IR process, but to point out that effective IR messaging is a customer-relationship-building process, and so is a branding process. In an integrated brand, a company's roadshow, analyst presentations, quarterly reports, earnings news releases, annual reports, and annual meetings should all convey the distinct aspects of a company's strengths, principle, and personality, as well as tell the company story.

Attracting and Retaining Investors throughout the Company's Life Cycle

Conventional wisdom is that investors (whether individuals, a mutual fund, or a pension plan) can be broken up into categories such as aggressive/high-growth, value, conservative, and income. What type of investor each is may depend on the objectives of the mutual fund or the age of the individual investor.

Branded IR, however, turns all investors into "buy and holders." IR done with a sense of the brand will attract more investors who are interested in a long-term relationship with the company. If an investor really likes a company's direction and actions, he or she will be more likely to continue to relate to the company's vision over time. This means that the investor may be more likely to accept the risk associated with a young start-up and continue to be comfortable with a company's direction as it becomes a stable performer.

For example, pasta company Annie's Homegrown did a direct offering in 1995 over the Internet to attract the same people as investors who are customers of its brand.[3] On the home page of the web site the company says: "We think that a small company can make a big difference on the planet. That's why we support Economic Democracy—in short, the idea that people take part in owning the companies whose products they buy."

These shareholders become loyal supporters of the company and further its mission. One of the company's unique programs is that it offers boxes of its products wholesale for charitable giving. Of Annie's Homegrown's twenty-five hundred shareholders, more than seven hundred gave boxes of product in 1997 to charitable organizations.

The Annual Report

The annual report is one of the great underused tools of a publicly held company. In terms of time spent by the executive staff and dollars allocated, annual reports are one of the major marketing pieces produced each year. Yet corporations rarely use them as an opportunity to enhance the relationship between them and their shareholders. With the advent of the web, the distribution of the annual report has grown to many times its previous level, as prospective customers, suppliers, the media, and alliance partners use it as a tool to get to know your company. In addition to talking about company financials and product strategies, the annual report is a great place to present the basics of what the company stands for (its mission and values), its unique approach to its mission (the brand principle), its face and voice (its personality), and its story. The annual report then becomes a way to bring newcomers into the brand message of your company.

Microsoft did this in a strong way in its 1997 annual report. Using the brand colors and elements from its brand toolbox, the annual report's theme was all based on the brand principle of *access*, to the point where the first headline read, "Microsoft is all about creating access." Subsequent headlines explained how access benefited each audience group, from IT professionals to home-based-business owners.

Investment Banker Push-Back

Be willing to rock the boat a little bit with investment bankers. Don't let them change your presentation to the point where it no longer shows the advantages of your brand. Remember that a successful IPO is not only about the initial offering price but also about where the stock goes afterward. Investment bankers are there to provide an exit strategy to original investors and an access point for additional capital to fund growth. They want you to do well, but their level of interest in the market for your stock wanes after capitalization. That means you need to take the reins in your hands from the beginning and consciously determine which shareholders, which actions, and which messages will be best for long-term company success.

Brand Valuation

If you do your job well, analysts will begin to mention and value your brand or brands as one critical component of your company's future earnings potential. Although U.S. Generally Accepted Accounting Principles (GAAP) does not allow brand equity on the balance sheet, analysts can and do figure a strong brand presence into a company's earnings potential. Your brand also becomes a factor they use when predicting a company's success in new product launches and market share growth.

NOTES

1. David Kaufman, "The IPO from Another Planet," *Fortune* (March 18, 1996), p. 19 or http://www.pathfinder.com/fortune/magazine/1996/960318/newstrends3.html.

2. Roger Lowenstein, "Intrinsic Value, Remember When Companies Made Things," *The Wall Street Journal* (September 18, 1997), p. C1.

3. Annie's Homegrown web site: http://www.annies.com.

17 Integrated Branding for Technology Companies

> One of the things that is very scary is technology-driven companies competing principally on price—offering constantly faster products with more features for less money. Few are out building an identity and relationship with customers.
> —Doss Struse, CEO, Research International USA

Branding technology products and services is different from branding anything else—but not because customers are somehow different in this market. Technology products are unique as a result of

- the rate of change demanded of technology brand leaders.
- the high degree of integration among many companies' products, hence brand overlap.
- the fact that standards often dictate which brands win.
- the distance between users and purchasers, resulting in a more detached brand experience.
- the types of people running technology companies.

THE FAST PACE OF INNOVATION

Those of us who have lived through the last half of the twentieth century are already more used to change than our parents or grandparents ever were. We have had the personal computer in the office for only eighteen years, and voice mail, email, and the Internet are very late arrivals in the scheme of things. However, experts tell us that the next twenty years will see an even greater explosion in technological and scientific breakthroughs. If Moore's law (that computer power doubles every eighteen months) continues to hold true, "by 2020 microprocessors will be as cheap and plentiful as scrap paper, scattered by the millions into the environment, allowing us to place intelligent systems everywhere. This will change everything around us, including the nature of commerce, the wealth of nations, and the way we communicate, work, play and live."[1]

Technology products and services are driving this change. They are creating new business categories seemingly every week, and customers are hard pressed to catch up to last year's innovations, much less last week's. In this environment, as soon as a company purchases a computer, it is out of date.

One big challenge for a technology brand is to *institutionalize change without adversely affecting the customer relationship*. The test for technology brands in the twenty-first century will be to maintain the meaning of their brands while morphing into wholly new products.

A great example of this change process is companies working in computer security. Conceivably, a company could have started by offering a product for data encryption and authentication and as a result of market forces moved (either willingly or unwillingly) into virtual private networks, firewalls, or the new breed of content security products, which protect companies from malicious content. Even focused, niche categories, such as content security, are evolving into other things. Content Technologies' product MIMEsweeper, for example, started as a way to *enhance antivirus programs* but has now moved into *protecting companies from legal liability* resulting from inappropriate employee email by filtering selected words and attaching disclaimers to each email message.

Although the organization and brand drivers outlined in this book will provide the calm center in the technology storms moving through the business world, there is a great risk that as a company's products and services change, management will be tempted to forget about its brand focus. This is why benchmarking brand awareness and analyzing customer interactions become so important. This type of information will demonstrate and reinforce to management what parts of their brand promise work.

Another important difference between technology products and those of other industries is the degree to which they must function as part of a larger system. This means that a brand's fate is often tied to outside factors, such as the operating system the product runs on. It also means that the customer perceives entire systems as the brand experience, rather than the discrete products that make up the system.

With many companies there is a disconnect between the end users and the brand experience, because the product's ultimate users and purchasers are often different people. That's why it's important to pay close attention to all customer segments that should be aware of you— from information technology managers to departmental power users. How do you determine whether the end user is a critical part of your brand focus? Use the guidelines that follow to make the determination.

How often do end users know they are using the product? If it is weekly or more often, they will probably have an opinion on the product and could be considered power users. This means that they have the power to knock out your product and replace it with a more strongly branded product; hence they share the brand relationship with IT.

What do you do if a power user's relationship with you is fairly limited? It is your job to use brand conveyors, such as public relations, advertising, and direct mail, and brand events, such as company-sponsored user groups, to enhance your relationship with power users. INTERLINQ, a leading provider of mortgage processing software, has a brand principle of *partner*. The company enjoys very high customer retention and customer loyalty statistics—which are partly due to an annual users group meeting that features ways to improve their mortgage processing systems and creates a close, personal bond between the company and the brand.

Because of the systems nature of high-technology products, savvy brand managers know that the brand experience extends beyond the customer to alliance partners. A good example of this extended brand is demonstrated by Microsoft. "Our hardware and software vendors are completely necessary for us to deliver our solutions,"[2] explains Gregory Maffei, CFO of Microsoft Corporation. Microsoft relies on its fourthousand-person software developer network, fifty thousand companies that distribute Microsoft software, and 4.3 million Windows developers. "We are only a small piece of the value chain," adds Maffei.

This is particularly true of products that stay in the background and run transparently on the desktop. So every technology company must first determine its level of importance in the total solution. Are you a greater part of the solution than customers and alliance partners give you credit for? If so, how do you demonstrate this through your brand?

You may be one step further removed from the customer if you are an original equipment manufacturer (OEM). In an OEM relationship, other manufacturers take your product and put their name on it. OEMs frequently decide that the only place they need awareness is with their direct customers. The problem with this approach is that it builds awareness only with a limited market and puts no pressure on the system integrator to use your component. Lack of broad market awareness by your final users puts all of the cards in someone else's hands and tends to dampen pricing. In addition to ingredient branding, a way to get around this is through becoming a market opinion leader and publicizing well-known case studies of product users in trade or business magazines.

Whether the product is invisible (as in the case of microprocessors), OEMed, or sold through a reseller, your objective is the same. You must find a way to develop a strong relationship with your customers. If you are successful, the relationship will create demand, increase sales, and put pressure on additional manufacturers or system integrators to use your product, giving you a better bargaining position and potentially higher margins.

It's also important to establish stronger relationships with your customers so that they understand what role you play in the entire system. When something goes wrong with the system, how much of the blame does your product deserve? How much does it get? Market leaders will try to solve a customer's problem whether their product is responsible for it or not.

THE PATH-DEPENDENT FACTOR

One of the dangers and opportunities that technology companies will continue to face is path dependency.[3] This theory says that technology products don't necessarily succeed because they are the best solution on the market. It suggests that a technology that the market perceives to be superior will attract a critical mass of users. Because so many people use it, it becomes a standard and attracts even more users. Examples of this phenomenon include the QWERTY positioning of typewriter keys, VHS videocassettes, and Windows. Although Windows has now equaled or surpassed Apple's Macintosh in many areas, it was not nearly as friendly an operating system for the first ten years or so of its life. Windows achieved superiority because it became the corporate standard and because Microsoft had the ability to court important software developers while providing excellent business software programs of its own.

From a technology branding point of view, path dependence means that you must expand your brand alliances to include all players who are likely to provide the critical path for a new technology. It also means that more than in other industries, you must keep a careful watch for structural changes in the marketplace. This is a service that global brand managers, with their focus on benchmarking and trends, can bring to the company. This method of institutionalizing flexibility can be seen in Microsoft's impressive response to the rise of the Internet, when it changed its focus from applications to the Internet, seemingly overnight.

TECHNOLOGY PEOPLE ARE DIFFERENT

Another difference found among high-technology companies is that leaders tend to be engineers and/or technophiles. People who run technology companies really get excited by new ideas, new ways of doing things, and new technologies. This is great for bringing innovation into the boardroom. However, it tends to take the focus away from the relationship with the customer and put it on short-lived technological advantages.

If a first product is successful, this behavior is reinforced and the company may go down the path to becoming a commodity manufacturer because it never differentiates beyond features. Or a technology focus may cause a company that has done a good job of bringing products to market in a certain area never to pinpoint the basis for its success with customers.

An example of this is Adobe Systems Inc. Adobe is the publisher of the well-regarded PageMaker and PhotoShop products. The company's products make personal computers into creative and publishing tools for such markets as graphic designers and in-house newsletter editors. Whereas other companies (such as Xerox) have focused their skills and messages, Adobe has not clearly represented its strengths through a comprehensive brand. Scott Thrum, a staff reporter for *The Wall Street Journal*, notes, "Today the World Wide Web has set off a global explosion of electronic publishing, making Adobe's vision more prescient than ever. But instead of surfing a growth wave, Adobe seems to be missing the boat."[4] Although Adobe has created a successful company, it has spent its sixteen-year history focusing on creating great products but without a strong brand focus.

What should a high-technology brand do differently than others? A Ziff-Davis High Tech Branding Study rated high-technology brands on the basis of researcher-defined factors.[5] The study presented basics that each brand must have and suggested directions for further differentiation of brand principles and personality. It concluded that purchase factors for technology products included many intangible factors, or combined tangible/intangible factors in the purchase decision. These key purchase factors included a progressive brand, a brand others try to imitate, a brand you respect, dedicated to making your business successful, technology leaders, good reputation for service and support, products that are worth the money, products that are fun to use, and a company that stands behind its customers.

You should add to this list locating and creating relationships with end users, standing out from the crowd through the use of associations and reseller/customer service, institutionalizing change, and hedging your technology standards bet. Although integrating the technology brand is a more complex process than nontechnology branding, it offers companies the best chance to maintain customer loyalty and keep focused in a very difficult business environment.

NOTES

1. Michio Kaku, *Visions* (New York: Doubleday, 1997), p. 14.

2. Washington Software Alliance, *NewsBytes* (July 1998), XII, no. 7, p. 4.

3. Peter Passall, "Why the Best Doesn't Always Win," *The New York Times Magazine* (May 5, 1996), p. 61.

4. Scott Thrum, "Once a Master of Fine Print, Adobe Slipped," *The Wall Street Journal* (August 27, 1998), p. B1.

5. ZD High-Tech Branding Study, conducted by IntelliQuest on behalf of ZiffDavis (March 1998), http://www.ziffdavis.com.

18 Comparing Well-Known Brand Models to Integrated Branding

The map is not the territory.[1]
—Alfred Korzybski, scholar and philosopher of language

Since people's definitions of brand often differ, it's difficult to compare brand models. The purpose here is to try to give those of you who have tried to understand different branding systems an apples-to-apples comparison. All of the models cited here are important contributions to the practice of modern branding.

The Integrated Brand Model differs from others in several ways. First, it is about integrating brand into every activity of the company in a deliberate and disciplined way—becoming a brand-driven company. This takes brand out of the realm of marketing, advertising, or design and places it in the company's strategic mainstream. Brand is not an image or bill of goods forced on the customer like some kind of mass hypnosis that causes them to shell out more cash for brand names. The quality of your brand direction and drivers, the consistency of your messages, and the skill with which employees relate to customers are where the power of brand shines through.

Second, brand is determined by the intersection of company strengths and what customers value—this two-sided focus means that what is really at the heart of the brand is the relationship between the brand and the customer. This is in counterpoint to those who look solely at company strengths or, on the other hand, those who base brand only on what customers say they want.

A third way in which the Integrated Brand Model differs is that it enables employees to use easy-to-understand drivers to create a rich, differentiating, and holistic customer experience. For example, the brand principle is an explicit agreement among all company employees as to how they will make decisions to build the brand. This takes brand out of the hands of the high priests and gives it to the people who can use it most. Brand does not need to be ambiguous or mysterious to be rich, deep, and effective.

Without a brand principle, a common focus is unlikely. The only exceptions are in those cases in which the brand has unconsciously been in existence for many decades and gradually all departments have come around to understanding and making decisions based on it. Even then, an unconscious brand is much more vulnerable to the whims of individuals or groups within a company (such as the decision to eliminate the RCA dog as an association in the early 1980s after eight decades of investment—a decision later revoked). The other exception occurs when a strong management team guides the organization into brand consciousness. Even then, if employees on the line had clear brand drivers, they would benefit from the clearer direction provided by them.

Fourth, in this model, the brand is created by experts—the people who live it everyday—company movers and shakers. Brand is not something brought in from outside consultants; it is something that is revealed from within the company.

The focus of integrated branding is to build solid, nearly unbreakable customer relationships. It does this by providing customers with the things they value about a brand (mission, principle), a shared perspectives on the world (values), a shared history (story), and personality- and sense-related cues (associations). These same drivers serve a second function of keeping employees focused on creating that value day in and day out. Solid customer relationships result in significant short- and long-term bottom line benefits, including consistent strategic focus, higher margins, higher valuations, higher loyalty (both employee and customer), higher retention, market prominence, and a cushion of customer goodwill against mistakes.

Another general difference of the Integrated Brand Model is its focus on building a strong brand rather than on building brand equity. Integrated branding results in strong equity, but only as a by-product of building customer relationships. Although this may sound like splitting hairs, it can be very significant. If you are focusing on building the brand, you are taking a holistic approach—creating a brand-driven company.

You will ask questions like, *What will be the best ways to deepen the relationship with the customer?* rather than *How can we increase brand equity?*

If a company focuses on brand equity, on the other hand, it may look at brand in a piecemeal fashion and focus only on those elements that will obviously build equity. This is like a publicly held company's focusing on building shareholder value rather than on building great products.

OTHER BRAND MODELS

The following are brand models that have made significant contributions to the understanding of brand development. If you are considering creating a brand-driven company, these are worth investigating.

Jean-Noel Kapferer's *Strategic Brand Management*

Kapferer bases brand identity on three qualities: durability, coherence, and realism. Drilling down deeper, Kapferer uses a brand identity prism (see figure 18.1) to understand various brand elements. He explains: "The identity prism allows us to examine the brand in detail in order to detect its strengths and weaknesses. . .and comes up with diagnoses which could never be obtained by stumbling blindly through a mass of image research data."

The external elements include the following:

- *Physique* describes certain features of prominent products, such as the crocodile for Lacoste or data processing systems for IBM.
- *Relationship* is the intangible exchange between the brand and it customers— Lacoste conveys social conformity and IBM offers security and reassurance.
- *Reflection* is the customer's image of who should use the product—Lacoste spans generations and is neither overly masculine nor overly feminine, and IBM is for those who take their business seriously.

Internal elements include the following:

- *Personality* is the brand as a person, the traits that customers see. Lacoste's personality is discreet without being fancy; IBM's is confident and square.
- *Culture* is an overriding social principle of the brand that may also be related to its country or place of origin or its values. Lacoste's is individualism, aristocratic ideals, and classicism, whereas IBM's is big business, Ivy League, order and collectiveness, East Coast, and Wall Street.

Figure 18.1
Brand Identity Prism

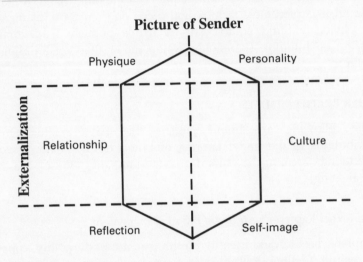

Brand identity may be represented diagrammatically by a six-sided prism.

Sources: Reprinted with the permission of The Free Press, a Division of Simon & Schuster, Inc. from *Strategic Brand Management: New Approaches to Creating and Evaluating Brand Equity* by Jean-Noel Kapferer. Copyright © 1992 by Les Editions d'Organisation. Translated by Philip Gibbs. First published in the English language in 1992 by Kogan Page Ltd., p. 43; reprinted also with the permission of Kogan Page from *Strategic Brand Management: New Approaches to Creating and Evaluating Brand Equity* by Jean-Noel Kapferer, London, 1992.

- *Self-image* is how customers see themselves in the brand. A Lacoste customer sees himself or herself as a member of an inclusive sporting club; IBM sees himself or herself as a pro.

Kapferer's perspective on brand shares several similarities with integrated branding, especially in the need for the brand to drive the company. He says, "Everyone from the highest to the lowest echelons of the firm, must consider the brand in a professional light, becoming an active living support, and an integral part, of its functioning."[2]

His brand personality attribute completely overlaps with the Integrated Brand Model definition. His idea of *culture* is related to the Integrated Brand Model's *values* driver; and *his physique, self-image, and reflection* are about customer perception, which is influenced by all brand drivers and conveyors in the Integrated Brand Model. His idea of "customer relationship" talks about one subset of the customer relationship, the intangible effect that a brand creates.

Kevin Lane Keller's Customer-Based Brand Equity (CBBE)[3]

Keller defines *customer-based brand equity* (CBBE) as the "differential effect that brand knowledge has on consumer response to the marketing of that brand."[4] In his model, brand knowledge is related to *brand awareness* and *brand image*, where *brand awareness* is broken down into recognition and recall, and *brand image* is broken down into associations. Brand equity is dependent on recognition, recall, and the favorability, strength, and uniqueness of brand associations.

Whether a brand will build *positive* equity is dependent on three factors:

• The initial choices for brand elements or identities: This includes brand names, logos, symbols, characters, packaging, and slogans.

• How well the brand is supported by and integrated into marketing programs: This includes product strategy, pricing strategy, channel strategy, and communications strategy.

• The strengths of other existing associations linked to the brand, such as company name, country of origin, channel of distribution, spokespeople, existing characters, or other brands.

Keller's CBBE model encompasses several elements of an effective brand. One major difference from integrated branding is that his system focuses on brand building through the marketing and marketing communications department only. It does not address the necessity for brand to be a companywide business strategy for brand actions to match brand communications.

David Arnold: Brand Mapping[5]

Arnold's model is based on *essence, benefits*, and *attributes*. *Brand essence* is the central value of a brand, called its personality, which "is meant to make customers feel good in using the brand."[6] The personality is also the source of brand equity. *Benefits* are the benefits of using the brand, and *attributes* are product attributes. The personality is typically expressed through a brand property such as the Marlboro Man. Finally, the brand is taken to the market through brand positioning, which places the brand in relation to competitors in the marketplace.

Arnold's model is also highly marketing communications-focused. Its focus on the personality as brand essence corresponds to the Integrated

Brand Model. It lacks the other aspect of brand essence used in integrated branding, the brand principle.

David A. Aaker

Aaker, who is one of the most widely published and cited brand experts today, ties brand identity to a *core identity, extended identity,* and *value proposition.*

The core identity is the associations of a brand that are most likely to be constant as the brand travels to new markets and products. An example of the core identity would be Black Velvet's *soft and smooth* product attribute.

The extended identity comprises the elements that provide texture and completeness. This could include important marketing elements such as visual associations. Black Velvet's extended identity includes the *Black Velvet lady with the black velvet dress; the black label on the bottle;* a personality of *class, elegant but friendly, and approachable; an imported brand; a spirits brand, not just a Canadian alternative;* and *a broad age spectrum of users (not restricted to older males).*

Value proposition is a statement of the functional, emotional, and selfexpressive benefits delivered by the brand that provide value to the customer. An effective value proposition should lead to a brand–customer relationship and drive purchase decisions. Black Velvet's functional benefits include *soft, smooth taste at a value price.* Its emotional benefits include feeling *relaxed, rewarded,* and *sensual.* And its self-expressive benefits include *serving a brand with a touch of class.*

Aaker's system can provide a helpful additional perspective for the integrated branding process. However, integrated branding's organization and brand drivers are easier to put into practice by all employees than this system.

Young and Rubicam, Brand Asset Valuator[7]

The Y&R model states that brands are built through four progressive stages: *differentiation, relevance, esteem,* and *knowledge.*

Differentiation and relevance are what define *brand strength,* which is an indication of future status based on a brand's appropriateness to the customer and difference from other brands.

Esteem and knowledge define *brand stature,* which is the brand's current status. Brands that have brand strength create esteem that builds knowledge with the customer.

Emerging brands will score highest in differentiation and progressively lower on relevance, esteem, and knowledge. Leading brands will score highly in all four areas, declining brands will score higher on knowledge than esteem and perhaps even lower on relevance and differentiation, and new brands will have low scores on all four measurements. Using this model, it's possible to predict who is an up-and-comer in a category, who is slipping, and who is remaining strong.

This type of model would be helpful as a benchmarking tool for integrated brands.

NOTES

1. http://www.newciv.org/isss_primer/quotes.html.

2. Reprinted with the permission of The Free Press, a Division of Simon & Schuster, Inc. from *Strategic Brand Management: New Approaches to Creating and Evaluating Brand Equity* by Jean-Noel Kapferer. Copyright © 1992 by Les Editions d'Organisation. Translated by Philip Gibbs. First published in the English language in 1992 by Kogan Page Ltd., p. 307.

3. Kevin Lane Keller, *Strategic Brand Management* (Upper Saddle River, NJ: Prentice-Hall, 1998), p. 75.

4. Ibid., p. 82.

5. David Arnold, *The Handbook of Brand Management* (Reading, MA: Addison Wesley, 1992), p. 17.

6. Ibid., p. 94.

7. Young and Rubicam, Annual Brand Asset Valuation (BAV) Survey, 1993.

Appendix: Conducting Organization and Brand Driver Interviews

In order for drivers to be effective, they must be based on both company strengths and what customers value. You can use research of various types including telephone, Internet, and face-to-face interviews to obtain the raw data for developing final drivers.

DEVELOPING A QUESTIONNAIRE

An effective questionnaire for one-on-one interviews should take no longer than fifteen minutes of a customer's time or forty-five minutes of an employee's time. A good questionnaire will ask questions about the who, what, when, where, and why of the company. It will also ask questions on a variety of levels, tapping into direct experience and metaphorical associations. This allows you to ask all around each issue and get a 360-degree perspective on it. When developing the integrated brand, it's also important to create questions that can be used to benchmark changes in the brand over time. Where possible, write the questions so they do not need to change from one research project to the next.

CONDUCTING BRAND INTERVIEWS

If possible, interview someone in a place with no distractions and no potential for interruption (away from phones, beepers, and computer monitors). Briefly explain that the purpose of the interview is to obtain the interviewee's buy-in.

For example in a story-specific interview process: *Your company is working on its corporate brand—bringing more effectiveness to its relationship with its customers. One driver of the brand is the company story. Telling your company story gives outsiders a big-picture perspective on the company. After we have finished these interviews we will create a composite story, which will then be reviewed and reworked by the corporate brand team. Once completed, the story will serve as a guide for all employees.* Ask them whether they have any questions once you have explained your purpose.

ORGANIZATION AND BRAND DRIVER QUESTION TEMPLATES—INTERNAL

Mission

- What business are you in?
- What gets you excited about coming to work?
- What changes do you expect to take place in company strategy in the next two years? Five years?
- Are there other businesses you are planning to enter in the future?
- What general customer need does the company answer?

Values

- What are the stated and unstated company beliefs about business, its marketplace, and employees?
- What values will remain constant regardless of what happens to the company?
- What would others say your company values are?
- What are the three most important values to the company?
- What values should you add as a company?

Story

- Who started the company and why did he or she decide to do it?
- What is the company's focus?
- What is most valuable about what they do?
- What's the history of the company?
- If the company were an animal, what kind would it be and why?

• Imagine we are sitting around a campfire under the stars. Tell me the story of the company.

Principle

• What are your brand strengths?
• Which ones are unique to the brand?
• Why do customers buy your brand over others?
• What are the consistent benefits of your brand?

Personality

• What is the business style of the brand?
• How do you feel when you hear [insert brand name]?
• If the brand were a person, what would that person be like?
• What other brands [or people] does it resemble?
• Imagine that the company has died. What is written on its gravestone?

Associations

• What is the first thing that comes to mind when I say [insert brand name]?
• What else comes to mind?
• Are there any visual images tied to the brand? Words? Sounds? Colors?
• [If it is a boxed product] Visualize the box. What do you see? What color is it? What does it tell you about the brand?

Creating the Brand Matrix

• What is the business scope of the brand?
• What are the assets of the brand?
• What are the products in each brand and what is each one's contribution to the brand?
• How does the brand relate to other brands and the company?
• Do the products using the brand name share the same business scope?
• Are the brand naming system and identity easy to understand and consistent with its drivers?

ORGANIZATION AND BRAND DRIVER QUESTION
TEMPLATES—EXTERNAL

Unaided Recall

- When you think of [insert category] which brand comes to mind first?
- What other brands come to mind?
- Which products come to mind?
- What other products come to mind?
- Which of the products are you familiar with?

Driver Creation

- What comes to mind when you hear brand name? Company name?
- What would it take to make you switch to [insert brand] as a primary vendor for one or more of the software products used?
- What is the business style of this company?
- What are the strengths of the brand?

Benchmarking

- Which brand is your primary supplier?
- How satisfied are you with this supplier on a scale of 1 to 5, with 5 being unsatisfied, 3 being neutral, and 1 being highly satisfied? Why?
- What is the first word or phrase that comes to mind when you think of this brand?
- Why would you choose this company over others?
- Do you consider yourself a favorable reference for this brand?
- On the basis of your past experience, are you most likely to continue to purchase this brand?

Other areas of questioning may include lists of purchasing criteria, associations, and personality traits that you ask the interviewee to respond to on a strongly agree to strongly disagree rating scale.

DURING THE INTERVIEW

Unless you are going for statistical results, don't follow the questionnaire rigidly; follow the interviewee's thoughts. Your interviewee may be the type of person who likes to tell stories—or just likes to digress. Follow his or her lead as long as it's something that feeds back into the learning process. Don't sweat it if the person answers questions 1–4 all at once. Simply go back later on and use answers where they most apply.

It's also a good idea to use a laptop computer to take notes. Most people can type much faster than they can write and it saves you from the tedious process of entering the information into your computer later on. Also, enter answers from multiple interviews under each question for easier comparison when you are finished.

Do not put names next to answers. Confidentiality is key to keeping the information relatively unbiased. Most people enjoy the process; everyone likes to be asked for his or her opinions and then be listened to attentively.

Selected Bibliography

Aaker, David A. *Building Strong Brands.* New York: The Free Press, 1996.

Aaker, David A. *Managing Brand Equity.* New York: Free Press, 1991.

Aaker, David A. and Robert Jacobson. "The Financial Information Content of Perceived Quality." *Journal of Marketing Research,* 31 (May 1994), pp. 191–201.

Annie's Homegrown web site: http://www.annies.com.

Arnold, David. *The Handbook of Brand Management.* Reading, MA: Addison Wesley, 1993.

Braitman, Stephen M.H., James L. Byram, Doug Millison, and Michael Moon. *Strategies for Building Digital Brands.* Cupertino, CA: Apple Computer, 1996.

Brandt, Marty and Grant Johnson. *Powerbranding.* San Francisco, CA: International Data Group, 1997.

Bridges, William. *The Character of Organizations.* Palo Alto, CA: Davis-Black, 1992.

Burrows, Peter. "Lew Platt's Fix-It Plan for Hewlett-Packard." *Business Week,* July 13, 1998.

Butterball Turkey web site: http://www.butterball.com.

"Can You Judge a Beer by Its Label." *Consumer Reports,* June 1996, pp. 10–15.

Case, John Inc. "Corporate Culture." *Business Week,* November 1996.

Chadderdon, Lisa. "How Dell Sells on the Web." *Fast Company,* September 1998.

Collins, James C. "Change Is Good—but First, Know What Should Never Change." *Fortune,* May 29, 1995.

Corporate Design web page: http://www.cdf.org/issue/fedex.html.

Data Dimensions, Inc. *Millennium³ 1998–1999 Journal/Calendar.* 1998.

Dennis, Kathryn. "The End of Brand Control." *Marketing Computers,* March 1998.

Doler, Kathleen. "Filthy Rich—Amazon.com Dusts the Competition." *Upside,* July 29, 1998.

Enrico, Dottie. "Marketers Learn to Teach Old Ad New Tricks." *USA Today*, November 4, 1996.

Farquhar, Peter H. "Managing Brand Equity." *Journal of Advertising Research*, 30, no. 4 (August/September 1990).

Frankel, Alex. "Name-o-Rama." *Wired 5.06*, June 1997.

Gurnett, Kate. "New Owner Pressured to Keep 4-Ton Dog." *Albany Times Union*, September 21, 1997.

Hammer, Michael. *Beyond Reengineering: How the Process-Centered Organization Is Changing Our Work and Our Lives*. New York: HarperCollins, 1996.

Hays, Constance L. "A Classic in Search of its Former Glory." *New York Times*, July 4, 1998.

Imperato, Gina. "Make a Name for Yourself." *Fast Company*, October–November 1997.

Intelliquest Brand Tech Forum, Seminar, October 24, 1998.

International Data Group. " 'Buying IT in the 90's'—the Channels Study," Laurentian Technomedia Inc., 1996–1998, handout.

Jacques, Chevron. "Branding, Marketing & Sausage Making." JRC&A: http://www.cl.ais.net/jchevron/art_sausage.html.

James, Jennifer. "Columns Were a Call for Teachers to Transform a Profession." *Seattle Times*, September 6, 1998.

Kaku, Michio. *Visions: How Science Will Revolutionize the 21st Century*. New York: Doubleday, 1997.

Kapferer, Jean-Noel. *Strategic Brand Management*. New York: Free Press, 1992.

Keller, Kevin Lane. *Strategic Brand Management*. Upper Saddle River, NJ: Prentice-Hall, 1998.

Kotter, John P. "Leading the Change: Why Transformation Efforts Fail." *Harvard Business Review*, March–April 1995.

Littman, Jonathan. "Driven to Succeed: The Yahoo Story." *Upside*, September 8, 1998.

Lix, Tom. "Building Brands on Web NPR Site Builder Complements On-Air Pressure." *Computerworld*, April 13, 1998, p. 41.

Lowenstein, Roger. "Intrinsic Value: Remember When Companies Made Things." *The Wall Street Journal*, September 18, 1997.

Lucent web site: http://www.lucent.com.

MacMillan, Ian C. and Rita Gunther McGrath. "Discovering New Points of Differentiation." *Harvard Business Review*, July–August 1997.

McCabe, Heather. "Battle over a Woman's Place on the Web." *Wired Magazine*, May 18, 1998.

McCall, William. "There's Mud on Nike's Swoosh." *Seattle Post-Intelligencer*, October 9, 1998.

Microsoft web site: www.Microsoft.com.

Montgomery Ward web site: http://www.mward.com.

Mooney, Bill and David Holt. *The Storyteller's Guide*. Little Rock, AR: August House, 1996.

Moore, Geoffrey A. *Inside the Tornado*. New York: HarperCollins, 1996.

Nass, Clifford and Byron Reeves. *The Media Equation: How People Treat Computers, Television and New Media Like Real People and Places*. Cambridge, England: Cambridge University Press, 1998.

Nike web site: http://www.nike.com.

Nipperscape web site: http://www.ais.org/lsa.

O'Malley, Chris. "RCA Seeks to Collar the Affinity Credit Card Market." *The Indianapolis Star*, March 3, 1997.

Passall, Peter. "Why the Best Doesn't Always Win." *The New York Times Magazine*, May 5, 1996.

Prognostics, WRQ commissioned research. October, 1997.

Ries, Al and Jack Trout. *Positioning: The Battle for Your Mind*. New York: Warner Books, 1993.

Reeves, Byron and Clifford Nass. *The Media Equation*. New York: Cambridge University Press, 1996.

Shedroff, Nathan. "Online Branding." *NewMedia.com*, July 1998.

Singer, Claude. "Branding Worlds Collide." *Wireless Review*, August 31, 1998.

Somasundaram, Meera. "Red Packages Lure Shoppers like Capes Flourished at Bulls." *The Wall Street Journal*, September 18, 1995.

Southern California Edison web site: http://www.edisonhome.com.

Stoddard, Bob. *Pepsi: 100 Years*. Los Angeles, CA: General Publishing Group, 1997.

Tabrizi, Behnam and Rick Walleigh. "Defining Next Generation Products: An Inside Look." *Harvard Business Review*, November–December 1997.

Thrum, Scott. "Once a Master of Fine Print, Adobe Slipped." *The Wall Street Journal*, August 27, 1998.

Trout, Jack and Steve Rivkin (contributor). *The New Positioning: The Latest on the World's #1 Business Strategy*. New York: McGraw-Hill, 1997.

Washington Software Alliance. "Microsoft Thrives on Partnership, Maeffei Tells 241 Venture Capitalists." *NewsBytes*, XII, no. 7 (July 1998), pp. 4–5.

Wiersema, Fred. *Customer Intimacy*. Santa Monica, CA: Knowledge Exchange, 1996.

Willigan, Geraldine E. "High-Performance Marketing: An Interview with Nike's Phil Knight." *Harvard Business Review*, July–August 1992.

Xerox web site: http://www.xerox.com.

Yahoo web site: http://www.yahoo.com.

Young and Rubicam, Annual Brand Asset Valuation (BAV) Survey, 1993.

ZD High-Tech Branding Study, Conducted by IntelliQuest on behalf of Ziff-Davis. March 1998. http://www.ziffdavis.com.

Zona Research web site: www.zona.com.

Index

About the Authors

F. JOSEPH LEPLA has worked with a broad range of companies for 20 years to help develop and manage their brands. Prior to co-founding Parker LePla, he was a corporate vice president of public relations, president of a full service marketing agency, and vice president of corporate relations for a national financial services company.

LYNN M. PARKER has more than 15 years' experience in technology marketing and brand development, and was one of the earliest practitioners of high tech public relations and product positioning. Prior to co-founding Parker LePla, she was a creative strategies director and a public relations senior writer. She has also worked as a journalist at three West Coast newspapers.